Robin Hood

Baking

Over 250 recipes from Robin Hood's *Baking Festival* and *Home Baking* cookbooks

Robert
ROSE

Robin Hood Baking
Text copyright © 2010 Smucker Foods of Canada Corp.
Photographs copyright © 2010 Robert Wigington & Robert Rose Inc.
Cover and text design copyright © 2010 Robert Rose Inc.

Disclaimer

For those people with food or other allergies, or who have special food requirements or health issues, please read the contents of each recipe carefully and determine whether or not they may be appropriate for you. You should also read the labels, specifically the ingredients, of any products called for in the recipes if you have any concerns.All recipes are used at the risk of the consumer. For those with special needs, allergies, requirements or health problems, in the event of any doubt, please contact your medical advisor prior to the use of any recipe.

Library and Archives Canada Cataloguing in Publication

Robin Hood baking : over 250 recipes from Robin Hood's baking festival and home baking cookbooks.

Includes index.
ISBN 978-0-7788-0257-0

1. Baking. 2. Confectionery. I. Title: Baking.

TX773.R624 2010   641.8'65   C2010-903177-6

Cover: Triple Chocolate Fudge Cake (page 204)
Photo page 4: Year-Round Shortbread (page 72), Raspberry Lattice Bars (page 110), Triple Chocolate Cookies (page 42) and Lickety-Split Lemon Bars (page 102)

Design & Production: Kevin Cockburn/PageWave Graphics Inc.
Editor: Carol Sherman
Copy Editor: Karen Campbell-Sheviak

Photography
Cover and pages 57, 135, 139, 161, 197, 201, 205, 213, 233, 255, 259, 365, 369, 373:
    Photographer: Colin Erricson
    Associate Photographer: Matt Johannsson
    Food Styling: Kathryn Robertson
    Prop Styling: Charlene Erricson

All other interior photography:
    Photographer: Robert Wigington
    Interior Food Styling: Jill Snider
    Interior Prop Styling: Maggi Jones & Sue Florian

We acknowledge the financial support of the Government of Canada through the Book Publishing Industry Development Program (BPIDP) for our publishing activities.

Published by: Robert Rose Inc.
120 Eglinton Ave. E., Suite 800, Toronto, Ontario, Canada M4P 1E2
Tel: (416) 322-6552   Fax: (416) 322-6936

Printed in China

1 2 3 4 5 6 7 8 9 10   PPLS   19 18 17 16 15 14 13 12 11 10

Contents

Robin Hood®

Robin Hood has been a household name in Canada since 1909, when our first flour mill went into operation in Moose Jaw, Saskatchewan. Since then, Robin Hood has become Canada's favorite flour, milled from the very best Canadian wheat in Quebec and Saskatchewan.

Much of our success has come from the long-term relationships we have developed with generations of Canadian home bakers. Our Robin Hood recipes have woven themselves into the fabric of daily life, creating memories and traditions for family and friends.

Robin Hood flour is made from the finest 100% Canadian wheat and is known for providing consistent results, every time. It's also the only national brand that offers a full line-up of flour varieties including All Purpose (unbleached, bleached, whole wheat), Best for Cake & Pastry, Best for Bread (whole wheat, white, multigrain), Best for Blending and our unique Nutri™ Flour Blend, which offers the taste of white flour with the goodness of whole wheat.

Robin Hood's dedicated baking Web site, www.robinhood.ca, offers more than 1,000 additional recipes and monthly newsletters featuring new recipes and tips.

Smucker Foods of Canada Corp.
A subsidiary of The J.M. Smucker Company

Founded in 1897, The J.M. Smucker Company has helped families celebrate memorable meals and moments for more than 110 years by providing consumers with great-tasting, high-quality products. Established with a commitment to Quality, People, Ethics, Growth and Independence, the Company continues to be guided by these Basic Beliefs and today owns and manufactures 10 number one food brands in the U.S. and Canada, with the Robin Hood brand joining Smucker Foods of Canada Corp. in 2004.

Robin Hood Baking

In this new cookbook, *Robin Hood Baking*, we have compiled a collection of our best recipes from the *Robin Hood Baking Festival* and *Robin Hood Home Baking* cookbooks, featuring recipes developed for novice and experienced bakers alike. With a comprehensive introduction to home baking, more than 250 easy-to-follow recipes ranging from snacks to desserts to savory dishes, as well as mouthwatering photographs, it's the perfect resource for helping you make memorable meals and moments.

Acknowledgments

We'd like to express our sincere thanks to the many talented and devoted people who helped put this book together: the publisher, Bob Dees, who convinced us to do this compilation cookbook, *Robin Hood Baking,* following the success of our *Baking Festival* and *Home Baking* cookbooks; Andrew Smith, Joseph Gisini and Kevin Cockburn, who designed and laid out the book; Brenda Venedam, who accurately input the recipes; and Carol Sherman and Karen Campbell-Sheviak for their eagle eyes in editing.

At Smucker Foods of Canada Corp., thanks to all the staff for their support, the large number of employees who critically tasted and evaluated every recipe until it was perfect; and our Consumer Services team, who pleasantly answer endless consumer calls regarding our recipes.

We also want to thank photographer Robert Wigington, food stylist Jill Snider, and prop stylists Sue Florian and Maggi Jones for the outstanding interior photography. Thanks to photographer Colin Erricson, associate photographer Matt Johannsson, prop stylist Charlene Erricson and food stylist Kathryn Robertson for the wonderful cover photograph and some of the interior photographs.

Introduction

Whenever thoughts turn to home, they inevitably gravitate toward baking. Nothing epitomizes domestic comfort more than freshly baked pies, breads, warm puddings, crisp buttery cookies or crunchy healthy snacks. But more than that, home baking is central to our everyday lives. From morning toast or muffins to coffee-break cake and evening dinner followed by a dessert, these ultimate comfort foods have woven themselves deeply into the fabric of daily life. Plain or fancy, old-fashioned or elegant, decadent or healthy — almost everyone cherishes a memory linked with freshly baked goods. So, not surprisingly, creating these mouthwatering treats to share with family and friends can be one of life's great pleasures.

Whether you are a novice or an experienced baker, *Robin Hood Baking* will inspire you to explore the wonderful world of baking. The basic ingredients couldn't be simpler, but the endless ways they can be varied make baking a great adventure. Fruit, nuts, grains, chocolate, dairy products and a wide range of flavorings can be mixed and matched with the essential components to create an array of delectable tastes and textures. Savory sensations cover a wide range, from vegetables to poultry, meats and fish.

With more than 250 easy-to-follow recipes and an abundance of mouthwatering photographs, this book is destined to become an indispensable resource in kitchens from coast to coast. There's something here for every occasion. Intended for home cooks, *Robin Hood Baking* is filled with dependable and delicious recipes that use basic ingredients. If they aren't already in your pantry, they will be readily available at your grocery store. We hope these recipes will inspire you to create delicious homemade treats that are uniquely yours.

Baking Basics

Baking is a science as much as an art, a basket of skills and techniques that create the foundation upon which artistry can build. With its orientation toward detail and dependence upon the chemical reactions of ingredients, baking is far less forgiving than cooking. Adding too much liquid to a stew may produce a watery result that lacks flavor, but the less-than-ideal dish may still be enjoyable. On the other hand, too much liquid in a cake batter is likely to produce a result that can't be salvaged.

Despite its exacting nature, it would be a mistake to assume that baking is, by definition, difficult. Some baked goods — for instance, drop cookies — are among the easiest home-cooked products to make, and many outstanding cooks got their start as toddlers baking cookies with Mom. The issue with baking is that, unlike cooking, it demands strict adherence to the rules. Because the basic ingredients are so simple — flour, mixed with some combination of salt, eggs, sweetener, leavening agent and fat, such as oil, butter or shortening — how they are combined and in what proportion are particularly important. Baking recipes are so rooted in science — the way ingredients react and the principles of how heat is transferred — they are more than guidelines: they are formulae that document how to measure, combine and cook ingredients to achieve particular results. Tinker with the formula and you're tempting disaster.

To achieve success, home bakers need four basic things: reliable recipes written to accommodate their level of skill, good equipment, quality ingredients and an attentive mindset. Usually, poor results can be traced back to a fault in one of these components.

All too often, the problem lies with the recipe. Some recipes are vaguely written and don't provide clear instructions that can be easily followed. Others assume a level of skill that a home baker is unlikely to have and use terms that are unintelligible to inexperienced cooks. All these factors increase the possibility of error. It has always been important to have confidence in your recipe source, but this is especially true today, when so many recipes are taken off the Internet, often from sites that lack quality control. The simple truth is that some recipes just don't work. And you don't want to invest valuable time and costly ingredients only to discover your recipe was a dud.

Because the recipes in this book originated in the Robin Hood Test Kitchen, you can be confident they have been properly formulated and thoroughly tested. In addition, we've included an abundance of tips to help you improve your baking skills and avoid potential pitfalls. We hope you will be able to achieve outstanding results every time you bake.

Baking Equipment

Using the right equipment is an important part of successful baking. In order to produce satisfactory results, good-quality dishes and pans, accurate measures, mixing bowls, spoons, spatulas and wire racks are essential. Depending upon how much you bake and what you're making, you may also need an electric mixer, a food processor, cutting boards, a strainer, a rolling pin, a pastry board and parchment paper.

Oven Temperature

Your oven is probably the single most important piece of baking equipment you own. Oven temperature plays a critical role in baking. If your oven is too hot, your baked goods will be overly brown on the surface and possibly not completely cooked through. If it is not hot enough, you will need to overcook the interior to achieve a desirable degree of browning.

Ideally, when you set the temperature, that's how hot your oven will be once it has finished preheating. The problem is, most ovens are 25°F (10°C) hotter or cooler than their setting. One solution is to have your oven calibrated by a professional to ensure that the setting and the temperature align. The flaw in this solution is that it's expensive to have

Watch for Hot Spots

Most ovens have "hot spots," which result in unevenly baked goods. Prevent uneven baking by placing the pans in the center of the oven and rotating them halfway through. Use just one oven rack — don't stack.

Check Early

Because oven temperatures vary so much, we recommend that you treat all recipe times as guidelines and begin checking what you are baking well before the recommended time.

Don't Peek

Minimizing the number of times you open the oven door and the amount of time you keep it open helps maintain the oven temperature, which is important to successful baking.

All Pans Aren't Equal

The material your pans are made from and whether their surface is shiny or dull affects the baking time. If you are using glass or nonstick pans, especially those that are dark, lower the oven temperature by 25°F (10°C).

an oven professionally calibrated, and unless you do it routinely, it's likely to fall out of alignment. A simpler and more cost-effective approach is to familiarize yourself with how your oven bakes. You will gain a sense of whether your oven is hotter or cooler than the setting by observing how quickly or slowly it cooks in relation to the recipes you use. A more accurate solution, which we recommend, is to purchase an oven thermometer. This simple, inexpensive device will tell you exactly what your oven temperature is and allow you to adjust the setting accordingly.

Convection Ovens

If you are using a convection oven to bake the recipes in this book, check your manual and follow the instructions. Because convection ovens are more energy efficient than traditional models, you can either reduce your baking time by about 25 per cent or lower the oven temperature by 25°F (10°C). As a rule of thumb, if you are baking anything for less than 15 minutes — cookies, for example — reduce the oven temperature rather than the baking time. Preheat your oven to the desired temperature before baking.

Pans

Good-quality, shiny metal pans and baking sheets are a great investment because they bake evenly and do not rust. However, heatproof glass pans also work well for many recipes. Since the quality of your pan can make a big difference to baking results, it's worth doing research before buying, particularly since expensive pans aren't necessarily the best. Ask for advice at a good kitchen-supply store or read cooking magazines, which test and rate equipment.

Pay Attention to Size

Today's baking pans are not as standardized as they once were; they differ in size and shape from older ones and also vary from one manufacturer to another. In addition, the labeling may show a mixture of imperial and metric measurements, which can be confusing. You'll likely have several standard-size pans in your pantry that you can readily identify for use in these recipes. But if you're using a pan that isn't a standard size, you'll need to estimate the volume and dimensions yourself. To confirm the volume of a pan, fill liquid measuring cups with water and pour liquid into the pan until it reaches the brim. The quantity you used is the volume measure of the pan. Use a ruler to measure the length and depth, taking measurements on the inside across the top of the pan. Measure depth on the outside of the pan, vertically from the bottom to the brim.

To achieve optimum results, we recommend using the pan size specified in the recipe. However, you can substitute a pan that is similar in dimension and volume — just make sure you don't use one that is smaller in volume because there may not be enough room to accommodate the expansion that takes place during baking. You can also interchange shapes (e.g., round instead of square) if the volume is the same and the pan is not much deeper, shallower, longer or shorter than the one recommended in the recipe.

Basic Pans

To prepare the recipes in this book, you will need the following pans:

- 8-inch (2 L) square cake pan
- 9-inch (2.5 L) square cake pan
- two or three 8-inch (1.2 L) round cake pans
- two or three 9-inch (1.5 L) round cake pans
- 10-inch (3 L) Bundt pan
- 10-inch (4 L) tube pan
- 8-inch (20 cm), 9-inch (23 cm) and 10-inch (25 cm) springform pans
- two 8½- by 4½-inch (1.5 L) or 9- by 5-inch (2 L) loaf pans
- six 5¾- by 3¼-inch (500 mL) mini-loaf pans
- two 12-cup muffin (cupcake) pans or one 24-cup muffin pan
- 13- by 9-inch (3.5 L) cake pan
- 15- by 10-inch (2 L) jelly roll pan
- three cookie sheets without sides
- 9-inch (23 cm) pie plate
- 9-inch (23 cm) deep-dish pie plate or quiche pan
- 10-inch (25 cm) pie plate
- 9-inch (23 cm) flan pan with removable side
- 9-inch (23 cm), 10-inch (25 cm) and 11-inch (27 cm) fluted flan pans with removable bottoms
- 7-inch (18 cm) soufflé dish
- 6-cup (1.5 L) baking dish
- 8-cup (2 L) baking dish
- 12-cup (3 L) shallow baking dish
- crêpe pan or nonstick skillet

Pans Matter

Don't use a pan that is a different size from the one recommended in the recipe you are using. If the recipe calls for a 9-inch (2.5 L) square pan and you use one that is 8 inches (2 L) square, the batter will spill over the sides during baking and much of your cake will end up on the floor of your oven. If you are using glass pans, decrease the oven temperature by 25°F (10°C) because glass pans bake more quickly than metal ones. If using nonstick pans, follow the manufacturer's directions. Most recommend decreasing the temperature by 25°F (10°C) since nonstick surfaces, especially those that are dark, bake faster.

Other Equipment

Bowls

Every kitchen needs a variety of bowls in different sizes for combining and mixing ingredients. Metal or glass bowls are preferable. Plastic does not work well for beating egg whites, as it retains oils, which can affect results. Have a few bowls of each size: small, medium and large.

The bowl needed for an electric mixer is a "mixer bowl." If the recipe doesn't specify a mixer bowl, other bowls will do.

Measuring Cups and Spoons

You will need glass or clear plastic measuring cups for liquid ingredients, a set of graduated dry-ingredient measures and a set of measuring spoons. (See Measure Accurately, page 13.)

Racks

Wire racks are essential for cooling cakes and cookies. Look for racks that have narrow spaces between the steel wires. It's a good idea to have a variety of sizes and shapes (round, square, rectangular) to suit whatever you're making. We recommend stainless-steel racks since they won't rust and have a long life.

Wire Whisks

Even if you use an electric mixer, you should have one medium-size all-purpose whisk for aerating dry ingredients or beating eggs before they are added to batters. If you don't have an electric mixer, a large balloon whisk is essential for jobs such as whipping cream or beating egg whites.

Zester and/or Fine Grater

Some recipes call for the zest of oranges, lemons or limes, which adds indispensable flavor to many dishes. A zester, an inexpensive gadget with tiny teeth, easily strips off the flavorful skin, separating it from the bitter white pith. Depending upon the recipe, it can be used as is or finely chopped. For finely grated zest, use a fine grater, which does the job in a single step.

Cookie Cutters

An assortment of cookie cutters in different shapes is both useful and fun. For many round cookies and biscuits, an inverted glass dipped in flour works very well.

Rolling Pin

A rolling pin is essential for making pie crusts and certain kinds of cookies. There are many different rolling pins on the market. Spend some time finding the one that works best for you.

Spatulas

You should have two rubber spatulas for tasks such as folding ingredients and scraping down the side of a mixing bowl. Offset spatulas made from metal are also required for lifting cakes and cookies from pans and racks. An icing spatula is used for applying frostings to cakes.

Pastry Brushes

Pastry brushes are useful for brushing pastry and bread dough with a wash or glaze, or for greasing pans.

Knives

A sharp serrated knife with a blade about 12 inches (30 cm) long makes cutting cakes horizontally a breeze. However, some people prefer to use dental floss for an even slice. Try both methods and pick your favorite.

Tip

If you don't like rack marks on the top of your cake, keep one rack covered with a thick tea towel pinned securely in place. When necessary, remove the towel for washing.

Tip

When purchasing wire cooling racks, look for ones that clear the countertop by at least 2 inches (5 cm). The height is necessary to prevent your baked goods from "sweating" on the bottom.

Tip

For tender pastry, it's worth investing in a pastry cloth and rolling pin cover. Available in most stores where kitchen equipment is sold, they eliminate sticking, which means you only need to use a minimum amount of additional flour when rolling out the pastry, which helps keep it tender.

Electric knives are excellent for cutting angel food cakes. A good-quality chef's knife is also essential for chopping ingredients.

Kitchen Shears

These are useful for many tasks, especially snipping herbs, such as chives, or dried fruits, such as apricots.

Pastry Bags and Tips

Although rarely essential, these devices, which can be used to shape batters and icings, give home baking a professional look. If you are writing names or greetings in frosting, a plastic squeeze bottle makes an acceptable substitute.

Mixer

Use an electric countertop mixer or a good-quality hand mixer, not the heavy-duty commercial type, which is too powerful for normal consumer-style baking. If you do a lot of baking, the countertop model is much more efficient and easier to use.

Food Processor

A food processor is a valuable kitchen tool that performs many tasks. It is useful for bakers, as it quickly chops ingredients such as fruits and nuts and purées mixtures. It also prepares an excellent pie crust, quickly cutting the fat into appropriately sized pieces and distributing them evenly throughout the dough.

Microwave Oven

Although a microwave oven is not essential, it is useful for baking functions such as melting chocolate or softening cold butter before it is creamed.

Baking Tips and Techniques

As mentioned earlier, baking is a science as well as an art, which helps to explain why things can so easily go wrong. Unless you understand the science behind recipes, which is reflected in baking techniques, it's all too easy to produce less-than-ideal results. Baking can get off track right from the get-go, as errors in measuring are one of the most common mistakes novice bakers make. Because so many things can go wrong in baking, it's important to understand the basic techniques and use carefully written, well-tested recipes.

Be Prepared

The first step to baking success is choosing a good recipe and reading it carefully, from beginning to end, before you start to bake. After you've read the recipe, measure all your ingredients and assemble them, along with the necessary equipment, on the counter. Few things are more frustrating than not being able to locate an ingredient when you're in the midst of mixing. You don't want to leave something out or be madly searching for a pan when your cake should be in the oven.

Allow adequate time to soften butter and bring cold ingredients, such as eggs, to room temperature. At least 15 minutes before you plan to bake, preheat your oven, being aware that some brands of ovens take

Tip

Most baked goods — cakes, muffins and cookies — are baked on the middle rack. For a well-browned bottom crust, bake yeast breads, pizzas and pies on the lower rack unless otherwise specified.

Tip

To ensure that goods don't overbake, check them early. Also use your nose. When things start to smell delicious, that's an indication that it's almost time to check for doneness.

Measure Then Sift

All the recipes in this book specify that dry ingredients such as icing sugar and cocoa powder be measured before being sifted. In the recipe ingredient list, this instruction appears as ½ cup (125 mL) icing sugar, sifted. If you are using a recipe from a different source, pay attention to how the sifting instruction reads. If it says ½ cup (125 mL) sifted icing sugar, it is telling you to sift before measuring, which results in less sugar.

longer to reach the desired temperature. Check your oven racks and adjust them, if necessary.

Prepare pans and baking sheets, if required, by greasing lightly with shortening or a vegetable cooking spray. Don't use butter or margarine, as they are more likely to stick and burn. If the pan needs to be floured as well, sprinkle the flour lightly over the greased surface. Shake the pan to distribute the flour evenly, then shake out the excess. Pans and baking sheets can also be lined with parchment paper, which ensures foolproof removal.

Why Your Recipe Was Overdone

There is no such thing as an exact baking time in any recipe because so many factors affect the time it takes to produce the desirable "golden brown" result. These include:

- the temperature of the ingredients — remember, unless otherwise specified, room temperature is ideal;
- the material your pans are made of and whether the finish is shiny or dull — if you are using glass or nonstick pans, reduce the temperature by 25°F (10°C);
- the accuracy of your oven setting — use an oven thermometer to get a sense of how much your oven is off; and
- the number of pans in the oven — unless you have a convection oven, your goods will bake unevenly if you are using multiple racks or too many pans, which can prevent the air from circulating properly around them.

Measure Accurately

Inaccurate measuring is one of the most common mistakes in baking. Every kitchen needs a set of graduated measures, both cups and spoons, specifically intended for dry ingredients. These have a straight rim so the ingredient being measured can be leveled off. To measure dry ingredients, spoon them lightly into the cup (you want them to be reasonably airy). Don't tap or pack. Then, using a spatula or the flat side of a knife, level off. Flour, cocoa powder and granulated and icing sugars should all be measured using this method, before sifting unless otherwise specified.

Brown sugar is measured differently from other dry ingredients. It is packed firmly into the measure, then leveled off. If you invert the measure and tap the bottom, brown sugar should unmold in the shape of the cup.

Liquids should be measured in clear glass or plastic liquid measuring cups, and the measurement should be read at eye level.

To accurately measure solid fats, such as butter, margarine or shortening, use the water displacement method. For example, if a recipe calls for ½ cup (125 mL) butter, fill a liquid measuring cup with ½ cup (125 mL) cold water. Add butter until the water level reaches the 1 cup (250 mL) mark. This ensures that you have exactly ½ cup (125 mL) butter.

Use measuring spoons for small amounts of both liquid and dry ingredients. Fill to the top, then level off.

When measuring, pay particular attention to how the instruction is written. One cup (250 mL) pitted cherries, chopped is a different quantity than 1 cup (250 mL) chopped pitted cherries. In the first amount, whole pitted cherries would be measured, then chopped. In the second amount, the chopped pitted cherries would be measured. They fit more tightly in the cup, meaning more cherries in your recipe.

For Liquids Only

A common mistake novice bakers make is using liquid measuring cups to measure dry ingredients. The problem is, scooping an ingredient such as flour into a measuring cup then tapping it on the counter to level it off to meet the line means more flour than the recipe calls for. Baking recipes are written with a view toward filling dry measures. Flour, for instance, should be spooned into the measure. This adds air, making it less dense. Then it is leveled off with a knife or spatula. Never tap to level off dry ingredients — you'll end up with more than the recipe calls for.

Sift as Required

Some ingredients, such as icing sugar, cocoa powder and cake flour, need to be sifted before being blended with other ingredients. If you don't have a sifter, a fine sieve will do. To ease cleanup, place a piece of waxed paper on the counter. Fill the sieve with the ingredients to be sifted and tap until all have sifted through to the paper. Using the paper as a funnel, transfer the dry ingredients to the rest of the mixture.

Have Ingredients at the Right Temperature

Ideally, ingredients for baking should be at room temperature unless otherwise specified. Eggs and cold butter (unless cold butter is called for in your recipe) should be removed from the refrigerator about 1 hour before baking. (If you're short on time, place eggs in a bowl of warm water for 5 minutes. You can soften cold butter in the microwave for a few seconds, but watch very carefully, as butter that is too soft will not cream effectively.)

One secret to producing flaky pastry is to ensure that all ingredients, including flour, are cold. (See Perfect Pie Crust and Pastry, page 22.)

Mix Carefully

Attention to mixing is as important for baking success as accurate measuring. For best results:

- Combine dry ingredients, such as flour, baking soda, baking powder and salt in a bowl or on a piece of waxed paper and mix together until they are well blended.
- Cream butter and sugar long enough to ensure that the mixture has achieved appropriate aeration (about 5 minutes on medium speed of an electric mixer if you are baking a cake). If using a mixer, stop it several times and scrape down the beaters and the side of the bowl.

Don't Substitute

Because recipes are chemical formulae, changing just one ingredient may destroy the delicate balance and ruin your result. If you want your recipe to work, use the specified ingredients only. Many of the recipes in this book suggest ingredient variations, which have been tested and will also produce the desired results.

Tip

If you aren't using a countertop mixer, place your mixing bowl on a folded damp towel to prevent it from slipping.

Assemble all the utensils you'll need, have your ingredients measured and prepare your pans before you start to mix.

Often the mixture looks curdled when the eggs are mixed in, but this will correct itself once the flour is added. If adding liquid along with the dry ingredients, alternate them, making three equal additions of the dry ingredients and adding the liquid in two equal parts. Adding these ingredients in alternate increments helps keep the fat emulsified in the liquid, which produces the desired texture.

- When combining sugar and eggs, beat the mixture until it increases in volume and falls in a ribbon when dropped from a spoon, unless the recipe specifies otherwise. This will usually take about 5 minutes on high speed of an electric mixer.
- Carefully fold lighter ingredients, such as beaten egg whites or whipped cream, into heavier ones to maintain the aeration.

Achieving Volume

Volume in baked goods is achieved in a variety of ways, depending upon the result desired. The most obvious method is the use of chemical leavens, such as yeast, baking powder and baking soda. Stiffly whipped egg whites, which contain trapped air bubbles, are another common volumizer. They give foam cakes, such as angel food or sponge cakes, their airy texture. Less well understood is the role of fats in achieving volume. Because solid fats such as butter or shortening coat the proteins in flour, they prevent it from absorbing water, which helps to build structure in baked goods. When butter and sugar are creamed together, the jagged edges of the sugar crystals create bubbles of air in the fat, which contributes to the aeration of the batter.

Bake Attentively

Attention to baking pans, oven temperature and timing are extremely important for baking success. For best results, keep the following in mind:

- Unless otherwise specified, the recipes in this book were developed using metal pans. Reduce the oven temperature by 25°F (10°C) if using glass pans instead of metal.
- Although most ovens have room for two or more oven racks, for best results, bake on only one rack at a time, unless you have a convection oven. Using multiple racks simultaneously produces unevenly baked goods.
- Always test baked goods to see if they are done 5 to 10 minutes before the end of the recommended baking time. This allows for variances in oven temperature. You can always bake longer if your product isn't done. If it is overcooked, it's too late to fix the mistake.

Convection Baking

One advantage to owning a convection oven is that you can use multiple oven racks simultaneously. Depending upon the model of your oven, you may be able to bake as many as six trays of cookies at the same time. So long as you're cooking at the same temperature, you can also bake casseroles or savory pies at the same time as sweets since the circulating air expels odors, preventing them from transferring to other foods. The recipes in this book have been tested in a conventional oven. If using a convection oven, reduce the temperature by 25°F (10°C).

Freezing

Because most — but not all — baked goods freeze well, we have included information on freezing capability along with every recipe. If your product can be frozen, follow these simple instructions. Wrap it tightly in plastic wrap and place in sealed containers or freezer bags. Write the date on the bag so you'll know when it was frozen. When ready to use, remove from the freezer and thaw in the sealed container. This ensures that the moisture lost during freezing will be reabsorbed when the goods have thawed.

Making Perfect Cakes

Tip

To help keep raisins, nuts, chocolate chips and candied fruit suspended in a batter, chop them finely (or use mini chocolate chips) and toss them in about 1 tbsp (15 mL) of the flour called for in the recipe before adding them to the other ingredients. Otherwise, they may sink because cake batters are not stiff enough to suspend them.

Many people find baking cakes intimidating because they require particularly close attention to detail. More than most other baked goods, cakes depend upon the exact proportion of ingredients and the proper execution of certain techniques to achieve their lift. Still, cakes don't need to be daunting; there are many ways to ensure cake-baking success, from using flour specially intended for cakes to making sure that ingredients are properly aerated.

Cake Types

There are two basic types of cakes: **butter cakes** and **foam cakes**. They are distinguished by their leavens and the method they use to add air to the batter. Butter cakes are based on the creaming technique — beating butter and sugar together long enough to create air bubbles in the mixture. They also employ chemical leavens, such as baking powder and baking soda, which produce carbon dioxide. Foam cakes get their lift from beating air into eggs.

Mixing Perfect Cakes

Butter Cakes: For butter cakes, cream the softened butter and sugar until the mixture is light and fluffy. This takes about 5 minutes on medium speed of an electric mixer. You'll need to stop the process several times and scrape down the beaters and the side of the bowl.
Foam Cakes: When making foam cakes, beat egg yolks with sugar on high speed of an electric mixer until they form a ribbon. This usually takes about 5 minutes. Pay close attention and follow the recipe instructions for beating egg whites. Overbeating will produce curdled whites and is as much of a problem as underbeating; neither has enough structure to support the cake. Fold beaten whites into the batter as soon as they reach the specified degree of firmness. If left to sit, they will soon disintegrate.

What Is Creaming?

Creaming, a volumizing technique used in butter cakes, is a common instruction in baking. When butter and sugar are beaten together until they become light and fluffy, the sharp edges of the sugar create air pockets in the mixture, which establishes a foundation to support the rising. Dense cakes may be the result of improper creaming.

Oven Position Matters

For best results, bake cakes on the middle oven rack. When baking two cake layers at the same time, be sure to place them on the same rack to ensure even baking. For proper heat distribution, cake pans should not touch each other or the sides of the oven during baking.

Light and Airy Cakes

To get the maximum volume in your cakes:

- Make sure that all ingredients are at room temperature.
- Follow the mixing instructions carefully.
- When using a chemical leaven, such as baking powder, make sure it is evenly distributed among the dry ingredients before they are added to the creamed mixture. Otherwise, your cake may develop tunnels as it bakes.
- Unless otherwise specified, add dry and liquid ingredients in increments, starting and ending with dry.
- Don't overmix. It's easy to create a tough cake just by overmixing.
- When folding ingredients into a recipe, particularly beaten egg whites, be careful not to overblend.
- Bake a cake as soon as it is mixed, as the leavening will start to work once it is moistened. A delay in baking after mixing will result in poor volume.

Preparing the Pans

When baking cakes, remember to prepare your pans before you begin to mix your batter. How the pan is greased determines how well the cake will release from the pan, a determinant of success. (You don't want pieces missing from your cake that were left behind in the pan.) How well you prepare your pans can also influence the degree of dome on top of the cake — for the best appearance, you want a flat rather than a domed cake.

When baking **layer cakes,** grease the pan with shortening or vegetable oil spray, then dust lightly with flour, tapping the pan to remove any excess. The flour gives the batter some traction and helps it climb up the side of the pan. For added insurance, place a round of parchment paper in the bottom of the pan. After the cake is cooked, it will peel of easily, leaving a smooth bottom.

Most **foam cakes** — a category that includes angel food, sponge and chiffon cakes, which achieve their volume through beaten eggs — are an exception. The pans are not greased so that the batter can cling to the pan and rise up the sides. In addition, the extra fat would weigh the airy batter down. All the recipes in this book have the appropriate instructions for preparing the pans.

Cake Flour

Cake flour is made from softer wheat than its all-purpose counterpart, and many cooks find that it helps them bake better cakes. Since it is lower in gluten and more finely ground, cake flour produces cakes with a more delicate crumb. Because most people always have a supply of all-purpose flour on hand, all our cake recipes have been written using this ingredient, which also produces a very satisfactory result. If you prefer to use cake flour, you will need to use a little bit more than the recipe calls for. When substituting Robin Hood Best For Cake & Pastry Flour for Robin Hood All-Purpose Flour, replace 1 cup (250 mL)

Tip

Line greased pans with parchment to ensure that your cake can be easily removed. Grease the parchment, too. After the cake has cooled for the recommended time, unmold and peel off the parchment.

Robin Hood All-Purpose Flour with 1 cup plus 2 tablespoons (280 mL) Robin Hood Best For Cake & Pastry Flour.

Is My Cake a Success?

If you're making a butter cake, look for:
- a level or just slightly rounded top (you don't want a dome);
- a fine-grained crumb; and
- an evenly browned crust.

The best foam cakes are:
- light, airy and moist;
- fine textured and tender; and
- deep golden brown.

Baking for Success

Incorrect oven temperature is one of the most significant factors affecting the success of cakes. As previously noted, use an oven thermometer to check the accuracy of your oven, preheat the oven for at least 15 minutes before you plan to bake and make sure the oven racks are properly positioned. Here are some additional tips.

Tip

Before baking, check your oven temperature with an oven thermometer to make sure it is as hot as it needs to be. Otherwise, your cake may not rise as much as you would like.

- Do not use a pan that is smaller in volume than the size recommended, as the cake may overflow. Slightly larger is usually safe, although the cake will be shallower and require less baking time.
- To eliminate any large air bubbles that may have formed in the batter, bang most cake pans firmly against the countertop before placing them in the oven. Do not do this with angel food cake, sponge cake or cakes containing fruit or nuts.
- Use recommended baking times as guidelines. Always set the timer for 5 minutes before the minimum time given to allow for oven variances. As previously noted, ovens are often hotter than the temperature indicated, and cakes can easily be overbaked, especially those high in sugar or baked in a dark pan. It's much safer to add more time in 5-minute increments if the cake isn't done.

Testing for Doneness

When cakes are done, a toothpick, wooden skewer or cake tester inserted in the center of the cake will come out clean. (However, this test won't work for some cakes with "gooey" ingredients.) Another indication that the cake is done is that the top springs back when lightly touched and the cake comes away from the sides of the pan. For lighter cakes, color is also a good indicator — the cake should be a nice golden brown.

Tip

When testing to see if your cake is done, be as quick and efficient as possible. Don't open the door all the way. The rush of cool air may cause your cake to fall.

Removing Cakes from Pans

Unless the recipe specifies otherwise, after they are taken out of the oven, layer cakes should cool in the pans for 10 minutes.

Deeper cakes, such as tube cakes and loaves, should be left for 20 minutes. After the required time has passed, turn the cake out and cool completely on a wire rack. To remove the cake from the pan, run

Tip
Don't cool a cake in
the pan on a rack
any longer than
the recommended
time. If left too long,
condensation will
form, making it
difficult to remove it
from the pan.

a knife around the edge (and also the center, if baking in a tube pan), then invert the pan and shake it gently to remove the cake. Most cakes are inverted twice so that they finish cooling in the same position (top side up) as they are baked. Bundt and angel food cakes are the two exceptions: after cooling initially for about 20 minutes in the pan, turn out a Bundt cake and finish cooling, fluted side up. Baked angel food cakes should cool completely in the pans. After removing from the oven, immediately turn the baked cake upside down on a funnel or bottle and let it cool completely.

Glazing and Frosting

Glazes differ from frostings in that they are usually a simpler way to finish a cake (for instance, drizzling with melted chocolate). Frostings are thicker and, when making from scratch, more complicated. Cakes are often glazed while still warm, but frostings aren't applied until cakes have completely cooled. Buttercream, a combination of softened butter, flavoring and icing sugar is the most common frosting used by home cooks. Flavored whipped creams also make easy and delicious frostings for cakes. Dusting cakes with sugar or drizzling them with syrup or melted chocolate are popular ways to finish cakes. We hope the following tips will inspire you to think creatively about how to finish your cakes and help you achieve successful results.

Glazing Tips

- Dusting plain cakes with icing sugar is the simplest and most calorie-conscious way to finish them. Just before serving (otherwise the moisture from the cake will quickly absorb the sugar), place icing sugar in a fine sieve and tap over the surface of the cake. For an elegant or festive look, place a paper doily over the unfrosted cake, then remove carefully after dusting, leaving a lacy decoration.
- When finishing cakes that are brushed with syrup while warm (usually tube and Bundt cakes), place the cake on a rack set over waxed paper to catch the drips.

Frosting Tips

- Frost cakes only after they are completely cool. If desired, place cakes to be frosted in the freezer for about 30 minutes to make them less fragile and easier to frost.
- When frosting, place a bit of frosting on the plate to hold the cake in place. To keep the plate clean, set four strips of waxed paper under the edge of the cake to form a square. Carefully remove the strips when you have finished.
- If you are using a filling that is different from the frosting, leave, a 1/2-inch (1 cm) margin from the edge to ensure that it doesn't run into and discolor the frosting.

Frosting Layer Cakes

Because layer cakes involve setting one cake on top of another, it may be necessary, if the layers are domed, to slice a bit off the top with a serrated knife to make them level before frosting. If there are burned spots on the cakes, cut them off. You can fill them with frosting. Set four strips of waxed paper on your plate to form a square and place a dab of icing in the middle of the plate to hold the cake in place. Place the first cake layer, top side down, on the plate. Spread $\frac{1}{2}$ to $\frac{3}{4}$ cup (125 to 175 mL) frosting over the layer using a spatula or table knife. Place the second cake layer, top side up, over the frosting. You now have the two flat surfaces together in the center so the cakes will sit evenly. Spread a very thin layer of frosting over the top and sides of the cake. (This seals in crumbs.) Then cover the cake with a second, thicker layer of frosting. You can smooth the surface with a long spatula or make swirls with a small spatula or the back of a spoon. If necessary, chill the cake to firm up the frosting. Remove the waxed paper strips before serving.

Storing Cakes

Properly wrapped, cakes keep very well. If the frosting does not contain eggs or dairy products, most cakes can be stored at room temperature, under a dome or a foil tent, for as long as three days. If storing your cake under a dome, add a slice of apple to help keep it moist. You can refrigerate most cakes for up to a week. Unfrosted layer cakes and foam cakes can be frozen for up to 6 months. Wrap them tightly in plastic wrap or place them in a freezer bag, removing as much air as possible.

To make slicing easy and develop the best flavor, make fruitcakes at least 4 weeks in advance. Wrap them and store in the refrigerator until you're ready to use them. Use a sharp, thin, nonserrated knife to make the nicest slices.

Thawing Frozen Cakes

When thawing unfrosted cakes, leave them covered for approximately three-quarters of the thawing time, then uncover for the remainder. This allows them to dry out slightly, which makes them easier to frost.

If you are thawing a frosted cake and the frosting contains either eggs or cream, thaw it overnight in the refrigerator. Other cakes may be thawed in this manner, or at room temperature, for about 3 hours.

Cookies, Bars and Squares

Almost everyone loves baking (not to mention eating) cookies, a designation which also includes bar cookies, such as brownies and squares. With their many different shapes, sizes and flavor variations, from crisp biscotti and soft chewy oatmeal cookies to rich blondies and apple squares, cookies are among the most versatile of baked goods. Because they are so easy, quick and delicious, cookies are a great starting place for novice bakers, including kids.

Like most cakes, many cookies use the creaming technique for combining butter and sugar. Since leavening is not as important in cookies as it is in cakes, it is not as necessary to beat volume into the mixture when making cookies. You can use a countertop mixer, a handheld mixer or a wooden spoon. Beat on medium speed, just until

Tip

It's a good idea to have a few plain cake layers in the freezer. Wrap unfrosted cake layers tightly in plastic wrap. You can thaw, fill and frost them in no time and quickly have a fabulous cake to serve to guests. Just be sure to cool unfrosted cakes completely before freezing.

Tip

An angel food cake will be easier to slice if you wrap it tightly and freeze it for 24 hours. Return to room temperature before serving.

Tip

When making cut and rolled cookies, dip the cookie cutter in flour so it won't stick to the dough. Cut the cookies as close together as possible. Although you can re-roll scraps of dough, the less the dough is handled, the more tender your cookies will be.

Tip

If you are not baking cookies within 1 hour of making the dough, refrigerate the batter, as the eggs and/or dairy products are likely to spoil at room temperature.

Cookie Types

Cookies are usually identified by how they are shaped and placed on the baking sheet. The following are common types of cookies.

Drop cookies, which are dropped by spoonfuls onto the baking sheet, are probably the easiest cookies to make. When making drop cookies, use a measuring spoon or small ice-cream scoop to ensure that all are equal in size so they will bake evenly.

Rolled and cut cookies are made from relatively firm dough that is rolled and cut into shapes; for instance, sugar cookies.

Sliced or refrigerator cookies are made from dough that is shaped into a roll and refrigerated for up to a week. These are among the most convenient cookies, as the dough can be sliced and baked whenever the mood strikes.

Shortbread, a tradition in many parts of the world, is a delicious combination of butter (a must) and flour worked together.

Biscotti are Italian biscuits that are traditionally used for dunking. Because they are baked twice, they are drier than most other cookies. They are particularly well suited to gift giving, as they keep well.

Bar cookies, the category that includes brownies and blondies as well as more-complex layered bars, can be a timesaving way to make bite-size treats. Instead of shaping each piece individually, they are baked in a pan, then cut into pieces.

Crisp or Chewy Cookies?

- If you prefer crisp cookies, press the dough flat with the bottom of a glass dipped in granulated sugar before baking.
- If you want soft, chewy cookies, remove them from the oven about 2 minutes before they are done, as they will continue to bake on the hot sheet. If you want crisp cookies, bake for 2 minutes longer.

Bake Great Cookies

Although cookies are among the simplest things to bake, these tips will help make yours even better.

- Use flat cookie sheets without sides for even baking.
- Place cookies about 2 inches (5 cm) apart on the cookie sheet to allow for spreading.
- Use cooking spray or a light coating of shortening to grease cookie sheets. It is not necessary to grease the sheets again, between batches, but use a paper towel to wipe off any sugar or crumbs from the surface before adding the next batch.
- Place the cookie sheet on the middle rack of your oven. Make sure that it is narrower than the oven rack and that it doesn't touch the sides of the oven, so the heat can circulate properly. For best results, bake only one sheet at a time to ensure proper heat circulation.
- Since cookies are usually small and bake quickly, pay particular attention to the baking time, as every extra minute can make a big

difference. Always aim to underbake rather than overbake, because cookies continue to bake after they are removed from the oven. Begin checking to see if your cookies are done a few minutes before the minimum time specified in the recipe.

Stop Cookie Spread

Sometimes your cookies can come out of the oven looking like a giant pancake because they have all run together on the baking sheet. Here are some ways to ensure that your cookies don't spread too much.

- Don't substitute butter or margarine in a recipe that calls for shortening. Shortening has a higher melting point than butter or margarine, so it doesn't liquefy as quickly, which means it does a better job of holding the dry ingredients together. Cookies made with butter or margarine will spread out more than those made with shortening.
- Grease cookie sheets only if the recipe specifies this and don't use an excessive amount. Unnecessary grease will cause some cookies to spread too much.
- Make sure your oven is preheated for at least 15 minutes before you bake and is set to the proper temperature. If the oven isn't hot enough, the fat will melt before the other ingredients have time to meld together, causing the cookies to spread.

Storing Cookies

Cool cookies completely before storing. Pack them in single layers in an airtight container, with waxed paper between layers to prevent sticking. Do not store crisp and soft cookies in the same container. To freeze cookies, place them in sealed plastic containers or freezer bags and store for up to 6 months.

Perfect Pie Crust and Pastry

While nothing defines excellence in home baking better than a freshly baked pie with a tender, flaky crust, few ventures inspire more trepidation. But making pie crust is not that difficult — it just takes practice. The fundamental ingredients couldn't be more basic: flour, fat and water. Once you understand how these ingredients work together, you'll be able to sense when the dough has the proper balance of flour and fat and the right consistency. Allow yourself a few failures and chalk them up as learning experiences. With a bit of practice, you'll be turning out perfect pies and pastry every time you bake.

Making Dough

Perfect pie crust is both tender and flaky, and achieving this balance is the challenge associated with making crust. Gluten, which is formed when flour comes into contact with moisture, is responsible for the flakiness in pie crust. The problem is, too much gluten makes pastry tough. The best pie crusts have just enough gluten to be flaky

Glazes to Enhance a Top Crust

- For a shiny, deep golden crust, brush with egg yolk beaten with a little water before baking.
- For a shiny crust, brush with lightly beaten egg white or milk.
- For a sugary, sweet crust, brush lightly with water, then sprinkle with sugar, preferably coarse.

without losing tenderness. Although it isn't flaky, pastry made with oil is particularly tender because, unlike a solid fat, such as butter or shortening, oil coats the flour, limiting the formation of gluten. Similarly, overblending a solid fat and flour (an easy mistake to make when using a food processor) will produce a crust that lacks flakiness. Ideally, when fat such as butter, shortening or lard, is cut into flour, it should be no smaller than the size of peas. This gives the flour space to bind with the water, thus creating the bit of gluten necessary to hold the crust together. The pieces of fat separate the strands of gluten, creating a flaky crust.

Excellent Results Every Time

The following tips will help you make excellent pastry every time.

- For the flakiest pastry, have all the ingredients, including the flour, well chilled. Freeze butter and/or shortening for 30 minutes before using. Use ice water (as little as possible) to bind the ingredients together. Water contributes to gluten formation, and adding too much liquid will produce a tough crust.
- Use the least amount of flour possible when rolling out the dough. The more flour you use, the tougher your pastry will be. Invest in a pastry cloth and rolling pin covered with stockinette, which help prevent the dough from sticking.
- Handle the dough as little as possible once the water is added. If you are re-rolling extra scraps of dough, do not knead them first. Kneading softens the fat, which creates a mealy crust.
- Chill the dough for at least 30 minutes before you roll it out. This allows the water to seep through the flour and ensures that the fat is firm, which contributes to flakiness.
- Start your pies in a hot oven (425°F/220°C). This generates steam in the pastry, creating air pockets that push up the flakes of fat-coated starch. Flakiness is the result.

Rolling out the Dough

When you're ready to roll out the dough, flour your work surface as lightly as possible. Unwrap one piece of dough and center it on the surface. You're now ready to begin rolling.

- Roll away from you, from the center out, in one direction only.
- Rotate the dough as you roll and use as few strokes as possible, until it is the required size, about 3 to 4 inches (7.5 to 10 cm) larger than the inside size of your pie plate. (Check to ensure that you have rolled the dough to the accurate size by holding the pie plate over the dough.)
- To transfer the rolled dough to the pie plate, carefully roll it onto the rolling pin and lift, positioning it properly over the pie plate. Gently set the crust on the plate, then, using your fingers, push it into the sides of the plate. Trim with scissors or a knife, allowing enough overhang to flute.
- If adding a top crust, fill the pie, roll out the pastry as for the bottom crust and center the crust over the filling. Seal the crusts together using a fork or by fluting.

Prevent a Soggy Bottom Crust

Tip

You can enhance a pastry to suit its filling by adding complementary ingredients. For dessert pies, try adding cinnamon, ginger, nutmeg, or lemon or orange zest to the dry ingredients before combining with the fat.

- Chill the crust for about 20 minutes before filling.
- Brush the crust with lightly beaten egg white, then chill for 15 minutes before filling.
- Bake on the bottom oven rack. For most pies, bake at a high temperature for 10 to 15 minutes, then continue baking at a lower temperature.
- Sprinkle toasted ground nuts on the pastry. Press lightly into the dough with the back of a spoon before filling. This also adds a nice flavor.

Storing Dough

Unrolled pastry dough can be stored in the refrigerator for up to 3 days or frozen for up to 6 months. Thaw dough overnight in the refrigerator before rolling it out.

Rolled pastry dough can be kept in the fridge for up to 3 days or frozen for up to 6 months. Wrap tightly in plastic before freezing. It isn't necessary to thaw rolled dough before baking.

Muffins and Biscuits

Tip

If you're not using all the cups in your muffin tins, don't grease the empty ones. The fat will burn, creating an unpleasant odor and possibly making a mess of your pan.

There is nothing quite like a warm muffin or hot scone in the morning or as a welcome afternoon break with a cup of coffee or tea. These tasty tidbits, which, like quick breads, use baking powder, baking soda or eggs rather than yeast to get their lift, are among the quickest and easiest baked goods to make. Additions such as nuts, chocolate chips and candied fruit, or even cheese and bacon if you're looking for a savory result, make them versatile enough for any occasion.

Making Muffins

There are two ways of preparing muffins. The simplest method combines the liquid and dry ingredients separately, then quickly whisks them together before baking (see Raspberry Muffins, page 152). The second uses the same technique as for butter cake: creaming the butter and sugar, then adding the other ingredients (see Chocolate Zucchini Muffins, page 171). No matter what method you are using, it is important not to overmix the batter once the liquid and dry ingredients are combined. Overmixing encourages the gluten to develop, which produces dense, tough muffins with unappealing holes known as tunnels.

Bake Better Muffins

- Mix muffin batter very lightly to avoid dense, tough results. Don't worry about small lumps; they will disappear during baking.
- For fast cleanup, bake muffins in paper cups set in ungreased pans.
- Use an ice-cream scoop with a wire release to scoop batter into the pans. Your muffins will be uniform in size and have a nicely shaped top.
- Always fill the tins at least two-thirds full.

Tip

When baking muffins and biscuits, whisk the dry ingredients together to blend. This aerates the flour and produces a lighter result.

- If you have not used all the cups in your pan, fill the empty ones with water before placing the pan in the oven. This helps the muffins bake more evenly.
- To retain freshness, store muffins in an airtight container. Alternatively, wrap them in plastic wrap and freeze. When thawing, leave the plastic on and bring the muffins to room temperature.

Biscuits

There is nothing quite like a sweet or savory biscuit fresh out of the oven. Savory biscuits are the perfect accompaniment to soup or stew. Among their other uses, sweetened biscuits can be the basis for delicious shortcakes during the summer months.

Better Biscuits

Biscuits are fast and simple to make. They take just 10 to 15 minutes, although getting the best results demands attention to technique. Here are some tips to improve your biscuit-making technique.

- Thoroughly combine the dry ingredients before cutting in the fat.
- Use cake-and-pastry flour for the most tender texture.
- For a rich flavor, make your biscuits with butter. If flakiness matters most, use shortening.
- Keep the cold ingredients, such as butter and milk, thoroughly chilled and work quickly with them. This helps to ensure flakiness.
- For flaky biscuits, the fat should be the size of small peas. Any smaller and you'll jeopardize flakiness.
- When combining the liquid and dry ingredients, mix with a light touch just until the dry ingredients are moistened. You want a tender biscuit, so keep gluten development to a minimum. Overmixing develops the gluten, which produces a tough result.
- Use a minimum of flour if you're turning out the dough, and handle it as gently and as little as possible to keep it tender.
- A hot oven is important to the success of biscuits. Make sure you have preheated the oven to the specified temperature.

Quick Breads and Yeast Breads

Quick Breads

Quick breads are the loaf versions of muffins. Unlike yeast breads, quick breads, which are made from a softer dough, are leavened with baking powder and baking soda. They do not require kneading. Most can be completed, start to finish, in not much more than an hour. Quick breads, such as Wheaten Bread (page 301) or Date-and-Nut Loaf (page 292), are delicious sliced and toasted.

Here are some things to look out for when making quick breads.

- Be quick when mixing the batter. Stir it as little as possible and bake immediately, as the leaven begins to work once it meets the liquid. Your bread will lose volume if the batter is left to sit.

Pancakes and Crêpes

You may be surprised to learn that pancakes and crêpes are forms of quick bread. Pancakes get their little bit of lift from baking powder or baking soda, whereas crêpes are flat, not leavened. Like with other quick breads, one key to success is to avoid overmixing.

Kneading Dough

There are different ways of kneading dough. Dough can be kneaded in a countertop mixer with a dough hook, by hand or by using a combination of these methods. You can also skip this process by using a bread machine, which does all the work for you.

Tip

If you're in a hurry, bake bread on a rainy day. Dough rises faster when the barometric pressure is falling.

- If your loaf is soggy and fallen in the middle, the dough may have had too much liquid in proportion to the dry ingredients. If it has a coarse texture, it may have had too much fat.
- It is normal for some quick breads to have a lengthwise crack down the top of the loaf, so don't worry if this happens to you.
- For easy removal, line the bottom and sides with greased aluminum foil or parchment paper. To remove the loaves, just lift them out of the pan. Remove the paper and let cool.

Yeast Breads

Homemade bread is one of life's great pleasures. Few things taste quite as good as a crusty loaf fresh from the oven or smell as appetizing as its yeasty aroma wafting through the house. Bread is one of the most versatile foods: it can be eaten on its own, as an accompaniment to a meal, toasted for breakfast or made into a sandwich for lunch. It is also an achievable goal. Making bread isn't complicated or time-consuming. It takes longer from start to finish than other baked goods, but most of that time is devoted to rising, which doesn't require your involvement.

Making Better Bread

Bear the following tips and techniques in mind when you're mixing and working with your dough and you'll improve your results.

- To achieve a supple, more elastic consistency, carefully measure the wet and dry ingredients. If the dough appears too wet, knead in more flour, a little at a time. If the dough appears too dry, knead in 1 tbsp (15 mL) of liquid at a time. If given a choice, start with a soft dough and add flour — it is much easier to knead flour into dough than a liquid.
- Test to see if your dough has enough flour when you are kneading. Slap your open hand against the ball of dough. If your hand comes away clean, the dough has enough flour. Also, if the dough is sticking to the kneading surface, knead in a little more flour, as required.
- To knead dough by hand, turn it out on a lightly floured surface. Kneading is the repetitive process of folding the dough and pushing down on it using the heels of your hands until the appropriate consistency is achieved. When kneading bread, it usually takes about 5 minutes to reach the right consistency.
- Allow dough to rise in a warm place (75 to 85°F/24 to 29°C) and away from drafts that can inhibit rising.
- Several factors can affect the volume of bread. Too much or too little flour or salt will inhibit the gluten's performance, and the dough will not rise to its full potential. To test if it has risen sufficiently on the first rise, insert your fingers into the dough. If an indentation remains, it is ready to punch down. If not, allow more time for the dough to finish rising.
- To prevent bread from sinking in the middle, do not allow the dough to rise too much. (Remember, it will rise more during baking.) Only allow dough to rise until it has doubled in volume. Otherwise, it may

collapse in the oven during baking. On the second rising, the center of the dough should be about $1\frac{1}{2}$ inches (4 cm) from the top of the pan.

- When shaping loaves, you can eliminate large air bubbles by rolling out the dough on a floured board. Roll the dough into a rectangle approximately 9 by 12 inches (23 by 30 cm), then, beginning with one shorter side, roll up jelly roll–style, sealing the roll with the heel of your hand after each turn.

Know Your Ingredients

Flour is key when making bread. When combined with water, the protein in wheat flour forms gluten, which, when kneaded, becomes elastic and supports the rise.

Although you can make excellent bread using Robin Hood All-Purpose Flour, Robin Hood Best For Bread Flour has been specially formulated for baking bread, not only from scratch but also in a bread machine. It will produce breads that are higher in volume with a lighter, more even texture. It is milled from hard wheat and is specially designed for yeast baking. If you prefer, you can replace Robin Hood All-Purpose Flour with an equivalent amount of Robin Hood Best For Bread Flour in any yeast bread recipe.

Yeast is the ingredient that gives bread its voluminous rise. Yeast produces carbon dioxide, which causes dough to rise; alcohol, which produces the wonderful aroma when bread bakes; and acids for flavor. Although working with yeast isn't tricky, it does require attention to detail. Store yeast in a cool, dry place or, for best results, in the freezer, and always check the best-before date prior to using. Using yeast that has passed its peak can limit how much your bread will rise.

Sugar adds flavor to breads and a golden color to the crust. It is also quick food for the yeast. Sugar helps produce the carbon dioxide gas that allows the yeast to activate. However, too much sugar can slow down the yeast action or prevent it from activating. Other sweeteners can be used, if desired. When baking fancy or whole grain breads, you can substitute brown sugar, molasses or honey for granulated sugar if you're feeling like a change. However, you may need to adjust your recipe if you're substituting a liquid for a dry ingredient.

Fats, such as butter, margarine, shortening or oil, help improve the flavor, tenderness and quality of bread. They also have a lubricating effect on the gluten's meshwork. In other words, adding fats will permit your dough to stretch more easily. However, adding too much fat will make your dough crumbly.

Bake for Success

No matter how carefully you've mixed, kneaded and risen your dough, your success can be undermined once it reaches the oven. The following baking tips will improve your results.

- Use shortening to grease your pans. Butter or margarine can cause the bread to stick to the pan or burn.

Tip

Too much flour produces a dry loaf. Don't overflour your hands or work surface when kneading.

Tip

When baking bread, try using Robin Hood Best For Bread Flour. It has a high protein content, which encourages the development of gluten.

Tip

Do not substitute oil for butter or margarine when baking bread. Oil is a liquid ingredient, and butter is a solid. Adjustments in dry and/or liquid ingredients would be necessary to achieve the correct dough consistency.

Tip

For nice light loaves, make sure your dough is just a tiny bit sticky. Too much flour in the dough produces bread that is dry and dense.

Tip

To know for sure if your loaf is done, insert an instant-read thermometer into the center of the loaf. Regular loaves are done when the temperature reads 190°F (90°C). If you're making a whole grain bread, which is more dense, the temperature should be 210°F (100°C).

- Make sure you use the pan size recommended in the recipe. Using an incorrect size pan can result in a flat loaf.
- Since aluminum pans reflect rather than transmit heat, they can result in a lighter-color loaf. For a darker loaf, try using a baking pan made from something other than aluminum.
- Score the loaf before putting it in the oven. Scoring improves the appearance of the finished loaf and allows the carbon dioxide to escape in a pattern. Otherwise, it will erupt randomly.
- For a different look, try baking loaves free-form on a baking sheet that has been sprinkled with cornmeal or greased. Cornmeal will prevent the bread from sticking and give it an interesting texture.
- Position pans in the oven so that the air can circulate between them and they are evenly exposed to the heat. Bread should be baked on a lower rack in the oven unless otherwise directed. If the crust is becoming too brown, cover the pan loosely with aluminum foil for the duration of the baking time.
- Doughs made with water generally yield a crisper crust than those made with milk. To achieve a crisp crust, spritz the loaf with water during baking. For a darker, richer color, brush with an egg wash before baking or brush finished loaves lightly with butter or margarine and return to the oven for 5 to 10 minutes.
- Too much flour, or too little sugar or fat, can toughen your crust. To soften a crust, brush the loaf with melted butter as soon as it comes out of the oven.

Store Breads Appropriately

For a crisp crust, keep bread in a paper bag for up to 2 days. Do not wrap bread in plastic wrap unless you want an especially soft crust. Store bread at room temperature or freeze (refrigeration tends to dry out bread). To freshen bread, heat it, unwrapped, in a 350°F (180°C) oven for 10 to 15 minutes.

If you're planning to freeze your bread, allow it to cool completely first. Frozen bread keeps and freshens well. To freeze, place the cooled loaf in a freezer bag. Remove all of the air from the bag or ice crystals will form during the freezing process. Thaw frozen bread inside the plastic freezer bag so it can absorb the moisture lost during the freezing process. To freshen previously frozen bread, place the thawed loaf on a baking sheet and heat for 10 to 15 minutes in a 350°F (180°C) oven.

Baking at High Altitudes

When baking at altitudes above 3,000 feet (915 m), you may need to adjust baking times and/or temperatures or fine-tune your recipe in other ways. The higher the altitude, the more the leavening gases in breads and cakes expand. Because water and other liquids boil at lower temperatures (which means that the internal heat needed to cook food takes more time to develop because the food is being cooked at a lower temperature), they also evaporate more quickly.

If you are baking at high altitude, you'll want to make sure that your cakes, breads, muffins and cookies are the best they can be, so please read the following tips carefully.

Breads

At high altitudes, the lower air pressure can cause flour to dry out, water takes longer to boil and yeast ferments faster, making dough rise more quickly.

The following tips will show you how to counteract the effects altitude can have on your finished loaf.

Quick Breads: Quick breads vary from muffin-like to cake-like in cell structure. Although the cell structure of biscuits and muffin-type quick breads is firm enough to withstand the increased internal pressure at high altitudes, a bitter or alkaline flavor may result because baking soda or baking powder is not adequately neutralized. In such cases, a slight decrease in the quantity of baking soda or baking powder will usually improve results.

Quick breads with a cake-like texture are more delicately balanced and can usually be improved at high altitudes by following the adjustment recommendations given below for cakes.

Cakes (General)

Most cake recipes perfected at sea level need no modification up to an altitude of 3,000 feet (915 m). Above that, decreased atmospheric pressure may result in excessive rising, which stretches the cell structure of the cake. This makes the texture coarse or breaks the cells, which causes the cake to fall. This can usually be corrected by decreasing the amount of leaven. Also, increasing the baking temperature by 15 to 25°F (5 to 10°C) "sets" the batter before the cells formed by the leavening gas expand too much.

Fast and excessive evaporation of water at high altitudes leads to a higher concentration of sugar, which weakens the cell structure. To counterbalance this problem, sugar is often decreased and liquid is increased.

Only repeated experiments with each recipe can determine the most successful proportions. The accompanying table is a helpful starting point. Try the smaller adjustment first — this may be all that is needed.

Fat, like sugar, weakens the cell structure. Therefore, rich cakes made at high altitudes may also need less fat (1 to 2 tbsp per cup/15 to 30 mL per 250 mL) than when made at sea level. On the other hand, because eggs strengthen cell structure, the addition of an egg may help prevent a "too-rich" cake from falling.

Angel Food and Sponge Cakes: These cakes present special problems at high altitudes. Since the leavening gas for these cakes is largely air, it is important not to beat too much air into the eggs. They should be beaten only until they form a peak that falls over, not until they are stiff and dry. Overbeating causes the air cells to expand too much and leads to their collapse. By using less sugar and more flour,

Cake Recipe Adjustment Guide for High Altitudes

Oven Temperature
Increase by 75°F (25°C) to compensate for faster rising in the oven and slower heating.

Liquids
Based on altitude, for each cup (250 mL), increase liquids by the amount indicated below.

Altitude	Increase Liquids By
more than 3,000 feet (915 m)	1 tbsp (15 mL)
5,000 feet (1,525 m)	2 to 3 tbsp (30 to 45 mL)
8,000 feet (2,440 m)	3 to 4 tbsp (45 to 60 mL)

Sugar
Based on altitude, for each cup (250 mL), decrease sugar by the amount indicated below.

Altitude	Decrease Sugar By
more than 3,000 feet (915 m)	1 tbsp (15 mL)
5,000 feet (1,525 m)	2 to 3 tbsp (30 to 45 mL)
7,000 to 8,000 feet (2,135 to 2,440 m)	3 to 4 tbsp (45 to 60 mL)

Flour
Based on altitude, for each cup (250 mL), decrease flour by the amount indicated below.

Altitude	Decrease Flour By
more than 3,000 feet (915 m)	1 tbsp (15 mL)
5,000 feet (1,525 m)	2 tbsp (30 mL)
6,500 feet (1,980 m)	3 tbsp (45 mL)

Baking Powder
Based on altitude, for each teaspoon (5 mL), decrease baking powder by the amount indicated below.

Altitude	Decrease Baking Powder By
more than 3,000 feet (915 m)	$\frac{1}{8}$ tsp (0.5 mL)
5,000 feet (1,525 m)	$\frac{1}{8}$ to $\frac{1}{4}$ tsp (0.5 to 1 mL)
6,500 feet (1,980 m)	$\frac{1}{4}$ tsp (1 mL)

and increasing the baking temperature, you will also strengthen the cell structure of foam-type cakes.

Cookies

Although many sea-level cookie recipes yield acceptable results at high altitudes, they can often be improved by a slight increase in baking temperature; a slight decrease in baking powder or soda, fat and sugar; and/or a slight increase in liquid ingredients and flour. Many cookie recipes contain a higher proportion of sugar and fat than necessary, even at low altitudes.

Ingredients

Flour, sugar and fat are the primary ingredients from which delicious baked goods evolve. Add eggs, leavening agents, chocolate, nuts and vanilla and you've opened the door to a cornucopia of mouthwatering delights: crusty bread, tender muffins and luscious cakes.

Flour

Flour is the most fundamental ingredient in baking, and the protein content of the flour you use plays a big role in your baking results. With so many different kinds of flours on the market, it's easy to become confused about what kind to use. The safest strategy is to always have all-purpose flour on hand since it can meet all your baking needs. Robin Hood All-Purpose Flour has a relatively high protein content and is made from a combination of soft and hard wheat. It can be used in any of the recipes in this book — from pastry, breads and crusty rolls to cakes, cookies and muffins — and will consistently produce excellent results.

If you prefer, you can substitute other kinds of flour that are appropriate for specific recipes. You can even mix and match flours if you're so inclined. Try altering the texture of cookies, muffins or quick breads by using half all-purpose flour and half whole wheat in a recipe that calls for all-purpose flour. When making biscuits, cakes, pastry and other more-tender baked goods, feel free to substitute 1 cup plus 2 tbsp (280 mL) of Robin Hood Best For Cake & Pastry Flour for every cup (250 mL) of all-purpose flour. Cake & Pastry flour has a lower protein content than all-purpose flour, so it will produce lighter biscuits and cakes with a finer crumb. When baking yeast breads, feel free to use 1 cup (250 mL) Robin Hood Best For Bread Flour for every cup (250 mL) of all-purpose flour. The high protein level of this flour encourages the development of gluten, which helps ensure sturdy dough.

Fats

Fats play many roles in baking, from adding flavor and influencing the texture and moistness of baked goods to creating creaminess and the smooth feel on the tongue known as "mouth appeal." They tenderize by coating the flour, preventing it from absorbing water and developing gluten. There are two kinds of fat: those that are solid at room temperature and those that are liquid. The more liquid the fat, the more thoroughly it coats the flour and the more tender the result. When creamed with sugar, solid fats, such as butter, contribute to leavening. Their different melting points and their composition determines how they interact with other ingredients.

Butter is the most popular fat in baking. However, from a technical standpoint, it is not the best fat to use. It is only 80 per cent solid fat and it has a low melting point, which means that all-butter pie crusts will be less flaky than those made with shortening or lard, and cookies made with butter rather than shortening won't hold their shape as well.

To Sift or Not to Sift

Unless otherwise specified, it is not necessary to sift flour before using it in a recipe. Just spoon it lightly into a dry measuring cup and level it off using the back of a knife. Do not pack the flour down in the cup (see Measure Accurately, page 13).

Tip

Store flour in a clean, airtight container in a cool, dry place. White flour lasts for approximately 1 year, and whole wheat lasts for approximately 6 months. To extend the shelf life of flour, store it in sealed containers in the refrigerator or freezer.

Tip

Because baked
goods are so
dependent upon their
ingredients, always
use the best you can
buy to ensure quality
results. Your baking
will only be as good
as the ingredients
you use.

Tip

If your shortbread
recipe calls for
granulated sugar,
for best results, use
superfine or fruit
sugar, both of which
are readily available
in supermarkets.

Tip

When storing icing
sugar, be sure to
keep the bag airtight
to prevent it from
clumping.

Tip

Because of its high
moisture content,
brown sugar tends
to lump. Store it in an
airtight jar or heavy
plastic bag in a cool,
dry place. If it does
harden, put it in a
plastic bag with a slice
of apple, seal tightly
and set aside. In a few
days it will be soft
enough to use.

Margarine is imitation butter made from vegetable oils. Like butter, it is only 80 per cent solid fat. It can be used instead of butter in any recipe, unless flavor is an issue; for instance, in Basic Butter Frosting (see recipe, page 216). When using margarine, be sure not to use brands classified as "spreads," which contain a high percentage of water and do not perform well in baking.

Vegetable shortening, which is made from vegetable oils, is 100 per cent fat and has a high melting point. This means it is excellent for producing flaky biscuits and pie crusts.

Lard, too, is 100 per cent fat and has a high melting point. Like shortening, it is a desirable fat to use when flakiness is valued. Because it is derived from meat, it is particularly good for use in savory recipes.

Vegetable oils, which are liquid at room temperature, are 100 per cent fat. They cannot be used in recipes that are based on creaming and do not contribute to leavening. Because they are liquid at room temperature, they thoroughly coat the flour when blended, which prevents gluten development. The results are tender but not flaky. Vegetable oil is often used in quick breads and muffins, and occasionally in pie crust, where it produces a tender but not flaky crust.

Sweeteners

Sweeteners, such as sugars and honey, give baked goods much of their appeal.

White granulated sugar is the most commonly used sugar in baking. It has a mild flavor, is free-flowing and doesn't require sifting. It works well for every baking need.

Icing sugar, also known as confectioner's sugar, is a powdered white sugar with added cornstarch, which prevents it from lumping and crystallizing. Icing sugar is used primarily in frostings and glazes. It dissolves almost instantly in liquids, which makes it wonderful for sweetening whipping cream.

Because of its tendency to clump, icing sugar should always be sifted before it is added to a recipe. When using, spoon it into a dry measure, level it off, then sift. All the recipes in this book have been based on this method rather than the reverse (sifting then measuring).

Although there are a few unrefined **brown sugars** on the market, such as Demerara, turbinado and sugar in the raw, traditional brown sugar is refined granulated sugar with added molasses. The darker the color, the more molasses and moisture refined brown sugar contains and, therefore, the stronger its flavor. In cooking, refined light and dark brown sugars and unrefined brown are interchangeable. Brown sugar is often used for toppings, streusels and some frostings. It isn't used much in tender cake batters because it makes them heavier and too moist. However, brown sugar works well in many recipes for cookies and bars, which benefit from its denser texture and caramel flavor.

Other sweeteners, such as molasses, honey, corn syrup and maple syrup, are effective, depending on the recipe used. Molasses, a by-product of refined sugar, is rich and dark and adds flavor and moisture to recipes. It has a strong flavor; if it is not to your liking, you can substitute an equivalent amount of honey, corn syrup or maple syrup in recipes. When making the recipes in this book, don't substitute liquid sweeteners for granulated or brown sugars, as they lack the texture and flavor of sugar and may break down when heated.

Eggs

Eggs are indispensable in baking and play many different roles in recipes. Eggs contribute to leavening, texture, color, flavor, volume and richness in baked goods. They also add nutritional value and act as an emulsifier, binding ingredients together.

Store eggs in their container in the refrigerator (not on the door, which is not cold enough). One hour before baking, remove the quantity you need from the refrigerator to allow them to come to room temperature. Temperature plays an important role in baking, as it changes the properties of many ingredients; for instance, adding cold eggs to a creamed mixture will solidify the butter you've worked so hard to make light and fluffy. This decreases the volumizing potential of the mixture and increases the likelihood of producing a flat, dense cake.

Separating Eggs

If you need to separate eggs for a recipe, do this as soon as you take them from the refrigerator, since eggs separate better when they are cold. After separating the yolks from the whites, cover them tightly with plastic wrap to keep them from drying out and leave them at room temperature for an hour. This also helps ensure that you achieve maximum volume after beating the whites. For food safety reasons, do not leave eggs at room temperature for longer than an hour.

Replacing Eggs

Egg replacement products can replace whole eggs in many recipes. Before using, check package information to make sure the product is appropriate for your use. If you are concerned about cholesterol — a large egg yolk contains about 5.6 g of fat and 274 mg of cholesterol — you can substitute $1\frac{1}{2}$ egg whites for one of the eggs in any recipe. We don't recommend eliminating the egg yolks entirely, as they contribute to tenderness.

Leavening Agents

Leavens are the ingredients that cause baked goods to rise. Some ingredients, such as eggs, contain leavening agents, but baked goods usually rely on biological or chemical leavens, such as yeast, baking powder or baking soda for their lift. Cream of tartar is another common leaven, which is most often used to stabilize meringue.

Yeast

Yeast is the leavening agent that gives bread its voluminous rise (see page 27 for more on yeast). In these recipes, we have used active dry yeast and quick-rise instant yeast.

Tip

All the recipes in this book have been tested using large eggs. When baking, always use this size, as recipes are traditionally tested with large eggs. If you need to substitute, assume that $1\frac{1}{2}$ medium eggs can be substituted for one large. To substitute for half an egg, beat a medium egg and measure out 2 tbsp (30 mL).

Active dry yeast is the most common form of yeast available in supermarkets, likely because in addition to being one of the first yeasts made for consumers, it is easy to store and has a relatively long shelf life. Active dry yeast needs to be "proofed," which means it is brought to life when mixed with lukewarm water. To test the vitality of active dry yeast, dissolve 1 tsp (5 mL) sugar in ¼ cup (50 mL) lukewarm water. Sprinkle in yeast and allow to stand for 10 minutes. This is known as "proofing yeast." If the yeast does not bubble within 10 minutes, it is no longer active.

Quick-rise instant yeast does not require proofing. It is simply mixed with the other dry ingredients. It also takes less time to rise than active dry yeast, so the traditional first rising is replaced by a 15-minute resting period.

Bread Machine Yeast

This form of yeast is specifically designed for use in bread machines. It is instant dry yeast and can be used in all your bread baking. Mix it directly into the dry ingredients.

Baking Soda

Baking soda is the chemical sodium bicarbonate. When combined with acids, such as yogurt, buttermilk, fruit juice or even chocolate, baking soda creates bubbles of carbon dioxide that cause batter and dough to rise. Batters that contain baking soda should be baked as soon as they are mixed because it starts to act as soon as it comes into contact with an acid. If left to sit, its leavening power will have exhausted itself by the time the batter reaches the oven.

Baking Powder

Baking powder is baking soda combined with an acid, so it works better as a leaven in batters that are low in acidity. Keep baking powder tightly covered in a cool, dry place and replace it every 6 months to ensure it maintains its potency.

Tip

Check your baking powder and baking soda regularly to make sure they are still active. Stir 1 tsp (5 mL) of baking powder into ½ cup (125 mL) hot water. If it does not bubble immediately, throw it out. To test baking soda, stir 1 tsp (5 mL) into 2 tbsp (25 mL) white vinegar. If it does not bubble, discard it.

Dairy Products

The recipes in this book were tested using 2% **milk**, the most commonly used dairy product. You can also use whole milk (homogenized), low-fat (1%) and nonfat (skim) milk, although your results will vary slightly because of the different fat contents. If you're lactose intolerant, substitute an equal amount of lactose-reduced milk.

Buttermilk, which is made from low-fat milk and a bacterial culture, is particularly useful in batters that require a bit of acidity, which helps produce a tender crumb. You can find buttermilk in the dairy case of your supermarket or you can make your own. For 1 cup (250 mL) buttermilk, mix 1 tbsp (15 mL) vinegar or lemon juice with enough milk to make 1 cup (250 mL); let stand for 5 minutes, then stir.

Two kinds of **cream** also appear in some of the recipes in this book: half-and-half cream, which has a 10% milk fat (M.F.) content, and whipping cream, which has 35% M.F. and is also called heavy cream. Table cream, which has 18% M.F., can be used in recipes that call for half-and-half or light cream, but it should not be substituted in recipes that call for whipping cream.

Tip
When buying dairy products, be sure to check the expiration date and buy those that are most current. Don't let dairy products sit out at room temperature. This reduces their storage life.

Evaporated milk is a canned product made by evaporating milk to half its volume. It has a mild caramel taste and comes in whole or low-fat versions. Mixed with an equal amount of water, evaporated milk can be substituted for milk.

Sweetened condensed milk is evaporated milk that has been reduced further and sweetened. It is available in whole and low-fat versions. All the recipes in this book were tested using the whole (or regular) version.

Regular **sour cream** is about 14% M.F., and all the recipes in this book have been tested using 14% M.F. sour cream. Sour cream is also available in low-fat and nonfat versions. Use regular or low-fat sour cream for baking. We don't recommend the nonfat variety, as it can sometimes result in poor texture and quality of baked goods.

Some of the recipes call for **yogurt,** which is available in plain and flavored varieties, with a range of fat contents. As with sour cream, don't use the nonfat type for baking.

Cream cheese is often used in baking, most commonly for cheesecake. These recipes have been tested using full-fat cream cheese. However, you can usually substitute a lower-fat version, if desired. For smooth blending, use blocks of cream cheese that have been softened to room temperature. Do not use tubs of soft, spreadable cream cheese unless specified in the recipe.

Chocolate

Chocolate is one of the most popular ingredients in baking. In fact, it is second only to vanilla as a flavoring and is a must-have ingredient that no baker should ever be without. Because it is so popular, consumers can now choose from a wide variety of chocolate products, which can make it difficult to know what to buy.

Basically, the quality of chocolate is determined by the blend of cocoa beans used to make it, the roasting and processing methods, and the percentage of chocolate liquor (not alcohol) it contains. The best varieties contain at least 70 per cent chocolate liquor. Chocolate varies dramatically in flavor and texture. Taste it to determine the brand that suits you best. Some cooks use different brands of chocolate for different products — one for cakes, another for cookies, a third for puddings and custards, and so on.

Always keep a supply of semi-sweet, bittersweet and unsweetened squares on hand for chopping, grating or melting in recipes. Chocolate chips, which are formulated to soften but hold their shape during baking, should also be a pantry staple. In general, chocolate chips are used in and on top of cakes and cookies, while squares are used for melting.

White chocolate, a blend of sugar, cocoa butter, milk solids and vanilla, is not really chocolate but has become a popular ingredient in baking. It is available in squares and chips.

Storing Chocolate
Unsweetened, semi-sweet and bittersweet chocolates will keep for up to 2 years in a cool place. White chocolate, which contains dairy solids, should be used more quickly than that. Store chocolate in the refrigerator only as a last resort.

Tip

Dutch-process cocoa, which is identified as such on the package, is treated with a mild alkali solution to neutralize the chocolate's natural acidity. It is less bitter than natural cocoa, and many people feel it produces superior results in baking. It is usually more expensive than natural cocoa, so you be the judge.

Tip

To make chocolate curls, heat a chocolate square in the microwave for 10 seconds, just until it's warm but not melted. Using a vegetable peeler, shave to make curls.

Cocoa Powder

Cocoa powder is a dry unsweetened powder made from chocolate liquor with most of the cocoa butter removed. There are several kinds of cocoa on the market. When baking, use natural cocoa or Dutch-process cocoa, not one of the sweetened versions, which are made for drinking. Because cocoa tends to clump during storage, it should be measured then sifted before using. If you run out of unsweetened chocolate, 1 oz (28 g) of unsweetened chocolate can be replaced with 3 tbsp (45 mL) cocoa powder plus 1 tbsp (15 mL) butter, margarine or shortening.

Melting Chocolate

Chocolate is fussy about how it is melted, and if it isn't treated appropriately, it will "seize," leaving you with an unusable glob. However, as long as you follow instructions and ensure that the chocolate does not come into contact with water in the process of melting, you should be successful. (It's OK to melt chocolate in a liquid such as cream as long as the hard chocolate is placed in the liquid before the melting process begins.)

Basically, chocolate can be melted three different ways. In all cases, coarsely chop the chocolate before heating. The safest (and slowest) way is to melt the pieces in the top of a double boiler or a bowl set over hot (not boiling) water, stirring frequently, until the chocolate is smooth and melted. Or you can place the pieces in a small saucepan and melt them over low heat, stirring constantly, until the mixture is smooth. Many cooks find a microwave oven useful for this job. Place the chopped chocolate in a microwaveable bowl and heat at Medium (50%) until almost melted, about 1 minute per ounce (28 g). (Times will vary with microwave power.) Remove from microwave and stir until the chunks are completely melted. Be sure not to cover chocolate when melting, as this will create steam, which will cause the chocolate to seize.

Nuts

Nuts add flavor and texture to many baked goods. However, because they are high in fat, we recommend you store them in the freezer to keep them fresh. When you're ready to use them, let them thaw and use as directed — or, for optimum flavor, toast before using in a recipe.

To toast nuts: Spread nuts in a single layer on a baking sheet. Bake at 350°F (180°C) for 5 to 10 minutes, stirring often, until golden and fragrant. Chopped nuts will take less time to toast than whole nuts. For hazelnuts, rub off skins in a tea towel while warm. The weight equivalent of 1 cup (250 mL) lightly toasted nuts is approximately 3.8 oz (100 g).

Measuring Nuts

When indicating quantities of nuts to be used, the recipes in this book specify that the nuts are chopped first, then measured. This means the ingredient reads: $\frac{1}{2}$ cup (125 mL) finely chopped almonds, not $\frac{1}{2}$ cup (125 mL) almonds, finely chopped. In the second notation, the nuts would be measured, then chopped. "Finely chopped" means the nuts should be chopped to a uniform size of less than $\frac{1}{8}$ inch (3 mm) in diameter.

Coconut

Like nuts, coconut should be stored in the freezer, and its flavor improves when it is toasted. Flaked or shredded coconut both work well in baking. Whether you use sweetened or unsweetened is a matter of choice — they are interchangeable in recipes.

To toast coconut: Spread in a single layer on a cookie sheet. Bake at 350°F (180°C) for about 5 minutes, stirring often, until it begins to brown. Watch carefully because coconut burns quickly.

Flavorings

The two most common flavorings used in baking are vanilla and almond extract. Although they are more expensive, we recommend the use of pure extracts, which produce much better results than their artificial counterparts. Extracts should be at room temperature when they are added to ingredients.

Spices

Spices are essential to the success of many recipes, and you should always have a good selection on hand. To make the recipes in this book, you'll need allspice, cinnamon, cloves, nutmeg and ginger. For the savories, make sure you have black pepper, oregano, paprika, rosemary, thyme and savory. Store your spices in tightly sealed glass containers in a cool dark place. Once spices are ground, they lose their potency quite quickly. Consequently, we recommend you buy them in small amounts and replace them within 6 to 9 months.

Fruit

Fruit is a great addition to many recipes. Fresh fruit in season is usually the ideal, but if it is unavailable, canned or frozen fruit can usually be substituted.

Keep a supply of the common types of **canned fruit,** such as pineapple (crushed, chunks and rings), apricots, peaches and mandarins, in your pantry. When using canned fruit, be aware that the proportion of solid fruit to liquid will vary from brand to brand, as will the size of fruit pieces, and this may affect the quantity required.

Frozen fruit, such as rhubarb and berries, can be purchased as needed. Cranberries are a great addition to many breads and desserts but they can be hard to find during the summer. As a result, we recommend that you keep a few bags in your freezer.

Keep **dried fruit,** such as raisins, apricots, cranberries and dates on hand for general baking and buy specialty items, such as candied fruit, for holiday baking or as needed.

Fresh Fruit Yields

Often recipes call for a quantity such as 1 tsp (5 mL) lemon zest or 1 cup (250 mL) mashed bananas. To make your baking easier, we've provided some measured yields for fresh fruits commonly used in baking.

- **Lemons:** One medium lemon yields about $\frac{1}{4}$ cup (50 mL) juice and 2 tsp (10 mL) grated zest.
- **Oranges:** Two or three medium oranges yield about 1 cup (250 mL) juice and 3 tbsp (45 mL) grated zest.
- **Apples:** One pound (500 g) or three medium apples yield about 2 cups (500 mL) chopped cored apples.
- **Bananas:** One pound or two or three large bananas yield about 1 cup (250 mL) mashed bananas.
- **Strawberries or raspberries:** One pound (500 g) contains about 4 cups (1 L) whole, 3 cups (750 mL) sliced or 2 cups (500 mL) crushed berries.

Emergency Substitution Tables

Whenever possible, use ingredients that the recipe calls for. But in a pinch, here are some substitutions you can use to avoid a last-minute trip to the store.

Leavens

1 tsp (5 mL) baking powder = $\frac{1}{4}$ tsp (1 mL) baking soda plus $\frac{1}{2}$ tsp (2 mL) cream of tartar

1 tsp (5 mL) double-acting baking powder = $1\frac{1}{2}$ tsp (7 mL) single-acting baking powder (phosphate or tartrate)

Flour

1 cup (250 mL) all-purpose flour, without sifting = 1 cup (250 mL) plus 2 tbsp (30 mL) cake & pastry flour, without sifting

1 cup (250 mL) cake & pastry flour, without sifting = 1 cup (250 mL) minus 2 tbsp (30 mL) all-purpose flour, without sifting

1 cup (250 mL) self-rising flour, without sifting = 1 cup (250 mL) all-purpose flour plus $1\frac{1}{2}$ tsp (7 mL) baking powder plus $\frac{1}{2}$ tsp (2 mL) salt

1 cup (250 mL) whole wheat flour = 1 cup (250 mL) all-purpose flour

Sweeteners

1 cup (250 mL) granulated sugar = 1 cup (250 mL) firmly packed brown sugar

corn syrup = equal amount of maple syrup

1 cup (250 mL) honey = $1\frac{1}{4}$ cups (300 mL) granulated sugar plus $\frac{1}{4}$ cup (50 mL) liquid

Chocolate

1 square (1 oz/28 g) unsweetened chocolate = 3 tbsp (45 mL) cocoa powder plus 1 tbsp (15 mL) shortening, butter or margarine

Dairy Products

1 cup (250 mL) butter = 1 cup (250 mL) firm margarine **or** 1 cup (250 mL) shortening plus 2 tbsp (30 mL) water

1 cup (250 mL) buttermilk or soured milk = 1 tbsp (15 mL) lemon juice or vinegar plus whole milk to make 1 cup (250 mL) (let stand for 5 minutes before using)

Dairy Products

1 cup (250 mL) whole milk = $\frac{1}{2}$ cup (125 mL) evaporated milk plus $\frac{1}{2}$ cup (125 mL) water **or** 1 cup (250 mL) skim milk plus 2 tbsp (30 mL) butter

1 cup (250 mL) buttermilk = 1 cup (250 mL) plain yogurt

1 cup (250 mL) sour cream = $\frac{7}{8}$ cup (225 mL) buttermilk or plain yogurt plus 3 tbsp (45 mL) butter

1 cup (250 mL) whipping (35%) cream (for use in cooking, not for whipping) = $\frac{3}{4}$ cup (175 mL) whole milk plus $\frac{1}{3}$ cup (75 mL) butter

Cereals and Grains

1 cup (250 mL) fine dry bread crumbs = $\frac{3}{4}$ cup (175 mL) cracker crumbs

$\frac{1}{4}$ cup (50 mL) dry bread crumbs = 1 slice of bread

$\frac{1}{2}$ cup (125 mL) soft bread crumbs = 1 slice of bread

$\frac{1}{4}$ cup (50 mL) dry bread crumbs (for mixing with ground meats) = $\frac{3}{4}$ cup (175 mL) rolled oats

Egg

1 whole egg = 2 egg whites

Tomato Products

4 medium tomatoes, chopped = $2\frac{1}{4}$ cups (550 mL) canned tomatoes, including juice

$1\frac{1}{3}$ cups (325 mL) chopped fresh tomatoes, lightly simmered = 1 cup (250 mL) canned tomatoes

1 cup (250 mL) tomato juice = $\frac{1}{2}$ cup (125 mL) tomato sauce plus $\frac{1}{2}$ cup (125 mL) water

2 cups (500 mL) tomato sauce = $\frac{3}{4}$ cup (175 mL) tomato paste plus 1 cup (250 mL) water

1 cup (250 mL) ketchup or chili sauce = 1 cup (250 mL) tomato sauce plus $\frac{1}{4}$ cup (50 mL) sugar plus 2 tbsp (30 mL) vinegar

1 tbsp (15 mL) tomato paste = 1 tbsp (15 mL) ketchup

Seasonings

1 medium onion = 1 tbsp (15 mL) minced dried onion **or** 1 tsp (5 mL) onion powder

1 clove garlic = $\frac{1}{8}$ tsp (0.5 mL) garlic powder **or** 1 tsp (5 mL) garlic salt (reduce salt in recipe by $\frac{1}{2}$ tsp/2 mL)

1 tbsp (15 mL) fresh herbs = 1 tsp (5 mL) crushed dried herbs

1 tbsp (15 mL) chopped fresh chives = 1 tbsp (15 mL) chopped green onion tops

1 tsp (5 mL) lemon juice = $\frac{1}{2}$ tsp (2 mL) vinegar

1 tbsp (15 mL) prepared mustard = 1 tsp (5 mL) dry mustard

1 drop hot pepper sauce = pinch cayenne or red pepper

2 tbsp (30 mL) soy sauce = 1 tbsp (15 mL) Worcestershire sauce plus 2 tsp (10 mL) water

$1\frac{1}{2}$ tsp (7 mL) Worcestershire sauce = 1 tbsp (15 mL) soy sauce plus dash hot pepper sauce

1 tsp (5 mL) allspice = $\frac{1}{2}$ tsp (2 mL) cinnamon plus pinch ground cloves

1 tbsp (15 mL) chopped gingerroot = 1 tsp (5 mL) dried ginger **or** 1 tbsp (15 mL) candied ginger with sugar washed off

Miscellaneous

1 tbsp (15 mL) cornstarch, for thickening = 2 tbsp (30 mL) all-purpose flour in sauces and gravies

$\frac{1}{2}$ cup (125 mL) raisins = $\frac{1}{2}$ cup (125 mL) dried cranberries **or** plumped pitted prunes **or** dates, chopped

$2\frac{1}{4}$ tsp (11 mL) active dry yeast = 1 package active dry yeast **or** 1 compressed yeast cake

Triple Chocolate Cookies and
Chocolate Almond Macaroon Logs

Cookies

Triple Chocolate Cookies

Three chocolates in one cookie! Try these cookies warm, then again after they have cooled — if there are any left.

Makes about 4 dozen cookies

Preparation: 20 minutes

Baking: 10 minutes

Freezing: excellent

TIPS

Chocolate chips can develop a whitish coating when stored. Don't worry — it disappears with baking.

Use cooking spray or a light coating of shortening to grease cookie sheets. Do not use butter, as it will burn. You don't have to regrease sheets between batches, but do wipe off any crumbs or sugar with a paper towel.

- *Preheat oven to 375°F (190°C)*
- *Cookie sheet, greased*

1 cup	butter, softened	250 mL
¾ cup	packed brown sugar	175 mL
½ cup	granulated sugar	125 mL
1	egg	1
2 tsp	vanilla	10 mL
1⅔ cups	Robin Hood All-Purpose Flour	400 mL
⅓ cup	unsweetened cocoa powder, sifted	75 mL
1 tsp	baking soda	5 mL
½ tsp	salt	2 mL
1 cup	semi-sweet chocolate chips	250 mL
1 cup	milk chocolate chips	250 mL
1 cup	coarsely chopped pecans	250 mL

1. Cream butter in a large bowl on medium speed of electric mixer until light. Gradually beat in brown and granulated sugars, egg and vanilla until smooth. Combine flour, cocoa powder, baking soda and salt. Gradually add to creamed mixture, beating on low speed until blended. Stir in semi-sweet and milk chocolate chips and pecans.

2. Drop dough by tablespoonfuls (15 mL), about 2 inches (5 cm) apart, on prepared cookie sheet. Bake for 8 to 10 minutes or until set. Cool for 5 minutes on sheet, then transfer to rack and cool completely.

Variation

Vary the kind of chips and nuts to suit your taste.

Chocolate Almond Macaroon Logs

If you like coconut, you'll love these cookies, which have the texture and taste of a mini candy bar.

Makes about 30 cookies

Preparation: 25 minutes

Baking: 12 minutes

Chilling: 5 minutes

Freezing: excellent (not dipped)

TIPS

Use flaked or shredded coconut for the best texture.

Store coconut in the freezer to keep it fresh. It tends to dry out quickly.

Don't be surprised: the egg whites are not beaten until stiff as they are in many macaroon recipes.

● *Preheat oven to 350°F (180°C)*
● *Cookie sheet, lined with parchment paper*

3 cups	flaked coconut	750 mL
1/2 cup	granulated sugar	125 mL
6 tbsp	Robin Hood All-Purpose Flour	90 mL
4	egg whites	4
1 tsp	vanilla	5 mL
1/2 cup	finely chopped almonds	125 mL
2	squares (each 1 oz/28 g) semi-sweet chocolate, melted	2

1. Combine coconut, sugar and flour in a large bowl. Add egg whites and vanilla. Mix well. Stir in almonds.
2. Shape heaping tablespoonfuls (20 mL) of mixture into logs and place on prepared cookie sheet.
3. Bake for 8 to 12 minutes or until golden around edges. Cool cookies completely on sheets, then remove from pan.
4. Dip ends of cooled cookies in melted chocolate. Place on waxed paper. Chill until chocolate is set, about 5 minutes.

Variation

Omit chocolate or dip one end of each cookie in white chocolate and the other in semi-sweet.

Chunky Chocolate Oatmeal Cookies

Sweet oatmeal dough loaded with chunks of chocolate produces a wholesome yet decadent cookie.

Makes about 4 dozen cookies

Preparation: 20 minutes
Baking: 12 minutes
Freezing: excellent

TIPS

Large-flake oats look and taste wonderful in these cookies. They give them a great homemade appearance that brings back childhood memories.

When baking a lot of cookies, it's helpful to have cookie sheets without sides and a supply of parchment paper. You can line the sheets with parchment paper, then slip the paper and cookies off once the cookies have finished baking. While one batch is baking, you can be preparing the next on a sheet of parchment spread on the counter. Slip it onto the first available cookie sheet and bake.

- *Preheat oven to 350°F (180°C)*
- *Cookie sheet, greased*

½ cup	butter, softened	125 mL
½ cup	granulated sugar	125 mL
½ cup	packed brown sugar	125 mL
1	egg	1
1 tsp	vanilla	5 mL
1 cup	Robin Hood Oats	250 mL
¾ cup	Robin Hood All-Purpose Flour	175 mL
½ tsp	baking soda	2 mL
¼ tsp	salt	1 mL
2 cups	coarsely chopped semi-sweet chocolate (10 squares, each 1 oz/28 g)	500 mL
1 cup	coarsely chopped pecans	250 mL

1. Beat butter, granulated and brown sugars, egg and vanilla until thoroughly blended.

2. Combine oats, flour, baking soda and salt. Gradually add to butter mixture, mixing until smooth. Stir in chocolate and pecans. Mix well.

3. Drop dough by heaping tablespoonfuls (20 mL), about 2 inches (5 cm) apart, onto prepared cookie sheet. Bake for 10 to 12 minutes or until golden. Cool for 5 minutes on sheet, then transfer to rack and cool completely.

Variations

Replace some or all of the chocolate with dried cranberries.

Almonds, walnuts and hazelnuts are nice alternatives to the pecans.

Oatmeal Chocolate Chip Cookies

Always a favorite with the young and the young at heart.

Makes about 3½ dozen cookies

Preparation: 15 minutes

Baking: 15 minutes

Freezing: excellent

TIP

Underbake for chewy cookies. Bake longer for crisp ones.

- *Preheat oven to 350°F (180°C)*
- *Cookie sheet, greased*

¾ cup	butter or margarine, softened	175 mL
¾ cup	packed brown sugar	175 mL
⅓ cup	granulated sugar	75 mL
1	egg	1
2 tbsp	water	30 mL
2 tsp	vanilla	10 mL
¾ cup	Robin Hood All-Purpose or Whole Wheat Flour	175 mL
¾ tsp	baking soda	3 mL
2½ cups	Robin Hood Oats	625 mL
1½ cups	semi-sweet chocolate chips	375 mL

1. Cream butter, brown and granulated sugars, egg, water and vanilla in large bowl on medium speed of electric mixer until light and creamy.

2. Combine flour and baking soda. Add to creamed mixture, beating on low speed until blended. Stir in oats and chocolate chips. Drop dough by heaping tablespoonfuls (20 mL) about 2 inches (5 cm) apart onto prepared cookie sheet. Bake for 12 to 15 minutes or until light golden. Cool for 5 minutes on sheet, then transfer to rack and cool completely.

Variation
Replace chips with raisins.

Chocolatey Chocolate Chip Cookies

The ultimate triple chocolate cookie! Warning: they're addictive, especially warm.

Makes about 4 dozen cookies

Preparation: 20 minutes
Baking: 10 minutes
Freezing: excellent

TIP

Chocolate chips can develop a whitish coating when stored. Don't worry — it disappears with baking.

- *Preheat oven to 375°F (190°C)*
- *Cookie sheet, greased*

1⅔ cups	Robin Hood All-Purpose Flour	400 mL
⅓ cup	cocoa powder	75 mL
1 tsp	baking soda	5 mL
½ tsp	salt	2 mL
1 cup	butter or margarine, softened	250 mL
¾ cup	packed brown sugar	175 mL
½ cup	granulated sugar	125 mL
1	egg	1
2 tsp	vanilla	10 mL
1 cup	semi-sweet chocolate chips	250 mL
1 cup	white chocolate chips	250 mL
1 cup	coarsely chopped pecans	250 mL

1. Stir together flour, cocoa powder, baking soda and salt. Set aside.
2. Cream butter in large bowl on medium speed of electric mixer until light. Gradually beat in brown and granulated sugars, egg and vanilla until smooth. Blend in dry ingredients on low speed. Mix well. Stir in chocolate chips and nuts.
3. Drop dough by tablespoonfuls (15 mL) about 2 inches (5 cm) apart on prepared cookie sheet. Bake for 8 to 10 minutes or until set. Cool for 5 minutes on sheet, then transfer to rack and cool completely.

Variation
Vary the kind of chips and nuts to suit your taste.

Chocolate Eclipse Cookies

The blend of light and dark dough gives these cookies tremendous eye appeal. They taste good, too.

TIPS

If you prefer a chewy texture, underbake these cookies by about 2 minutes. They will become quite crisp if you extend the baking time by about 2 minutes.

Don't forget to leave room on the cookie sheet for spreading. Cookies, particularly those made with butter, flatten and spread during baking.

Don't improvise when trying a new recipe. Read it through carefully and follow the instructions to the letter. You can make it your own way next time.

- Preheat oven to 375°F (190°C)
- Cookie sheet, ungreased

1 cup	butter, softened	250 mL
1 cup	granulated sugar	250 mL
1 cup	packed brown sugar	250 mL
2	eggs	2
1 tsp	vanilla	5 mL
2½ cups	Robin Hood All-Purpose Flour	625 mL
1 tsp	baking soda	5 mL
¼ tsp	salt	1 mL
¾ cup	semi-sweet chocolate chips, melted	175 mL
1 cup	semi-sweet chocolate chips	250 mL
1 cup	white chocolate chips	250 mL

1. Beat butter, granulated and brown sugars, eggs and vanilla until light and creamy.

2. Combine flour, baking soda and salt. Gradually add to creamed mixture, beating until blended. Divide dough in half. Stir melted chocolate and semi-sweet chocolate chips into one portion of dough. Stir white chocolate chips into the other.

3. To shape, take small spoonful of each dough and roll together into a 1-inch (2.5 cm) ball. Place about 2 inches (5 cm) apart on cookie sheet.

4. Bake for 8 to 12 minutes or until set. Cool for 5 minutes on sheet, then transfer to rack and cool completely.

Variations
Add 1 tsp (5 mL) grated orange zest to one portion of dough.

Add ½ cup (125 mL) chopped nuts to one portion of dough.

Chocolate Chunk Pecan Cookies

Don't count on these lasting very long.

TIP

For storage, pack cookies in single layers between waxed paper in airtight container.

- *Preheat oven to 375°F (190°C)*
- *Cookie sheet, ungreased*

1 cup	butter or margarine, softened	250 mL
¾ cup	packed brown sugar	175 mL
½ cup	granulated sugar	125 mL
1	egg	1
1 tsp	vanilla	5 mL
2 cups	Robin Hood All-Purpose Flour	500 mL
1 tsp	baking soda	5 mL
¼ tsp	salt	1 mL
6	squares (each 1 oz/28 g) semi-sweet chocolate, chopped	6
¾ cup	coarsely chopped pecans	175 mL

1. Cream butter, brown and granulated sugars, egg and vanilla in large bowl on medium speed of electric mixer until light and creamy.

2. Combine flour, baking soda and salt. Add to creamed mixture, beating on low speed until blended. Stir in chocolate and pecans.

3. Drop dough by heaping tablespoonfuls (20 mL) about 2 inches (5 cm) apart onto prepared cookie sheet. Bake for 9 to 12 minutes or until light golden. Cool for 5 minutes on sheet, then transfer to rack and cool completely.

Variation
Choose your favorite nut and chocolate.

White Chocolate Crisps

A chewy cookie with a crunch. Chunks of chocolate make cookies look quite decadent.

Makes about 4 dozen cookies

Preparation: 15 minutes
Baking: 10 minutes
Freezing: excellent

TIP

You can use 1 cup (250 mL) white chocolate chips in place of the chopped chocolate.

- Preheat oven to 375°F (190°C)
- Cookie sheet, greased

1 cup	shortening	250 mL
¾ cup	packed brown sugar	175 mL
½ cup	granulated sugar	125 mL
1	egg	1
2 tbsp	milk	30 mL
1½ tsp	vanilla	7 mL
1¾ cups	Robin Hood All-Purpose Flour	425 mL
1 tsp	baking soda	5 mL
½ tsp	salt	2 mL
6	squares (each 1 oz/28 g) white chocolate, coarsely chopped	6
1½ cups	crisp rice cereal	375 mL

1. Cream shortening, brown and granulated sugars, egg, milk and vanilla in large bowl on medium speed of electric mixer until light and creamy.
2. Combine flour, baking soda and salt. Add to creamed mixture, beating at low speed until blended. Stir in chocolate and cereal. Mix well.
3. Drop dough by heaping tablespoonfuls (20 mL) about 2 inches (5 cm) apart onto prepared cookie sheet. Bake for 8 to 10 minutes or until light golden. Cool for 5 minutes on sheet, then transfer to rack and cool completely.

Variation
Try milk chocolate chips in place of white.

Chocolate Caramel Pecan Cookies

Try to resist eating these while they're still warm!

TIP

The caramels will melt and tend to stick. Use parchment paper for easy removal from pan.

- Preheat oven to 375°F (190°C)
- Cookie sheet, lined with parchment paper or well greased

1 cup	butter or margarine, softened	250 mL
¾ cup	packed brown sugar	175 mL
½ cup	granulated sugar	125 mL
1	egg	1
1½ tsp	vanilla	7 mL
2 cups	Robin Hood All-Purpose Flour	500 mL
1 tsp	baking soda	5 mL
¼ tsp	salt	1 mL
6	squares (each 1 oz/28 g) semi-sweet chocolate, chopped	6
25	individual vanilla caramels, quartered	25
¾ cup	coarsely chopped pecans	175 mL

1. Cream butter, brown and granulated sugars, egg and vanilla in large bowl on medium speed of electric mixer until light and creamy.

2. Combine flour, baking soda and salt. Add to creamed mixture, beating on low speed until blended. Stir in chocolate, caramels and pecans.

3. Drop dough by tablespoonfuls (15 mL) about 2 inches (5 cm) apart onto prepared cookie sheet. Bake for 8 to 12 minutes or until light golden. Cool for 5 minutes on sheet, then transfer to rack and cool completely.

Variations

Try white chocolate and almonds for another great taste.

Use chocolate caramels for a more chocolatey taste.

Chocolate Butterscotch Almond Crisps

This crispy, crunchy cookie has a great butterscotch taste. What more could you want?

Makes about 4 dozen cookies

Preparation: 20 minutes

Baking: 14 minutes

Freezing: excellent

TIPS

Crisp rice cereal works well in cookies. It stays crisp during baking and adds an appealing crunch to every bite. Crushed cornflakes produce a similar result.

Be sure to use fresh chips. They melt much more easily than stale ones.

Cool cookies completely before storing, and pack similar cookies together. You don't want to mix moist and dry cookies, as dry cookies will absorb moisture and become soft, and you don't want strong flavors like ginger to mix with subtle, buttery shortbread.

- *Preheat oven to 375°F (190°C)*
- *Cookie sheet, ungreased*

1/2 cup	milk chocolate chips	125 mL
1/2 cup	butter, softened	125 mL
2/3 cup	packed brown sugar	150 mL
1	egg	1
1 tsp	vanilla	5 mL
1 1/3 cups	Robin Hood All-Purpose Flour	325 mL
1 tsp	baking soda	5 mL
1/4 tsp	salt	1 mL
1 1/2 cups	crisp rice cereal	375 mL
1 cup	butterscotch chips	250 mL
1/2 cup	slivered almonds	125 mL

1. Heat milk chocolate chips in small saucepan over low heat, stirring constantly, until smooth and melted.
2. Beat butter, brown sugar, egg and vanilla until thoroughly blended. Stir in melted chocolate.
3. Combine flour, baking soda and salt. Gradually add to butter mixture, mixing until smooth. Stir in cereal, butterscotch chips and almonds. Mix well.
4. Shape dough into 1-inch (2.5 cm) balls. Place on cookie sheet, about 2 inches (5 cm) apart. Flatten slightly with a fork dipped in sugar. Bake for 10 to 14 minutes or until light golden. Cool for 5 minutes on sheet, then transfer to rack and cool completely.

Variation

Use butterscotch chips in place of the milk chocolate chips for a stronger butterscotch flavor.

Chunky Chocolate Almond Cookies

These chunky, nutty cookies are a delightful treat. Don't count on them lasting too long.

Makes about 3½ dozen cookies

Preparation: 20 minutes

Baking: 12 minutes

Freezing: excellent

TIPS

Bake cookies in the center of the oven to ensure that the tops and bottoms are evenly browned. If the cookies at the back of the oven are browning more quickly than those in front, your oven bakes unevenly. Turn the sheet around halfway through baking.

To store cookies, cool completely, then pack in single layers in an airtight container, spreading waxed paper between each layer to prevent sticking.

- *Preheat oven to 375°F (190°C)*
- *Cookie sheet, ungreased*

1 cup	butter, softened	250 mL
¾ cup	packed brown sugar	175 mL
½ cup	granulated sugar	125 mL
1	egg	1
1 tsp	vanilla	5 mL
2 cups	Robin Hood All-Purpose Flour	500 mL
1 tsp	baking soda	5 mL
¼ tsp	salt	1 mL
10	squares (each 1 oz/28 g) semi-sweet chocolate, chopped	10
¾ cup	slivered almonds	175 mL

1. Beat butter, brown and granulated sugars, egg and vanilla in a large bowl on medium speed of electric mixer until light and creamy.
2. Combine flour, baking soda and salt. Add to creamed mixture, beating on low speed until blended. Stir in chocolate and almonds.
3. Drop dough by heaping tablespoonfuls (20 mL), about 2 inches (5 cm) apart, onto prepared cookie sheet. Bake for 10 to 12 minutes or until light golden. Cool for 5 minutes on sheet, then transfer to rack and cool completely.

Variations

Replace chopped chocolate with 2 cups (500 mL) chocolate chips.

Replace almonds with pecans or walnuts.

Chocoholic's Dream Cookies

The next time you need a gift for a chocolate lover, bake a batch of these mouthwatering cookies instead of buying a box of chocolates.

Makes about 4½ dozen cookies

Preparation: 20 minutes

Baking: 14 minutes

Freezing: excellent

TIPS

Be careful not to overbake these cookies. They will firm up as they cool.

Toasting nuts before baking improves their flavor. Spread nuts out in a single layer on a baking sheet and bake at 350°F (180°C) for 10 minutes, or less if using chopped nuts, watching carefully and stirring often. Cool before using.

Pack completely cooled cookies in single layers in an airtight container with a sheet of parchment or waxed paper between each layer.

- *Preheat oven to 325°F (160°C)*
- *Cookie sheet, ungreased*

6	squares (each 1 oz/28 g) semi-sweet chocolate, chopped	6
4	squares (each 1 oz/28 g) unsweetened chocolate, chopped	4
6 tbsp	butter	90 mL
1¼ cups	granulated sugar	300 mL
3	eggs	3
1 tsp	vanilla	5 mL
1 cup	Robin Hood All-Purpose Flour	250 mL
1 tsp	baking powder	5 mL
¼ tsp	salt	1 mL
2 cups	coarsely chopped nuts	500 mL

1. Heat semi-sweet chocolate, unsweetened chocolate and butter in a medium saucepan over low heat, stirring, until smooth. Remove from heat. Stir in sugar. Add eggs, one at a time, beating after each addition. Stir in vanilla.

2. Combine flour, baking powder and salt. Gradually add to chocolate mixture, mixing until blended. Stir in nuts.

3. Drop dough by tablespoonfuls (15 mL), about 2 inches (5 cm) apart, onto cookie sheet. Bake for 12 to 14 minutes or until set. Cool for 5 minutes on sheet, then transfer to rack and cool completely.

Variations

Any nuts work well in this recipe.

Omit nuts if desired, but remember you'll end up with fewer cookies.

Peanut Butter Cookies

No cookbook is complete without this old-fashioned favorite.

Makes about 5 dozen cookies

Preparation: 25 minutes

Baking: 15 minutes

Freezing: excellent

TIPS

Use smooth, creamy peanut butter for baking cookies. If you prefer a nutty texture, add chopped peanuts (see Variation).

For a change, use a potato masher to make an attractive design on top of the cookies, instead of the traditional crisscross fork pattern.

Top each cookie with a peanut before baking.

Make cookie sandwiches by spreading raspberry jam or Peanut Butter Frosting (see recipe, right) on the bottom of one cookie and placing a second cookie on top, bottom side down.

If you have leftover frosting, store it in the refrigerator for up to 2 weeks. Bring to room temperature before using.

If you're using this frosting on a cake, sprinkle chopped peanuts on the top and/ or sides of the cake for added crunch.

- *Preheat oven to 375°F (190°C)*
- *Cookie sheet, ungreased*

1 cup	butter, softened	250 mL
1 cup	smooth peanut butter	250 mL
1 cup	granulated sugar	250 mL
1 cup	packed brown sugar	250 mL
2	eggs	2
2½ cups	Robin Hood All-Purpose Flour	625 mL
2 tsp	baking soda	10 mL
¼ tsp	salt	1 mL

1. Cream butter, peanut butter and granulated and brown sugars until light and creamy. Beat in eggs, one at a time, mixing well after each addition.
2. Combine flour, baking soda and salt. Add to creamed mixture, beating until blended. Shape dough into 1-inch (2.5 cm) balls. Place on cookie sheet. Press flat with a fork dipped in sugar or flour.
3. Bake for 12 to 15 minutes or until set and golden. Cool for 5 minutes on sheet, then transfer to rack and cool completely.

Variation
Stir ½ cup (125 mL) finely chopped peanuts into the dough after the dry ingredients have been added.

Peanut Butter Frosting

- *Makes about 3 cups (750 mL) frosting*
- *Enough to fill and frost a 9-inch (23 cm) 2-layer cake*

⅔ cup	creamy peanut butter	150 mL
3½ cups	icing sugar, sifted	875 mL
½ to ⅔ cup	milk	125 to 150 mL

1. In a large mixer bowl, on medium speed of electric mixer, beat peanut butter until creamy. Gradually add icing sugar alternately with milk, beating until smooth and creamy.

Peanut Butter Oatmeal Cookies

An abundance of nuts makes these cookies a great choice for the whole family.

Makes about 5 dozen cookies

Preparation: 25 minutes
Baking: 12 minutes
Freezing: excellent

TIPS

To add more fiber, substitute Robin Hood Whole Wheat Flour for the all-purpose.

For a different flavour, substitute dried fruit, such as raisins or cranberries, for the chips.

Choose light-color cookie sheets with low or no sides for even baking. Dark ones absorb more heat and may cause cookies to overbrown on the bottom.

- *Preheat oven to 375°F (190°C)*
- *Cookie sheet, ungreased*

¾ cup	butter, softened	175 mL
½ cup	creamy peanut butter	125 mL
1 cup	granulated sugar	250 mL
½ cup	packed brown sugar	125 mL
2	eggs	2
1 tsp	vanilla	5 mL
1¼ cups	Robin Hood All-Purpose Flour	300 mL
1 tsp	baking powder	5 mL
½ tsp	baking soda	2 mL
2 cups	Robin Hood Oats	500 mL
1 cup	semi-sweet chocolate chips	250 mL
1 cup	coarsely chopped pecans	250 mL

1. Beat butter, peanut butter, granulated and brown sugars, eggs and vanilla until thoroughly blended.

2. Combine flour, baking powder and baking soda. Add to butter mixture gradually, beating until blended. Stir in oats, chocolate chips and pecans. Mix well.

3. Drop dough by heaping tablespoonfuls (20 mL), about 2 inches (5 cm) apart, onto cookie sheet. Bake for 10 to 12 minutes or until golden. Cool for 5 minutes on sheet, then transfer to rack and cool completely.

Variations

Replace semi-sweet chocolate chips with butterscotch or peanut butter chips.

Replace pecans with peanuts.

Chewy Peanut Butter Chocolate Chip Cookies

The combination of peanut butter and chocolate is always hard to resist.

Makes about 3 dozen cookies

Preparation: 20 minutes

Baking: 12 minutes

Freezing: excellent

TIPS

Honey-roasted peanuts give great flavor to cookies.

Cool cookies completely on a wire rack or they will soften when stored.

For a crisper cookie, increase the baking time by 2 minutes.

If you accidentally overbake a batch of cookies but haven't burned them, crumble them and sprinkle over fruit, ice cream or yogurt.

- *Preheat oven to 350°F (180°C)*
- *Cookie sheet, ungreased*

½ cup	butter, softened	125 mL
½ cup	smooth peanut butter	125 mL
½ cup	granulated sugar	125 mL
½ cup	packed brown sugar	125 mL
1	egg	1
1 tsp	vanilla	5 mL
¾ cup	Robin Hood All-Purpose Flour	175 mL
½ tsp	baking soda	2 mL
½ cup	coarsely chopped peanuts	125 mL
½ cup	chocolate chips	125 mL

1. Beat butter, peanut butter, granulated and brown sugars, egg and vanilla until thoroughly blended.

2. Combine flour and baking soda. Add to butter mixture, beating until thoroughly blended. Stir in peanuts and chocolate chips.

3. Drop dough by heaping tablespoonfuls (20 mL), about 2 inches (5 cm) apart, on cookie sheet. If desired, press down lightly with a fork dipped in flour for a patterned look. Bake for 10 to 12 minutes or until golden. Cool for 5 minutes on sheet, then transfer to rack and cool completely.

Variation
For an extra hit of peanut, use peanut butter chips.

White Chocolate Macadamia Nut Cookies

Crisp or chewy, these cookies are every bit as delectable as their photo on page 61 suggests.

Makes about 6 dozen cookies

Preparation: 20 minutes

Baking: 12 minutes

Freezing: excellent

TIPS

Store flour in the freezer if you don't use it often to keep it fresh.

Baked cookies can be frozen for up to 6 months.

- Preheat oven to 375°F (190°C)
- Cookie sheet, greased

1½ cups	butter, softened	375 mL
1½ cups	packed brown sugar	375 mL
1 cup	granulated sugar	250 mL
2	eggs	2
1 tsp	vanilla	5 mL
3¼ cups	Robin Hood All-Purpose Flour	800 mL
1 tsp	baking soda	5 mL
1 tsp	salt	5 mL
12	squares (each 1 oz/28 g) white chocolate, chopped	12
2 cups	coarsely chopped macadamia nuts	500 mL

1. Beat butter, brown and granulated sugars, eggs and vanilla until thoroughly blended. Combine flour, baking soda and salt. Add to butter mixture, mixing until thoroughly blended. Stir in chocolate and nuts.

2. Drop dough by heaping tablespoonfuls (20 mL), about 2 inches (5 cm) apart, on prepared cookie sheet. Bake for 8 to 12 minutes or until light golden. Cool for 5 minutes on sheet, then transfer to rack and cool completely.

Variation

Use any of your favorite nuts in this recipe. If nut allergies are a problem, omit the nuts completely and add more chocolate (about 1 cup/250 mL, or 5 squares, each 1 oz/28 g, coarsely chopped).

Super Chunky Peanut Butter Chocolate Cookies

Here's a cookie that looks and tastes just great. The mild peanut butter flavor is enhanced with an abundance of peanuts and chocolate.

Makes about 4 dozen cookies

Preparation: 20 minutes
Baking: 12 minutes
Freezing: excellent

TIPS

Buy good-quality chocolate to chop for cookies. Cookies are only as good as the ingredients you use to make them.

Bittersweet chocolate has a more intense flavor than semi-sweet, but the two can be used interchangeably.

If you're using nonstick bakeware, be sure to use a spatula that won't scratch the surface, such as one made of plastic, when you remove the cookies.

- *Preheat oven to 350°F (180°C)*
- *Cookie sheet, greased*

½ cup	butter, softened	125 mL
⅓ cup	smooth peanut butter	75 mL
¾ cup	packed brown sugar	175 mL
¼ cup	granulated sugar	50 mL
1	egg	1
1 tsp	vanilla	5 mL
1 cup	Robin Hood All-Purpose Flour	250 mL
½ tsp	baking soda	2 mL
¼ tsp	salt	1 mL
2 cups	coarsely chopped semi-sweet chocolate (12 oz/375 g)	500 mL
1 cup	coarsely chopped peanuts	250 mL

1. Beat butter, peanut butter, brown and granulated sugars, egg and vanilla until thoroughly blended.
2. Combine flour, baking soda and salt. Gradually add to butter mixture, mixing until smooth. Stir in chocolate and peanuts.
3. Drop dough by heaping tablespoonfuls (20 mL), about 2 inches (5 cm) apart, onto prepared cookie sheet. Bake for 10 to 12 minutes or until golden. Cool for 5 minutes on sheet, then transfer to rack and cool completely.

Variation
Use dark brown sugar rather than golden for a more intense butterscotch taste.

Nice 'n' Nutty Refrigerator Cookies

With a roll or two of this dough in your fridge, you'll be able to bake delicious cookies at a moment's notice.

Makes about 8 dozen cookies

Preparation: 20 minutes
Chilling: overnight
Baking: 12 minutes
Freezing: excellent

TIPS

Small plastic-wrap boxes work well for shaping square cookies. Line the box with plastic wrap and pack the dough firmly into it.

For perfectly round cookies, wash and dry frozen juice containers and fill with dough. When you're ready to bake, remove the bottom of the container, push the chilled dough out and slice.

If nut allergies are a problem, replace the nuts in this recipe with candied fruit or mini chocolate chips.

Dark and nonstick cookie sheets bake faster. Always set your timer for the minimum time. You can return the cookies to the oven if they are underbaked.

Store rolls of dough in the refrigerator for up to 3 months or the freezer for up to 6 months.

- *Preheat oven to 375°F (190°C)*
- *Cookie sheet, ungreased*

1 cup	butter, softened	250 mL
1 cup	granulated sugar	250 mL
2	eggs	2
1½ tsp	vanilla	7 mL
2½ cups	Robin Hood All-Purpose Flour	625 mL
1 tsp	baking powder	5 mL
½ tsp	baking soda	2 mL
¼ tsp	salt	1 mL
½ cup	chopped almonds	125 mL
½ cup	chopped pecans	125 mL
½ cup	chopped hazelnuts	125 mL

1. Beat butter, sugar, eggs and vanilla until light and creamy. Combine flour, baking powder, baking soda and salt. Add to creamed mixture gradually, mixing until smooth. Stir in almonds, pecans and hazelnuts.

2. Shape dough into two rolls, each about 1½ inches (4 cm) in diameter. Wrap in waxed paper or plastic wrap and chill overnight.

3. Cut roll into ¼-inch (0.5 cm) slices. Place 2 inches (5 cm) apart on cookie sheet. Bake for 8 to 12 minutes or until light golden. Cool for 5 minutes on sheet, then transfer to rack and cool completely.

Variation

Any nut works well in this recipe. Use your favorites, keeping the total amount at 1½ cups (375 mL).

Crisp Butterscotch Oatmeal Cookies

These cookies are ideal for the cookie jar. They stay crisp and make a treat the whole family can enjoy.

Makes about 4 dozen cookies

Preparation: 20 minutes

Baking: 20 minutes

Freezing: excellent

TIPS

If you prefer, use Robin Hood Unbleached or Whole Wheat Flour in cookie recipes in the same quantity as all-purpose flour. If you have never used whole wheat flour, you may want to begin by blending it with an equal amount of all-purpose flour. Whole wheat flour gives baked goods a pleasant nutty flavour and a slightly coarse and drier texture.

Crisp cookies are good for shipping. They travel well and stay fresh longer than soft ones. A gift of homemade cookies is always welcome.

There is no egg in this recipe, making these cookies a good choice for people with egg allergies.

- *Preheat oven to 350°F (180°C)*
- *Cookie sheet, greased*

1 cup	butter, softened	250 mL
1 cup	packed brown sugar	250 mL
1/4 cup	water or milk	50 mL
1 tsp	vanilla	5 mL
1 3/4 cups	Robin Hood All-Purpose Flour	425 mL
1/2 tsp	baking soda	2 mL
1/4 tsp	salt	1 mL
2 cups	Robin Hood Oats	500 mL
1 1/2 cups	butterscotch chips	375 mL
1/2 cup	flaked coconut	125 mL

1. Beat butter, brown sugar, water and vanilla in large bowl on medium speed of electric mixer until thoroughly blended.
2. Combine flour, baking soda and salt. Gradually add to butter mixture, beating on low speed until blended. Stir in oats, butterscotch chips and coconut.
3. Drop dough by tablespoonfuls (15 mL), about 2 inches (5 cm) apart, onto prepared cookie sheet. Press flat with fork dipped in sugar or flour. Bake for 15 to 20 minutes or until crisp and golden. Cool for 5 minutes on sheet, then transfer to rack and cool completely.

Variation

Replace butterscotch chips with semi-sweet chocolate chips, dried cranberries or raisins.

Butterscotch Honey Cereal Crunchies

Kids will try to convince you they love their breakfast cereal this way.

Makes about 6 dozen cookies

Preparation: 20 minutes

Baking: 10 minutes

Freezing: excellent

TIP

Replace baking powder and soda every six months.

- *Preheat oven to 375°F (190°C)*
- *Cookie sheet, ungreased*

2 cups	Robin Hood All-Purpose Flour	500 mL
1 tsp	baking soda	5 mL
½ tsp	baking powder	2 mL
1 cup	butter or margarine, softened	250 mL
½ cup	granulated sugar	125 mL
½ cup	packed brown sugar	125 mL
⅓ cup	liquid honey	75 mL
1	egg	1
1¾ cups	butterscotch chips	425 mL
2 cups	cornflakes cereal, slightly crushed	500 mL
2 cups	crisp rice cereal	500 mL
1 cup	flaked coconut, optional	250 mL

1. Combine flour, baking soda and baking powder.
2. Cream butter, granulated and brown sugars, honey and egg thoroughly. Add dry ingredients to creamed mixture, mixing well. Stir in chips, cornflakes, rice cereal, and coconut, if using.
3. Drop dough by tablespoonfuls (15 mL) about 2 inches (5 cm) apart onto cookie sheet. Bake for 8 to 10 minutes or until golden. Cool for 5 minutes on sheet, then transfer to rack and cool completely.

Variation
Replace butterscotch chips with peanut butter chips.

Toffee Almond Crunch Cookies

Chewy but crunchy — a delectable treat!

Makes about 4½ dozen cookies

Preparation: 20 minutes
Baking: 12 minutes
Freezing: excellent

- *Preheat oven to 375°F (190°C)*
- *Cookie sheet, greased*

1 cup	shortening	250 mL
¾ cup	packed brown sugar	175 mL
½ cup	granulated sugar	125 mL
1	egg	1
2 tbsp	milk	30 mL
2 tsp	vanilla	10 mL
1¾ cups	Robin Hood All-Purpose Flour	425 mL
¾ cup	Robin Hood Oats	175 mL
1 tsp	baking soda	5 mL
¼ tsp	salt	1 mL
4	(each 1.4 oz/39 g) crunchy toffee chocolate bars, coarsely crushed (1 cup/250 mL)	4
1 cup	slivered almonds	250 mL

1. Cream shortening, brown and granulated sugars, egg, milk and vanilla in large bowl on medium speed of electric mixer until light and creamy.

2. Combine flour, oats, baking soda and salt. Add to creamed mixture, beating on low speed until blended. Stir in chocolate bars and almonds.

3. Drop dough by tablespoonfuls (15 mL) about 2 inches (5 cm) apart onto prepared cookie sheet. Bake for 8 to 12 minutes or until light golden. Cool for 5 minutes on sheet, then transfer to rack and cool completely.

Sesame Snap Wafers

Try different seeds for a new look and taste (see photo, page 69).

Makes about 6 dozen cookies

Preparation: 10 minutes

Baking: 9 minutes

Freezing: not recommended

TIPS

Store in airtight containers.

Black sesame seeds are available in Asian grocery stores.

- *Preheat oven to 350°F (180°C)*
- *Cookie sheet, lined with parchment paper or lightly greased aluminum foil*

$^2/_3$ cup	Robin Hood All-Purpose Flour	150 mL
$^1/_4$ tsp	baking powder	1 mL
$^1/_2$ cup	butter or margarine, softened	125 mL
1 cup	packed brown sugar	250 mL
1	egg	1
1 tsp	vanilla	5 mL
$1^1/_4$ cups	sesame seeds, toasted	300 mL

1. Combine flour and baking powder.
2. Cream butter, sugar, egg and vanilla. Add flour mixture. Mix until combined. Stir in seeds.
3. Drop by teaspoonfuls (5 mL) about 2 inches (5 cm) apart onto prepared cookie sheet. Bake for 6 to 9 minutes or until lightly browned. Cool for 5 minutes on sheet, then transfer to rack and cool completely.

Variation
Try with half black sesame seeds or flaxseeds and half white sesame seeds.

Oatmeal Jam Sandwich Cookies

An easy-to-make turnover. Fill with your favorite flavor of jam.

Makes about 2½ dozen sandwich cookies

Preparation: 25 minutes

Baking: 13 minutes

Freezing: excellent filled or unfilled

TIPS

Filled cookies become soft and chewy with standing.

Cookies can be stored unfilled, then assembled when desired.

- Preheat oven to 350°F (180°C)
- Cookie sheet, greased

¾ cup	butter, softened	175 mL
1 cup	packed brown sugar	250 mL
½ cup	granulated sugar	125 mL
1	egg	1
2 tbsp	water	30 mL
2 tsp	vanilla	10 mL
⅔ cup	Robin Hood All-Purpose or Whole Wheat Flour	150 mL
¾ tsp	baking soda	3 mL
½ tsp	cinnamon	2 mL
3 cups	Robin Hood Oats	750 mL
1½ cups	raspberry jam	375 mL

1. Cream butter, brown and granulated sugars, egg, water and vanilla in large bowl on medium speed of electric mixer until light and fluffy.

2. Combine flour, baking soda and cinnamon. Add to creamed mixture, beating on low speed until blended. Stir in oats. Drop dough by tablespoonfuls (15 mL) about 2 inches (5 cm) apart onto prepared cookie sheet. Bake for 10 to 13 minutes or until edges are golden brown. Cool for 5 minutes on sheet, then transfer to rack and cool completely.

3. Spread jam on flat side of half of the cookies. Top with another cookie to form sandwiches.

Year-Round Shortbread

Although shortbread is a holiday tradition, it is delicious any time of the year.

Makes about 3 dozen cookies

Preparation: 25 minutes

Baking: 25 minutes

Freezing: not recommended

TIPS

Shortbread is best stored in a cool place or the refrigerator for up to 1 month. Freezing alters its texture.

Always use butter when making shortbread. Margarine just doesn't have the flavor.

Shortbread is great for any holiday. Use a variety of cutters to suit different holidays, such as bunnies, hearts or trees.

For best results when making shortbread, use superfine or fruit sugar instead of granulated.

- *Preheat oven to 300°F (150°C)*
- *Cookie sheet, ungreased*

1 cup	butter, softened	250 mL
½ cup	superfine sugar	125 mL
2 cups	Robin Hood All-Purpose Flour	500 mL
2 tbsp	cornstarch	30 mL

1. Cream butter and sugar in a mixing bowl until light and creamy. Stir in flour and cornstarch. Mix well, then knead with hands, blending in flour thoroughly to form a smooth dough.

2. Roll out dough on lightly floured surface to ¼-inch (0.5 cm) thickness. Cut into desired shapes using cookie cutter dipped in flour. Place on cookie sheet. Sprinkle with colored sugar or decorate as desired with cherries and nuts.

3. Bake for 15 to 25 minutes or until cookies just start to brown around edges. (The time will depend on the size of the cookies.) Cool for 5 minutes on sheet, then transfer to rack and cool completely.

Variation

Add ½ cup (125 mL) finely chopped nuts to the dough.

Apricot Oat Chews

This chewy apricot version of oatmeal cookies is simply yummy.

Makes about 4 dozen cookies

Preparation: 20 minutes

Baking: 12 minutes

Freezing: excellent

TIPS

Oatmeal cookies tend to dry out when they are stored. Freeze extras for up to 3 months to keep them fresh.

Use scissors to cut apricots easily. Spray blades with cooking spray so the fruit doesn't stick.

- Preheat oven to 375°F (190°C)
- Cookie sheet, ungreased

1 cup	butter, softened	250 mL
¾ cup	packed brown sugar	175 mL
½ cup	granulated sugar	125 mL
1	egg	1
½ tsp	almond extract	2 mL
2½ cups	Robin Hood Oats	625 mL
1 cup	Robin Hood All-Purpose Flour	250 mL
1 tsp	baking soda	5 mL
1 cup	chopped dried apricots	250 mL

1. Beat butter, brown and granulated sugars, egg and almond extract until thoroughly blended.
2. Combine oats, flour and baking soda. Add to butter mixture gradually, beating until well blended. Stir in apricots.
3. Drop dough by heaping tablespoonfuls (20 mL), about 2 inches (5 cm) apart, onto cookie sheet. Bake for 8 to 12 minutes or until golden. Cool for 5 minutes on sheet, then transfer to rack and cool completely.

Variation

Add a drizzle of icing for an attractive presentation. Leave these cookies plain for everyday eating or if you're planning to store them.

Golden Molasses Gems

Crunchy on the outside, chewy on the inside, these spicy cookies will bring back memories of early childhood and Grandma's homemade treats.

Makes about 4 dozen cookies

Preparation: 20 minutes

Baking: 14 minutes

Freezing: excellent

TIP

The cookies flatten and spread during baking, forming an interesting cracked top.

- Preheat oven to 350°F (180°C)
- Cookie sheet, greased

¾ cup	shortening	175 mL
1 cup	granulated sugar	250 mL
¼ cup	molasses	50 mL
1	egg	1
2 cups	Robin Hood All-Purpose Flour	500 mL
2 tsp	baking soda	10 mL
1 tsp	ground cinnamon	5 mL
½ tsp	ground cloves	2 mL
½ tsp	ground ginger	2 mL
¼ tsp	salt	1 mL
1 cup	raisins	250 mL
	Granulated sugar	

1. Cream shortening and sugar in large bowl on medium speed of electric mixer until light and fluffy. Add molasses and egg. Mix well.

2. Combine flour, baking soda, cinnamon, cloves, ginger and salt. Add to creamed mixture. Mix well. Stir in raisins. If desired, cover and refrigerate for about 1 hour for easy shaping.

3. Shape dough into 1-inch (2.5 cm) balls. Roll in sugar to coat well. Place about 2 inches (5 cm) apart on prepared cookie sheet. Bake for 10 to 14 minutes or until set. Cool for 5 minutes on sheet, then transfer to rack and cool completely.

Variation
Adjust the spice level to suit your own taste.

Hazelnut Biscotti

Enjoy biscotti dipped in a steaming cup of coffee or hot chocolate for a great treat any time of the day.

Makes about 30 biscotti

Preparation: 20 minutes
Baking: 50 minutes
Freezing: excellent

TIPS

If using ground nuts in a dough or batter, grind them with a small amount of the flour called for in the recipe. This helps keep them from clumping together.

The hard texture of biscotti makes them ideal for storage, which means you can bake them ahead for convenience.

Be sure to bake biscotti thoroughly to achieve the right hard, dry texture. Otherwise, they will soften and become slightly chewy when stored.

Biscotti make a wonderful hostess gift. Pack them standing up in a large mug or glass jar tied with a colorful ribbon.

For added taste and presentation flair, dip both ends of the biscotti in melted chocolate.

- Preheat oven to 350°F (180°C)
- Cookie sheet, greased

2	eggs	2
¾ cup	granulated sugar	175 mL
½ cup	vegetable oil	125 mL
1 tbsp	grated lemon zest	15 mL
1 tsp	vanilla	5 mL
2 cups	Robin Hood All-Purpose Flour	500 mL
⅓ cup	ground hazelnuts	75 mL
1¼ tsp	baking powder	6 mL
¼ tsp	salt	1 mL
1 cup	coarsely chopped hazelnuts	250 mL

1. Beat eggs, sugar, oil, lemon zest and vanilla until smooth and blended.

2. Combine flour, ground hazelnuts, baking powder and salt. Add to egg mixture, stirring until blended. Add chopped nuts. Knead until dough is smooth and holds together. (There are a lot of nuts, so work them in well with your hands. The dough comes together quite easily.)

3. Divide dough in half. Shape each half into a log about 6 inches (15 cm) long. Place about 4 inches (10 cm) apart on prepared cookie sheet. Flatten logs until they are 3 inches (7.5 cm) wide, leaving top slightly rounded.

4. Bake for 30 minutes or until light golden. Remove from oven. Cool on rack for 15 minutes. Transfer to a cutting board. Cut into ½-inch (1 cm) thick slices. Arrange cut side up on cookie sheet and bake for 10 minutes longer. Turn slices over and bake for 5 to 10 minutes longer or until golden and crisp. Cool for 5 minutes on sheet, then transfer to rack and cool completely. Store in an airtight container for up to 2 weeks.

Variation
Replace hazelnuts with almonds, and vanilla with ½ tsp (2 mL) almond extract.

Ice Cream Sandwiches

Always keep a supply of these on hand for a wonderful snack.

Makes about 30 sandwich cookies or 60 plain cookies

Preparation: 25 minutes

Baking: 13 minutes

Freezing: excellent

TIP

Freeze sandwiches or plain cookies to fill when desired. Add chocolate chips or other favorites to the ice cream.

- *Preheat oven to 350°F (180°C)*
- *Cookie sheet, greased*

1¼ cups	shortening	300 mL
1 cup	granulated sugar	250 mL
⅔ cup	packed brown sugar	150 mL
1	egg	1
¼ cup	liquid honey	50 mL
¼ cup	milk	50 mL
2½ cups	Robin Hood All-Purpose Flour	625 mL
1½ cups	Robin Hood Oats	375 mL
1 tsp	baking soda	5 mL
½ tsp	salt	2 mL
1½ cups	flaked coconut	375 mL
1 cup	chopped nuts (walnuts, pecans or peanuts)	250 mL
	Ice cream or frozen yogurt	

1. Cream shortening, granulated and brown sugars, egg, honey and milk in large bowl on medium speed of electric mixer until light and creamy.

2. Combine flour, oats, baking soda and salt. Add to creamed mixture gradually, beating at low speed until thoroughly blended. Stir in coconut and nuts.

3. Drop dough by heaping tablespoonfuls (20 mL) about 2 inches (5 cm) apart onto prepared cookie sheet. Bake for 10 to 13 minutes or until golden. Cool for 5 minutes on sheet, then transfer to rack and cool completely.

4. Assembly: Spread one cookie with generous amount of ice cream. Top with another cookie; press down lightly. Repeat with remaining cookies and ice cream. Wrap individually and freeze.

Candied Ginger Rounds

If you like ginger, this is the cookie for you.

Makes about 4 dozen cookies

Preparation: 20 minutes
Chilling: 1 hour
Baking: 12 minutes
Freezing: excellent

TIPS

Buy crystallized ginger when you are ready to use it, as it hardens quickly. Candied ginger is best when it is slightly soft and has a strong ginger flavor. It's usually sold in the baking section with other candied fruit.

- *Preheat oven to 375°F (190°C)*
- *Cookie sheet, ungreased*

1 cup	butter, softened	250 mL
¾ cup	granulated sugar	175 mL
¾ cup	packed brown sugar	175 mL
2	eggs	2
2¾ cups	Robin Hood All-Purpose Flour	675 mL
1 tsp	baking soda	5 mL
1 tsp	cream of tartar	5 mL
½ tsp	ground ginger	2 mL
¼ tsp	salt	1 mL
½ cup	finely chopped crystallized ginger	125 mL
	Granulated sugar	

1. Cream butter and ¾ cup (175 mL) granulated sugar and brown sugar until light and creamy. Add eggs, one at a time, beating after each addition.

2. Combine flour, baking soda, cream of tartar, ground ginger and salt. Add to creamed mixture gradually, beating until blended. Stir in crystallized ginger. Cover and chill dough for 1 hour for easy shaping.

3. Shape dough into 1-inch (2.5 cm) balls. Roll in granulated sugar. Place on cookie sheet, about 2 inches (5 cm) apart. Bake for 8 to 12 minutes or until golden. Cool for 5 minutes on sheet, then transfer to rack and cool completely.

Variation
Add ½ cup (125 mL) finely chopped almonds for extra crunch.

Lemon Sugar Wafers

A hint of lemon in a tender-crisp sugar cookie.

Makes about 6 dozen cookies

Preparation: 20 minutes

Refrigeration: 1 hour

Baking: 20 minutes

Freezing: excellent

TIP

Store crisp cookies in container with loose-fitting lid. If cookies become soft, place in single layer on ungreased baking sheet and heat in 300°F (150°C) oven for 5 minutes.

- *Preheat oven to 325°F (160°C)*
- *Cookie sheet, greased*

1 cup	butter, softened	250 mL
2 cups	granulated sugar	500 mL
2	eggs	2
1 tbsp	grated lemon zest	15 mL
¼ cup	lemon juice	50 mL
1 tsp	vanilla	5 mL
3½ cups	Robin Hood Best For Cake & Pastry Flour	875 mL
1 tsp	baking soda	5 mL
1 tsp	salt	5 mL
1 tsp	cream of tartar	5 mL
	Granulated sugar	

1. Cream butter, sugar, eggs, lemon zest, juice and vanilla in large mixing bowl until smooth. Stir in flour, baking soda, salt and cream of tartar until well blended. Refrigerate for 1 hour.

2. Shape dough into 1-inch (2.5 cm) balls. Roll in sugar. Place 2 inches (5 cm) apart on prepared cookie sheet. Bake for 15 to 20 minutes or until light golden brown. Cookies will be soft in center. Cool for 5 minutes on sheet, then transfer to rack and cool completely.

Butterscotch No-Bakes

Quick to mix, these cookies taste like candy (see photo, page 81).

(see photo, page 81).

Makes about 5 dozen cookies

Preparation: 15 minutes

Cooking: 1 minute

Cooling time: 10 minutes

Refrigeration: 1 hour

Freezing: excellent

TIP

Refrigerate cookies in airtight container.

● *Baking sheet, lined with waxed paper*

1½ cups	granulated sugar	375 mL
½ cup	butter or margarine	125 mL
⅔ cup	evaporated milk	150 mL
1 cup	butterscotch chips	250 mL
3½ cups	Robin Hood Oats	875 mL
½ cup	flaked coconut	125 mL

1. Combine sugar, butter and evaporated milk in saucepan. Bring to a boil and boil for 1 minute, stirring constantly. Remove from heat and add butterscotch chips. Stir until smooth. Stir in oats and coconut. Mix thoroughly. Cool for 5 to 10 minutes. Drop by rounded teaspoonfuls (5 mL) onto waxed paper. Refrigerate until firm, about 1 hour.

Date 'n' Nut Drops

A spicy old-fashioned favorite drop cookie that's loaded with good taste.

Makes about 6 dozen cookies

Preparation: 20 minutes
Baking: 10 minutes
Freezing: excellent

TIP

Store chewy cookies in airtight containers.

- Preheat oven to 375°F (190°C)
- Cookie sheet, greased

2 cups	Robin Hood All-Purpose Flour	500 mL
1 tsp	baking soda	5 mL
1 lb	dates, chopped	500 g
1 cup	shortening	250 mL
1 1/2 cups	packed brown sugar	375 mL
2	eggs	2
2 tsp	vanilla	10 mL
1 cup	Robin Hood Oats	250 mL
3/4 cup	flaked coconut	175 mL
1/2 cup	chopped nuts	125 mL
1 1/4 tsp	ground cinnamon	6 mL
1/4 tsp	ground nutmeg	1 mL

1. Toss together flour, baking soda and dates to coat dates.

2. Cream shortening, brown sugar, eggs and vanilla in large bowl on medium speed of electric mixer until light and creamy. Stir in oats, coconut, nuts, cinnamon and nutmeg along with date mixture. Mix well.

3. Drop dough by tablespoonfuls (15 mL) about 2 inches (5 cm) apart onto prepared cookie sheet. Bake for 8 to 10 minutes or until light golden. Cool for 5 minutes on sheet, then transfer to rack and cool completely.

Variation
Omit nuts if desired.

Oats 'n' Seeds Cookies

These cookies taste as good as they look, making them a wholesome choice for the whole family.

Makes about 5 dozen cookies

Preparation: 20 minutes

Baking: 12 minutes

Freezing: excellent

TIPS

Store wheat germ and whole wheat flour in the freezer to keep the flavor fresh.

Use large-flake oats for a more wholesome look and taste.

Honey makes a softer cookie than one made with granulated sugar. It also has great flavor and keeps well.

- *Preheat oven to 375°F (190°C)*
- *Cookie sheet, greased*

1 cup	butter, softened	250 mL
1 cup	packed brown sugar	250 mL
½ cup	liquid honey	125 mL
2	eggs	2
1 tsp	vanilla	5 mL
1½ cups	Robin Hood Whole Wheat Flour	375 mL
½ cup	wheat germ	125 mL
1 tsp	baking soda	5 mL
½ tsp	salt	2 mL
1½ cups	Robin Hood Oats	375 mL
1½ cups	raisins	375 mL
1 cup	chopped walnuts	250 mL
¾ cup	sunflower seeds	175 mL
¼ cup	flaxseeds	50 mL
¼ cup	sesame seeds	50 mL

1. Beat butter, brown sugar, honey, eggs and vanilla until thoroughly blended.

2. Combine flour, wheat germ, baking soda and salt. Add to butter mixture gradually, beating until blended. Stir in oats, raisins, walnuts, sunflower seeds, flaxseeds and sesame seeds. Mix well.

3. Drop dough by heaping tablespoonfuls (20 mL), about 2 inches (5 cm) apart, onto prepared cookie sheet. Bake for 8 to 12 minutes or until golden. Cool for 5 minutes on sheet, then transfer to rack and cool completely.

Variation

Replace raisins with chocolate chips for a more decadent treat.

Cranberry Cereal Crisps

If you find it difficult to imagine a cookie that is delicate enough to melt in your mouth but chunky and chewy at the same time, try these delectable fruit crisps which are pictured on page 85.

which are pictured on page 85.

Makes about 6 dozen cookies

Preparation: 20 minutes
Baking: 18 minutes
Freezing: excellent

TIPS

You can use either unsalted or salted butter when baking cookies and achieve the taste you are accustomed to. The advantage to using unsalted butter is that it allows you to control the amount of salt in the recipe.

This recipe makes a big batch of cookies. They keep well, so enjoy some now and keep the rest to satisfy cravings later.

Emphasize cereals, breads and other grain products, as well as vegetables and fruits, in your diet.

- *Preheat oven to 325°F (160°C)*
- *Cookie sheet, ungreased*

1 cup	butter, softened	250 mL
1 cup	granulated sugar	250 mL
1 cup	packed brown sugar	250 mL
1	egg	1
1 cup	vegetable oil	250 mL
1 tsp	vanilla	5 mL
3½ cups	Robin Hood All-Purpose Flour	875 mL
1 tsp	baking soda	5 mL
½ tsp	salt	2 mL
1 cup	Robin Hood Oats	250 mL
2 cups	crisp rice cereal	500 mL
1 cup	dried cranberries	250 mL

1. Beat butter, granulated and brown sugars and egg on medium speed of electric mixer until light and creamy. Stir in oil and vanilla.

2. Combine flour, baking soda and salt. Add to creamed mixture along with oats, mixing on low speed until blended. Stir in cereal and cranberries.

3. Drop dough by heaping tablespoonfuls (20 mL), about 2 inches (5 cm) apart, onto cookie sheet. Bake for 13 to 18 minutes or until golden. Cool for 5 minutes on sheet, then transfer to rack and cool completely.

Variation
Substitute chopped dried apricots for the cranberries.

Breakfast Cereal Crunchies

The goodness of oats and raisins, with the crunch of crisp cereal, makes these cookies a particularly appetizing morning snack.

Makes about 3 dozen cookies

Preparation: 20 minutes

Baking: 15 minutes

Freezing: excellent

TIPS

When baking cookies, to ensure perfect results, test-bake two cookies. If they spread out too much, stir in a little more flour, about 1 tbsp (15 mL) at a time. If they are dry and crumbly, a little water stirred into the dough, about 1 tbsp (15 mL) at a time, will do the trick.

After opening a package of raisins, put leftovers in a jar with a few pieces of orange or lemon peel. Close the lid tightly and refrigerate. The raisins will stay moist and absorb the pleasant citrus flavor, too.

- *Preheat oven to 350°F (180°C)*
- *Cookie sheet, greased*

¾ cup	butter, softened	175 mL
1¼ cups	packed brown sugar	300 mL
1	egg	1
1 tsp	vanilla	5 mL
1½ cups	Robin Hood All-Purpose Flour	375 mL
½ tsp	baking soda	2 mL
¼ tsp	salt	1 mL
1½ cups	Robin Hood Oats	375 mL
1 cup	raisins	250 mL
¾ cup	crisp rice cereal	175 mL

1. Beat butter, brown sugar, egg and vanilla in a large bowl on medium speed of electric mixer until light and creamy.
2. Combine flour, baking soda and salt. Add to butter mixture gradually, beating on low speed until blended. Stir in oats, raisins and cereal.
3. Drop dough by heaping tablespoonfuls (20 mL), about 2 inches (5 cm) apart, on prepared cookie sheet. Flatten slightly with a fork dipped in flour. Bake for 12 to 15 minutes or until golden. Cool for 5 minutes on sheet, then transfer to rack and cool completely.

Variation
Replace raisins with your favorite dried fruit or a combination of several kinds.

*Chunky Caramel Nut Squares
and Chewy Chocolate Brownies*

Bars & Squares

Chunky Caramel Nut Squares

If you can bear to part with them, these chewy squares, which are chock-full of nuts, make a perfect gift.

Makes about 4 dozen squares

Preparation: 20 minutes

Baking: 25 minutes

Chilling: 1 hour

Freezing: excellent

TIPS

The look and taste of these squares depends entirely on the nuts you use. You can buy mixed nuts, with or without peanuts, or you can make your own mix.

Be sure your butterscotch chips are fresh for easy melting.

- Preheat oven to 350°F (180°C)
- 13- by 9-inch (3.5 L) cake pan, greased

Crust

2 cups	Robin Hood All-Purpose Flour	500 mL
1 cup	packed brown sugar	250 mL
¼ tsp	salt	1 mL
1 cup	butter, softened	250 mL
1	egg yolk	1

Topping

1½ cups	butterscotch chips	375 mL
¾ cup	corn syrup	175 mL
3 tbsp	butter	45 mL
2½ cups	salted mixed nuts (12 oz/375 g)	625 mL

1. **Crust:** Combine flour, brown sugar and salt. Using two knives, a pastry blender or your fingers, cut in butter until mixture resembles coarse crumbs. Stir in egg yolk. Press into prepared pan.
2. Bake for 20 to 25 minutes or until golden. Cool.
3. **Topping:** Combine butterscotch chips, corn syrup and butter in a small saucepan. Cook over low heat, stirring occasionally, until smooth and melted. Cool slightly. Spread over cooled crust and sprinkle with nuts; press nuts gently into topping. Refrigerate until topping is firm, about 1 hour. Cut into squares.

Variation

Chocolate lovers may prefer semi-sweet chocolate chips in place of the butterscotch.

Chewy Chocolate Brownies

A dense, moist brownie with a rich chocolate taste is every chocolate lover's dream. For a great dessert, cut into larger squares and serve slightly warm, topped with ice cream, and chocolate or caramel sauce.

TIPS

Use the pan size called for in the recipe when making bars and squares. If the pan is too large, the bars will be thin and dry. If the pan is too small, they will not bake through properly.

Add a chocolate frosting (see recipes, page 216) for an indulgent treat. Spread it on after the brownies have cooled but before you cut them into squares.

- Preheat oven to 350°F (180°C)
- 9-inch (2.5 L) square cake pan, greased

½ cup	butter	125 mL
3	squares (each 1 oz/28 g) unsweetened chocolate	3
1¼ cups	granulated sugar	300 mL
1 tsp	vanilla	5 mL
3	eggs	3
⅔ cup	Robin Hood All-Purpose Flour	150 mL
½ tsp	baking powder	2 mL
½ tsp	salt	2 mL
½ cup	chopped pecans or walnuts, optional	125 mL

1. Melt butter and chocolate over low heat in a medium saucepan, stirring until smooth. Remove from heat. Add sugar and vanilla and beat well. Add eggs, one at a time, beating lightly after each addition.

2. Combine flour, baking powder and salt. Add to chocolate mixture, stirring until well blended. Stir in nuts, if using. Spread in prepared pan.

3. Bake for 25 to 30 minutes or until set. Cool completely in pan on rack, then frost, if desired, and cut into squares.

Variation

If you prefer a more cake like brownie, add an extra egg to the batter.

Chocolate Caramel Pecan Squares

Rich, sweet, gooey, these squares are worth every bite.

TIPS

Choose caramel sauce carefully for use in this recipe. If it seems thin, you may need to add a little more flour.

Because the caramel sauce will stick, the pan should be lined completely with aluminum foil or baking parchment and the sides well greased. After the squares are completely cool, you can remove them from the pan and cut them easily.

If your brown sugar gets lumpy, add a slice of apple, seal tightly and leave for a few days to soften. For instant softening, put brown sugar in a covered bowl with an apple slice and microwave on High for 20 seconds.

- Preheat oven to 350°F (180°C)
- 9-inch (2.5 L) square cake pan, greased

1 cup	Robin Hood All-Purpose Flour, divided	250 mL
½ cup	Robin Hood Oats	125 mL
⅓ cup	packed brown sugar	75 mL
½ tsp	baking soda	2 mL
⅓ cup	butter, melted	75 mL
1 cup	caramel sauce	250 mL
1 cup	semi-sweet chocolate chips	250 mL
¾ cup	chopped pecans	175 mL

1. Combine ¾ cup (175 mL) flour, oats, brown sugar and baking soda; stir well to blend. Add melted butter; mix well. Press evenly into prepared pan. Bake for 10 minutes.

2. Combine caramel sauce and ¼ cup (50 mL) flour, mixing until smooth. Sprinkle chocolate chips and chopped pecans over warm crust. Drizzle caramel mixture evenly over top. Bake for 20 to 25 minutes longer or until bubbly and browned. Cool completely in pan on rack, then cut into squares.

Variations

For an extra caramel taste, replace chocolate chips with butterscotch chips.

Replace chocolate chips and pecans with peanut butter chips and peanuts, and caramel sauce with chocolate sauce.

Downright Decadent Truffle Brownies

Every bite of these mouthwatering brownies is worth the calories. Each piece is like a truffle and will satisfy any chocolate craving.

Makes about 30 squares

Preparation: 20 minutes

Baking: 35 minutes

Chilling: 3 hours

Freezing: excellent

TIPS

Bittersweet chocolate can be substituted for semi-sweet in baking. The flavor will be slightly richer and more intense.

People have been known to enjoy rich chocolate brownies straight from the freezer. Stash a few away and give it a try. It's easier to eat just one when they are stored out of sight!

- *Preheat oven to 350°F (180°C)*
- *9-inch (2.5 L) square cake pan, greased*

Brownie

6	squares (each 1 oz/28 g) semi-sweet chocolate	6
¾ cup	butter	175 mL
4	eggs	4
1 cup	granulated sugar	250 mL
1½ tsp	vanilla	7 mL
¾ cup	chopped walnuts	175 mL
½ cup	Robin Hood All-Purpose Flour	125 mL
½ tsp	ground cinnamon, optional	2 mL
¼ tsp	salt	1 mL

Ganache Topping

6	squares (each 1 oz/28 g) semi-sweet chocolate	6
2 tbsp	butter	30 mL
2 tbsp	whipping (35%) cream	30 mL

1. **Brownie:** Heat chocolate and butter in a small saucepan over low heat, stirring, until smooth and melted. Remove from heat; set aside.

2. Beat eggs and sugar in a small bowl on high speed of electric mixer until thick, about 5 minutes. Stir in reserved chocolate mixture and vanilla. Add walnuts, flour, cinnamon (if using), and salt, stirring just until combined. Spread evenly in prepared pan. Bake for 30 to 35 minutes or until set. Cool completely in pan on rack, then chill for 1 hour.

3. **Ganache Topping:** Combine chocolate, butter and whipping cream in a small saucepan. Heat over low heat, stirring often, until smooth and melted. Pour over chilled brownie. Chill until ganache is set, about 2 hours. Cut into squares.

Marbled Cream Cheese Brownies

A creamy white filling marbled through a decadent chocolate brownie makes these squares an extra-special treat.

Makes about 30 squares

Preparation: 25 minutes

Baking: 40 minutes

Freezing: excellent

TIPS

The top layer of brownie batter won't completely cover the filling. Don't worry — after marbling and baking, it will be beautiful.

The frosting is more like a chocolate glaze than an icing. You can omit it entirely if time is of the essence.

- Preheat oven to 350°F (180°C)
- 9-inch (2.5 L) square cake pan, greased

Filling

4 oz	cream cheese, softened	125 g
2 tbsp	butter, softened	30 mL
¼ cup	granulated sugar	50 mL
1 tbsp	Robin Hood All-Purpose Flour	15 mL
1	egg	1
1 tsp	vanilla	5 mL

Brownie

4	squares (each 1 oz/28 g) semi-sweet chocolate	4
3 tbsp	butter	45 mL
¾ cup	granulated sugar	175 mL
2	eggs	2
½ cup	Robin Hood All-Purpose Flour	125 mL
½ cup	chopped nuts, optional	125 mL
1 tsp	baking powder	5 mL
1 tsp	vanilla	5 mL
¼ tsp	salt	1 mL

Frosting, optional

1 cup	icing sugar	250 mL
1 tbsp	unsweetened cocoa powder	15 mL
2 tbsp	half-and-half or light (10% or 18%) cream	30 mL
1 tbsp	butter, softened	15 mL

1. **Filling:** Beat cream cheese, butter and sugar in a small bowl on low speed of electric mixer until smooth and blended. Add flour, egg and vanilla, beating until blended. Set aside.

2. **Brownie:** Heat chocolate and butter in a small saucepan over low heat, stirring until melted. Remove from heat. Stir in sugar and eggs. Mix thoroughly. Add flour, nuts (if using), baking powder, vanilla and salt, stirring to blend. Spread half of batter in prepared pan. Spread filling on top. Cover evenly with spoonfuls of remaining batter. Swirl mixtures with the tip of a knife just enough to marble. Bake for 35 to 40 minutes or until set. Cool in pan on rack for 20 minutes.

3. **Frosting (optional):** Sift icing sugar and cocoa into a small saucepan. Add cream and butter. Cook over medium-high heat just until mixture starts to boil around the edge of the pan. Remove from heat. Beat with a wooden spoon until mixture starts to dull and is a thin, spreadable consistency. (It will harden when cool.) Spread evenly over warm brownies. Cool completely, then cut into squares.

Decadent Chocolate Macaroon Bars

These bars have a soft, chewy coconut filling sandwiched between layers of chocolate and are crowned with a rich chocolate topping.

Makes about 4 dozen bars

Preparation: 25 minutes

Baking: 40 minutes

Chilling: 30 minutes

Freezing: excellent

TIPS

Because these bars are so rich, one pan goes a long way. Cut the bars small. People can always come back for more.

Sweetened condensed milk should not be confused with evaporated milk. It is considerably sweeter and much thicker in consistency.

The recipes in this book were tested with whole, or regular, sweetened condensed milk. Lower-fat versions are also available and make a satisfactory substitute.

Drop the filling on the top layer of chocolate batter by small spoonfuls to ensure that it spreads evenly.

- *Preheat oven to 350°F (180°C)*
- *13- by 9-inch (3.5 L) cake pan, greased*

Base

4	squares (each 1 oz/28 g) unsweetened chocolate	4
1 cup	butter	250 mL
2 cups	granulated sugar	500 mL
3	eggs	3
1¼ cups	Robin Hood All-Purpose Flour	300 mL

Filling

3 cups	flaked coconut	750 mL
1	can (10 oz/300 mL) sweetened condensed milk	1
1 tsp	vanilla	5 mL

Topping

1½ cups	semi-sweet chocolate chips, melted	375 mL
½ cup	finely chopped nuts, optional	125 mL

1. **Base:** Heat chocolate and butter in a medium saucepan over low heat, stirring until smooth and melted. Remove from heat. Stir in sugar until blended. Add eggs, one at a time, mixing lightly after each addition. Add flour; mix well. Spread half of the batter in prepared pan.
2. **Filling:** Combine coconut, condensed milk and vanilla in a medium bowl. Mix well. Drop by small spoonfuls over base. Carefully spread remaining chocolate batter over filling. Bake for 35 to 40 minutes or until set. Cool completely in pan on rack.
3. **Topping:** Spread melted chocolate chips evenly over baked bar. Sprinkle nuts on top, if using. Chill until chocolate is set, about 30 minutes, then cut into bars.

Variation

The nut garnish is a matter of preference. Use your favorite nut or omit it completely. Replace chocolate chips and pecans with peanut butter chips and peanuts, and caramel sauce with chocolate sauce.

Coffee Chocolate Cheesecake Squares

Great for entertaining. One pan goes a long way.

TIP

Don't overbake cheesecake. It should be soft-set when done or it may crack on top.

- *Preheat oven to 350°F (180°C)*
- *13- by 9-inch (3.5 L) cake pan, greased*

Brownie Layer

¾ cup	butter or margarine	175 mL
6	squares (each 1 oz/28 g) semi-sweet chocolate	6
1 tbsp	instant coffee granules	15 mL
2	eggs	2
¾ cup	packed brown sugar	175 mL
¾ cup	Robin Hood All-Purpose Flour	175 mL
½ tsp	baking powder	2 mL

Cheesecake Layer

1	package (8 oz/250 g) cream cheese, softened	1
½ cup	granulated sugar	125 mL
2	eggs	2
2 tbsp	Robin Hood All-Purpose Flour	30 mL
2 tbsp	strong brewed coffee	30 mL

Sour Cream Layer

1½ cups	sour cream	375 mL
3 tbsp	granulated sugar	45 mL
	Chocolate-covered coffee beans, optional	

1. **Brownie Layer:** Melt butter and chocolate together in large saucepan until smooth. Stir in coffee granules. Cool. Add eggs and brown sugar. Mix well. Add flour and baking powder, mixing until smooth. Spread in prepared pan. Refrigerate for 10 minutes.

2. **Cheesecake Layer:** Beat cream cheese, sugar and eggs in large bowl on medium speed of electric mixer until creamy. Gradually add flour and coffee, beating until smooth. Spread over brownie layer. Bake for 20 to 25 minutes or until set.

3. **Sour Cream Layer:** Combine sour cream and sugar. Spread over cheese layer. Bake for 10 minutes longer. Cool completely, then cut into small squares. Decorate with coffee beans, if desired.

Variation

Bittersweet chocolate is interchangeable with semi-sweet.

Chocolate Butterscotch Almond Crunch

A candy-like cookie that's sure to be a hit!

Makes about 100 pieces

Preparation: 15 minutes

Baking: 18 minutes

Freezing: excellent

TIP

A jelly roll pan is a baking sheet with sides.

- *Preheat oven to 350°F (180°C)*
- *15- by 10-inch (2 L) jelly roll pan*

1¾ cups	Robin Hood All-Purpose Flour	425 mL
¾ cup	granulated sugar	175 mL
¾ cup	packed brown sugar	175 mL
1 cup	butter or margarine, softened	250 mL
2	egg yolks	2
1½ tsp	vanilla	7 mL
1¾ cups	milk chocolate chips, melted	425 mL
1 cup	sliced almonds, toasted	250 mL

1. Combine flour and granulated and brown sugars. Mix in butter until thoroughly blended. Add egg yolks and vanilla. Mix until smooth. OR blend in food processor until mixture comes together. Press with floured fingers into pan. Bake for 13 to 18 minutes or until light golden. Cool slightly, about 20 minutes. Spread melted chocolate over base. Sprinkle nuts on top and press in lightly. Cool until chocolate sets. Cut into squares or triangles.

Variation

Substitute semi-sweet or white chocolate chips for milk chocolate chips.

Cranberry Pecan Bars

Combine sweet pecan pie with tart cranberries for an easy-to-eat, bite-size bar that's a sure winner (see photo, page 99).

Makes about 3 dozen bars

Preparation: 25 minutes

Baking: 58 minutes

Freezing: excellent

TIP

Combine crust mixture in food processor.

- Preheat oven to 350°F (180°C)
- 13- by 9-inch (3.5 L) cake pan, greased

Crust

2 cups	Robin Hood All-Purpose Flour	500 mL
1/2 cup	granulated sugar	125 mL
3/4 cup	butter or margarine	175 mL

Topping

4	eggs	4
1 cup	granulated sugar	250 mL
1 cup	corn syrup	250 mL
3 tbsp	butter or margarine, melted	45 mL
1 1/4 cups	coarsely chopped pecans	300 mL
3/4 cup	coarsely chopped cranberries	175 mL

1. **Crust:** Combine flour, sugar and butter until crumbly. Press firmly into prepared pan. Bake for 15 to 18 minutes or until light golden.
2. **Topping:** Beat together eggs, sugar, corn syrup and melted butter until blended. Stir in pecans and cranberries. Pour evenly over crust. Bake for about 40 minutes or until set and golden. Cool completely, then cut into bars.

Variation
This is also delicious made with sweetened dried cranberries in place of fresh.

Cranberry Apricot Almond Squares

Although delicious any time of the year, these tasty squares are particularly nice to have on hand during the holiday season, when they can make a colorful addition to a cookie tray.

Makes about 30 squares

Preparation: 20 minutes

Cooking: 10 minutes

Baking: 55 minutes

Freezing: excellent

TIPS

Since ovens are often not accurate in their temperature, a good oven thermometer is a worthwhile investment. Just leave it in the oven, check the temperature and adjust the temperature control accordingly.

When baking, set the timer for the minimum time recommended in a recipe. You can always bake longer but you can't fix items that are overbaked.

If using a glass pan, decrease the oven temperature by 25°F (10°C).

- Preheat oven to 325°F (160°C)
- 9-inch (2.5 L) square cake pan, greased

Crust

1/2 cup	butter, softened	125 mL
1/4 cup	granulated sugar	50 mL
1 cup	Robin Hood All-Purpose Flour	250 mL

Topping

1/2 cup	dried cranberries	125 mL
1/2 cup	chopped dried apricots	125 mL
	Water	
2	eggs	2
1 cup	packed brown sugar	250 mL
1/3 cup	Robin Hood All-Purpose Flour	75 mL
1/2 tsp	baking powder	2 mL
1 tsp	vanilla	5 mL
1/2 cup	chopped almonds	125 mL

1. **Crust:** Cream butter and granulated sugar until light and creamy. Add flour; mix well. Press into prepared pan.
2. Bake for 15 to 20 minutes or until light golden.
3. **Topping:** Combine cranberries, apricots and enough water to cover in small saucepan. Bring to a boil over low heat and simmer for 10 minutes. Drain well; set aside.
4. Beat eggs and brown sugar until smoothly blended. Stir in flour, baking powder and vanilla. Mix well. Stir in almonds and cranberry-apricot mixture. Spread over warm crust.
5. Bake for 30 to 35 minutes longer. Cool completely in pan on rack, then cut into squares.

Variations

Replace almonds with hazelnuts.

If you prefer an all-apricot version, replace cranberries with apricots.

Lickety-Split Lemon Bars

If you like the flavor of lemon, you'll love the hint of tartness in these luscious bars.

Makes about 30 bars

Preparation: 15 minutes

Baking: 50 minutes

Freezing: excellent

TIPS

Bars are cookies that are particularly easy to make, as they are baked in one pan, then cut into pieces.

Most bars freeze well.

Use fresh lemon juice for the best flavor.

To obtain almost twice as much juice from a lemon, submerge it in hot water for 15 seconds before squeezing.

When grating the zest, try to use only the yellow part. The white pith has a bitter taste.

Add a dusting of confectioner's (icing) sugar just before serving for a finishing touch.

- Preheat oven to 350°F (180°C)
- 8-inch (2 L) square cake pan, greased

Crust

1 cup	Robin Hood All-Purpose Flour	250 mL
1/4 cup	granulated sugar	50 mL
1/2 cup	butter	125 mL

Topping

1 cup	granulated sugar	250 mL
3 tbsp	Robin Hood All-Purpose Flour	45 mL
3	eggs	3
1 1/2 tsp	grated lemon zest	7 mL
1/2 cup	fresh lemon juice	125 mL

1. **Crust:** Combine flour and sugar. Using two knives, a pastry blender or your fingers, cut in butter until mixture resembles coarse crumbs. Press into prepared pan. Bake for 15 to 20 minutes or until light golden.

2. **Topping:** Beat sugar, flour, eggs, and lemon zest and juice in a small bowl just until smooth. Don't overbeat. Pour over warm crust. Bake for 25 to 30 minutes longer or until set. Cool completely in pan on rack, then cut into bars.

Variation

Replace 1/4 cup (50 mL) of the flour in the crust with 1/2 cup (125 mL) ground almonds.

Lemon Almond Cranberry Squares

A thick, lemony square dotted with wonderful sweetened dried cranberries.

Makes about 3 dozen squares

Preparation: 25 minutes

Baking:
1 hour 10 minutes

Freezing: excellent

TIP

Sprinkle top lightly with confectioner's (icing) sugar before serving for an attractive presentation.

- Preheat oven to 350°F (180°C)
- 13- by 9-inch (3.5 L) cake pan, greased

Crust

2 cups	Robin Hood All-Purpose Flour	500 mL
1/3 cup	confectioner's (icing) sugar, sifted	75 mL
1 cup	butter or margarine	250 mL

Topping

4	large lemons	4
7	eggs	7
2 1/4 cups	granulated sugar	550 mL
1/4 cup	butter or margarine, melted	50 mL
1/2 cup	Robin Hood All-Purpose Flour	125 mL
2 tsp	baking powder	10 mL
1 1/4 cups	ground or finely chopped almonds	300 mL
6 oz	sweetened dried cranberries (1 cup/250 mL)	170 g

1. **Crust:** Combine flour, sugar and butter until crumbly. Press firmly into prepared pan. Bake for 15 to 20 minutes or until light golden.

2. **Topping:** Reduce oven temperature to 325°F (160°C). Grate zest from two lemons. Squeeze out 3/4 cup (175 mL) juice. Beat eggs and sugar until light and slightly thickened. Stir in zest, juice and melted butter. Add flour and baking powder. Stir in almonds and cranberries. Mix well. Pour over baked crust. Bake for 40 to 50 minutes or until set and golden. Cool completely, then cut into squares.

Variation
Replace almonds with hazelnuts.

Citrus Almond Slices

Choose your favorite flavor — orange, lime or lemon.

Makes about 80 slices

Preparation: 25 minutes

Baking: 15 minutes

Freezing: excellent

TIP

These are also delicious without the frosting, if you prefer.

- *Preheat oven to 325°F (160°C)*
- *Baking sheet, ungreased*

Cookie

½ cup	butter or margarine, softened	125 mL
1 cup	granulated sugar	250 mL
1	egg	1
	Grated zest of 1 orange, lime or lemon	
1¾ cups	Robin Hood All-Purpose Flour	425 mL
2 tsp	baking powder	10 mL
¼ tsp	salt	1 mL
	Milk	
¾ cup	sliced almonds	175 mL

Frosting

1 cup	confectioner's (icing) sugar, sifted	250 mL
4 to 5 tsp	orange, lime or lemon juice	20 to 25 mL

1. **Cookie:** Cream butter, sugar, egg and zest in large bowl on medium speed of electric mixer until light and creamy. Combine flour, baking powder and salt. Add to creamed mixture on low speed, mixing just until smooth. Divide dough into four pieces. Shape each into a roll 12 inches (30 cm) long. Place two rolls 4 inches (10 cm) apart on baking sheet. Flatten to 2½ inches (6 cm) wide. Brush with milk. Sprinkle almonds on top, pressing in lightly. Bake for 12 to 15 minutes or until edges are lightly browned. Cool completely.

2. **Frosting:** Mix confectioner's sugar and enough juice to make a smooth drizzling consistency. Drizzle over strips. Let frosting set. Cut on diagonal into ½-inch (1 cm) slices.

Key Lime Cheesecake Squares

A pleasant combination of tart and tangy but light and creamy. Garnish with a colorful touch of fresh fruit, if desired.

Makes about 3 dozen squares

Preparation: 20 minutes
Baking: 30 minutes
Refrigeration: 1 hour
Freezing: excellent

TIP

Decorate top with a small piece of lime, halved small strawberry or maraschino cherry.

- Preheat oven to 350°F (180°C)
- 8-inch (2 L) square cake pan

Crust

¾ cup	Robin Hood All-Purpose Flour	175 mL
¼ cup	packed brown sugar	50 mL
¼ cup	ground almonds	50 mL
¼ cup	butter or margarine	50 mL

Filling

1	package (8 oz/250 g) cream cheese, softened	1
½ cup	granulated sugar	125 mL
1	egg	1
2 tsp	grated lime zest	10 mL
4 tsp	lime juice	20 mL

1. **Crust:** Combine flour, sugar and almonds in mixing bowl. Cut in butter until mixture is crumbly. Press firmly into pan. Bake for 15 minutes.

2. **Filling:** Beat together cream cheese, sugar, egg and lime zest and juice in small bowl on medium speed of electric mixer until smooth and creamy. Spread evenly over baked crust. Bake for 12 to 15 minutes or until set. Cool on wire rack. Refrigerate until chilled before cutting into small squares, about 1 hour. Serve plain or decorate as desired just before serving.

Variation

Replace lime juice and zest with lemon.

Lemon Almond Strips

A lemon lover's delight. You can't go wrong with a supply in your freezer.

TIP

Bars are popular items as they're really many cookies baked in one pan. They are easy to prepare and also easy to cut, wrap, store and transport.

- Preheat oven to 350°F (180°C)
- 13- by 9-inch (3.5 L) cake pan, greased

Almond Crust

1¾ cups	Robin Hood All-Purpose Flour or 2 cups (500 mL) Robin Hood Best For Cake & Pastry Flour	425 mL
⅓ cup	granulated sugar	75 mL
½ cup	ground almonds	125 mL
1 cup	butter or margarine	250 mL

Lemon Filling

4	eggs	4
2 cups	granulated sugar	500 mL
⅓ cup	lemon juice	75 mL
¼ cup	Robin Hood All-Purpose or Best For Cake & Pastry Flour	50 mL
1 tsp	baking powder	5 mL
	Confectioner's (icing) sugar, optional	

1. **Almond Crust:** Combine flour, sugar and ground almonds in mixing bowl. Cut in butter until mixture is crumbly. Press into prepared pan. Bake for 15 minutes or until light golden. Cool for 10 minutes.

2. **Lemon Filling:** Beat together eggs, sugar and lemon juice. Combine flour and baking powder; stir into egg mixture. Pour over baked crust. Bake for 25 to 30 minutes or just until set and light golden. Cool completely, then cut into bars. Sprinkle with confectioner's sugar before serving, if desired.

Ginger Date Bars

If you like lots of gingery flavor, try these cake-like bars.

Makes about 18 bars

Preparation: 20 minutes

Baking: 30 minutes

Freezing: excellent

TIPS

Candied ginger should be slightly soft. If yours has hardened, don't use it — invest in fresh.

Honey dates are wonderful for baking. They have great flavor and a soft, buttery texture, which makes them easy to chop.

Store dates in a tightly covered airtight container. If they are exposed to air, they become dry and sugary.

To make it easier to remove these — and many other — bars from the pan, line it completely with parchment paper or greased aluminum foil.

- Preheat oven to 350°F (180°C)
- 8-inch (2 L) square cake pan, lined with parchment paper or greased aluminum foil

³⁄₄ cup	chopped pitted dates	175 mL
¹⁄₂ cup	boiling water	125 mL
¹⁄₃ cup	chopped candied ginger	75 mL
¹⁄₃ cup	butter, softened	75 mL
¹⁄₂ cup	granulated sugar	125 mL
1	egg	1
1 cup	Robin Hood All-Purpose Flour	250 mL
1¹⁄₂ tsp	baking powder	7 mL
1 tsp	ground cinnamon	5 mL
¹⁄₄ tsp	salt	1 mL

1. Combine dates, water and candied ginger in a small bowl; set aside to soften for 10 minutes.
2. Beat butter, sugar and egg in a large bowl until light and creamy. Stir in date mixture.
3. Combine flour, baking powder, cinnamon and salt. Stir into date mixture. Mix well. Spread batter evenly in prepared pan.
4. Bake for 25 to 30 minutes or until set and golden. Cool completely in pan on rack, then cut into bars.

Variations

A mixture of confectioner's (icing) sugar and cinnamon sprinkled over these bars just before serving adds a nice finishing touch.

For a change, try finishing these bars with Lemon Glaze (see recipe, page 219).

Raspberry Lattice Bars

These dainty bars are attractive to look at and wonderful to eat!

<table>
<tr><td colspan="2">Makes about 30 bars</td></tr>
<tr><td colspan="2">Preparation: 20 minutes</td></tr>
<tr><td colspan="2">Baking: 30 minutes</td></tr>
<tr><td colspan="2">Freezing: excellent</td></tr>
</table>

TIPS

The strength and flavor of almond extract varies considerably among brands. It's best to use a smaller amount the first time you bake with an extract, then gradually increase the quantity to suit your taste.

Both salted and unsalted butter work well in baking. In most cases, they are interchangeable — it just depends on what you are accustomed to.

Choose a jam that is thick for this recipe.

Using a fork, rather than a spoon, to mix the dough helps keep it crumbly. If you use a spoon, it is tempting to make it smooth, which you don't want.

- Preheat oven to 375°F (190°C)
- 9-inch (2.5 L) square cake pan, greased

1½ cups + 2 tbsp	Robin Hood All-Purpose Flour, divided	405 mL
½ cup	packed brown sugar	125 mL
¼ cup	granulated sugar	50 mL
½ tsp	baking powder	2 mL
½ tsp	salt	2 mL
½ tsp	ground cinnamon	2 mL
½ cup	butter	125 mL
1	egg, beaten	1
1 tsp	almond extract	5 mL
1 cup	raspberry jam	250 mL
1	egg yolk	1
4 tsp	water, divided	20 mL

1. Combine 1½ cups (375 mL) flour, brown and granulated sugars, baking powder, salt and cinnamon in mixing bowl. Mix well. Using two knives, a pastry blender or your fingers, cut in butter until mixture resembles coarse crumbs. Add egg and almond extract. Mix with a fork. Transfer ½ cup (125 mL) of mixture to a small bowl and set aside. Press remaining mixture into prepared pan. Spread jam evenly over top.

2. Add 2 tbsp (30 mL) flour to reserved mixture and stir to blend. Stir in water (about 1 tbsp/15 mL) until the dough holds together. (It will resemble pastry dough.) Divide dough into 12 portions and roll into pencil-like strips. Crisscross strips diagonally over jam to form a lattice. Mix egg yolk and 1 tsp (5 mL) water in a small bowl. Brush over lattice.

3. Bake for 25 to 30 minutes or until golden. Cool completely in pan on rack, then cut into bars.

Raspberry Coconut Dream Bars

These chewy bars are a favorite with kids. They are a bit on the gooey side, but that's part of the appeal.

Makes about 30 bars
Preparation: 20 minutes
Baking: 35 minutes
Freezing: excellent

TIPS

When making bars, line pans with parchment paper or greased aluminum foil. After cooling, chill bars until firm, remove them from the pan and peel off paper. Place on a board for easy cutting.

Mix crust in a food processor for convenience.

Stir jam before using. This makes it easier to spread over the crust.

- Preheat oven to 425°F (220°C)
- 9-inch (2.5 L) square cake pan, greased

Crust

1 ⅓ cups	Robin Hood All-Purpose Flour	325 mL
⅓ cup	granulated sugar	75 mL
½ tsp	baking powder	2 mL
½ cup	butter	125 mL
1	egg, beaten	1
⅓ cup	raspberry jam	75 mL

Topping

1 cup	packed brown sugar	250 mL
¾ cup	chopped walnuts	175 mL
¾ cup	shredded coconut	175 mL
2 tbsp	Robin Hood All-Purpose Flour	30 mL
1 tbsp	lemon juice	15 mL
1 tsp	baking powder	5 mL
2	eggs, beaten	2

1. **Crust:** Combine flour, sugar and baking powder in a mixing bowl. Using two knives, a pastry blender or your fingers, cut in butter until mixture resembles coarse crumbs. Add egg; mix thoroughly. Press mixture evenly into prepared pan.

2. Bake for 10 minutes. Reduce heat to 350°F (180°C). Spread jam over partially baked crust.

3. **Topping:** Combine brown sugar, walnuts, coconut, flour, lemon juice, baking powder and eggs in a bowl. Mix well. Spread evenly over jam.

4. Bake for 20 to 25 minutes longer or until set and golden. Cool completely in pan on rack, then cut into bars.

Variation

If you prefer, substitute strawberry, peach or pineapple jam for the raspberry.

Raspberry Hazelnut Squares

*Three delights —
shortbread, raspberry jam
and hazelnuts — stack up
attractively in one square.*

Makes about 25 squares

Preparation: 30 minutes

Baking: 40 minutes

Freezing: excellent

TIP

Hazelnuts and filberts are
the same nut. In these
squares, you can also use
ground pecans or almonds.

- Preheat oven to 350°F (180°C)
- 9-inch (2.5 L) square cake pan, greased

Crust

½ cup	butter or margarine, softened	125 mL
½ cup	confectioner's (icing) sugar, sifted	125 mL
2	egg yolks	2
1¼ cups	Robin Hood All-Purpose Flour	300 mL

Topping

⅔ cup	raspberry jam	150 mL
2	egg whites	2
Pinch	cream of tartar	Pinch
½ cup	granulated sugar	125 mL
1 cup	toasted hazelnuts, ground	250 mL
1	square (1 oz/28 g) semi-sweet chocolate	1
1 tbsp	butter or margarine	15 mL

1. **Crust:** Cream butter, sugar, egg yolks and flour until smooth. Press into prepared pan. Bake for 15 minutes or until light golden.
2. **Topping:** Spread jam over base. Beat egg whites and cream of tartar to soft peaks. Gradually add sugar, beating until stiff peaks form. Fold in nuts. Spread over jam. Bake for 20 to 25 minutes or until lightly browned. Cool.
3. Melt together chocolate and butter. Drizzle over squares. Let chocolate set. Cut into squares.

Variation

Although not as pretty, apricot jam tastes delicious, too.

Raspberry Almond Bars

The best granola bar your children will ever eat.

Makes about 2 dozen bars

Preparation: 15 minutes

Baking: 30 minutes

Freezing: excellent

TIP

These bars are also a favorite cut in bite-size pieces for your holiday gift cookie boxes.

- *Preheat oven to 350°F (180°C)*
- *9-inch (2.5 L) square cake pan, greased*

1¾ cups	Robin Hood Oats	425 mL
1 cup	Robin Hood All-Purpose or Whole Wheat Flour	250 mL
1 cup	packed brown sugar	250 mL
1 tsp	baking powder	5 mL
¼ tsp	salt	1 mL
¾ cup	butter, melted	175 mL
¾ cup	raspberry jam	175 mL
½ cup	sliced almonds	125 mL

1. Combine oats, flour, brown sugar, baking powder and salt. Mix well. Stir in melted butter. Press two-thirds of the crumb mixture into prepared pan. Spread with jam. Add almonds to remaining crumb mixture and sprinkle over jam, patting down lightly. Bake for 25 to 30 minutes or until golden. Cool completely, then cut into bars.

Caramel Pecan Bars

These look fabulous and taste even better. Bet your tasters can't eat just one! (See photo, page 115.)

(See photo, page 115.)

Makes about 50 bars

Preparation: 15 minutes

Boiling time: 7 minutes

Baking: 30 minutes

Freezing: excellent

TIP

Take time to place pecans right side up.

- *Preheat oven to 350°F (180°C)*
- *15- by 10-inch (2 L) jelly roll pan*

Crust

1 cup	butter	250 mL
1/2 cup	packed brown sugar	125 mL
3 cups	Robin Hood All-Purpose Flour	750 mL
1	egg, beaten	1

Filling

3 cups	pecan halves	750 mL
3/4 cup	butter	175 mL
1/2 cup	liquid honey	125 mL
3/4 cup	packed brown sugar	175 mL
1/4 cup	whipping (35%) cream	50 mL

1. **Crust:** Combine butter, brown sugar, flour and egg in food processor or with electric mixer until blended. Press evenly into pan. Bake for 15 minutes.

2. **Filling:** Spread pecans evenly over crust. In large, heavy saucepan over medium-high heat, melt butter with honey. Add brown sugar. Boil for 5 to 7 minutes, stirring constantly, until a rich caramel color. Remove from heat. Stir in whipping cream. Mix well and pour over pecans. Bake for 15 minutes longer. Cool completely, then cut into bars.

Pecan Cheesecake Squares

While cheesecake is typically topped with fruit, topping with pecans result in a tasty dessert.

TIPS

To ensure a smooth texture, make sure your cream cheese is at room temperature.

To cut butter into a dry mixture, you can use your fingers, a food processor, a pastry blender, two knives or a fork. Cold butter is necessary if you're using a food processor.

Use real vanilla extract in all your baking. The flavor is far better than that of artificial vanilla.

- Preheat oven to 350°F (180°C)
- 8-inch (2 L) square cake pan, greased

Crust

1 cup	Robin Hood All-Purpose Flour	250 mL
1/4 cup	packed brown sugar	50 mL
1/3 cup	butter	75 mL

Topping

1	package (8 oz/250 g) cream cheese, softened	1
1/3 cup	packed brown sugar	75 mL
1	egg	1
2 tsp	milk	10 mL
1 tsp	vanilla	5 mL
1/3 cup	finely chopped pecans	75 mL

1. **Crust:** Combine flour and brown sugar. Using two knives, a pastry blender or your fingers, cut in butter until mixture resembles coarse crumbs. Press firmly into prepared pan.
2. Bake for 10 minutes or until light golden.
3. **Topping:** Beat cream cheese in a small bowl on medium speed of electric mixer until creamy. Add brown sugar, egg, milk and vanilla, beating until smooth, about 2 minutes. Spread evenly over crust. Sprinkle with pecans. Bake for 25 to 30 minutes longer, or until the edges are lightly browned. Cool completely in pan on rack, then refrigerate for at least 2 hours before cutting into bite-size squares.

Variation
Replace pecans with finely chopped hazelnuts.

Caramel Macadamia Nut Squares

What could be more appetizing than a layer of whole macadamia nuts stuck together with caramel on a shortbread crust? These squares are amazing to look at and even better to eat.

Makes about 2 dozen squares

Preparation: 20 minutes

Cooking: 3 minutes

Baking: 50 minutes

Freezing: excellent

TIPS

Use salted macadamia nuts in this recipe. The combination of sweet and salty is fantastic!

For best results, when you are baking, have all the ingredients at room temperature. This makes them easier to mix, as well.

Unless you line the pan completely with parchment paper or well-greased aluminum foil, you will have trouble cutting these bars because the caramel will stick to the pan.

- Preheat oven to 350°F (180°C)
- 8-inch (2 L) square cake pan, lined with parchment paper or greased aluminum foil

Crust

⅔ cup	butter, softened	150 mL
⅓ cup	granulated sugar	75 mL
1¼ cups	Robin Hood All-Purpose Flour	300 mL

Topping

6 tbsp	butter	90 mL
¼ cup	packed brown sugar	50 mL
¼ cup	liquid honey	50 mL
1¾ cups	salted whole macadamia nuts	425 mL
2 tbsp	whipping (35%) cream	30 mL

1. **Crust:** Cream butter and sugar until smooth and creamy. Gradually add flour, mixing until smooth. Knead lightly, if necessary, to make a smooth dough. Press evenly into prepared pan.
2. Bake for 20 to 25 minutes or until light golden.
3. **Topping:** Combine butter, brown sugar and honey in a medium saucepan. Cook over medium-high heat, stirring constantly, until mixture comes to a full rolling boil. Cook, without stirring, for 1 minute or until slightly thickened and bubbles are large. Remove from heat. Immediately stir in nuts and cream. Mix well. Spread over crust.
4. Bake for 20 to 25 minutes longer or until set and caramel is bubbly. Cool completely in pan on rack, then cut into squares.

Variation

Replace macadamia nuts with cashews, pecans, pine nuts or a mixture of nuts.

White Chocolate Raspberry Squares

The combination of white chocolate, raspberry and crunchy almonds is a knockout that's guaranteed to receive compliments.

Makes about 2 dozen squares

Preparation: 20 minutes

Baking: 65 minutes

Freezing: excellent

TIPS

White chocolate can be tricky to melt. The temperature must be low, and it needs to be stirred constantly.

Use butter, not margarine, for the best flavor in this creamy delight.

In this recipe, sliced almonds with the skins on are preferable to blanched almonds, as the contrast between the dark and light colors has more eye appeal.

Drizzle some white chocolate over the top to dress these up.

Cut into triangles for a different look. Different shapes add interest and variety to an assorted cookie tray.

- Preheat oven to 325°F (160°C)
- 9-inch (2.5 L) square cake pan, greased

2 cups	white chocolate chips, divided	500 mL
½ cup	butter	125 mL
2	eggs	2
½ cup	granulated sugar	125 mL
1 cup	Robin Hood All-Purpose Flour	250 mL
1 tsp	vanilla	5 mL
¾ cup	raspberry jam	175 mL
¼ cup	sliced almonds	50 mL

1. Heat 1 cup (250 mL) white chocolate chips and butter in a small saucepan over low heat, stirring until melted and smooth; set aside.

2. Beat eggs and sugar in small bowl on high speed of electric mixer until thick and light, about 5 minutes. Stir in melted chocolate mixture, flour and vanilla. Mix on low speed until well blended. Spread half of the batter in prepared pan.

3. Bake for 20 to 25 minutes or until light golden. Cool for 5 minutes. Spread jam on top. Stir 1 cup (250 mL) white chocolate chips into remaining batter. Drop by small spoonfuls evenly over jam. Spread out gently. Sprinkle with almonds.

4. Bake for 40 minutes longer or until set. Cool completely in pan on rack, then cut into squares.

Variation
Replace the raspberry jam with apricot and the almonds with hazelnuts.

Chocolate Caramel Raspberry Bars

How can you go wrong with a combination of creamy chocolate-coated caramels and raspberry?

Makes about 2 dozen squares

Preparation: 20 minutes

Baking: 35 minutes

Freezing: excellent

TIP

Chocolate-covered caramel balls are sold in packages like chocolate chips.

- Preheat oven to 375°F (190°C)
- 8-inch (2 L) or 9-inch (2.5 L) square cake pan, greased

Topping

⅔ cup	Robin Hood All-Purpose Flour	150 mL
½ cup	chopped pecans	125 mL
⅓ cup	packed brown sugar	75 mL
6 tbsp	butter, softened	90 mL

Crust

1¼ cups	Robin Hood All-Purpose Flour	300 mL
½ cup	granulated sugar	125 mL
½ cup	butter	125 mL
⅓ cup	raspberry jam	75 mL
8 oz	milk chocolate-covered caramel balls	225 g

1. **Topping:** Combine flour, pecans, brown sugar and butter, mixing until crumbly. Set aside.

2. **Crust:** Combine flour, sugar and butter, mixing until crumbly. Press firmly into prepared pan. Bake for 12 to 15 minutes or until light golden. Spread with jam and sprinkle chocolate caramel balls evenly on top. Sprinkle with topping. Bake for 15 to 20 minutes longer or until lightly browned. Cool completely, then cut into bars.

Variation

Try strawberry or apricot jam for another great taste.

Chocolate Chip Walnut Bars

A decadent bar for the holiday season.

Makes about 2½ dozen bars

Preparation: 20 minutes

Baking: 45 minutes

Freezing: excellent

TIP

Have eggs at room temperature for baking.

- Preheat oven to 350°F (180°C)
- 9-inch (2.5 L) square cake pan, greased

Crust

1 cup	Robin Hood All-Purpose Flour	250 mL
¼ cup	granulated sugar	50 mL
⅓ cup	butter or margarine	75 mL

Topping

2	eggs	2
½ cup	granulated sugar	125 mL
½ cup	corn syrup	125 mL
2 tbsp	butter or margarine, melted	30 mL
1 cup	semi-sweet or white chocolate chips	250 mL
¾ cup	chopped walnuts	175 mL

1. **Crust:** Combine flour, sugar and butter, mixing until crumbly. Press firmly into prepared cake pan. Bake for 12 to 15 minutes or until light golden.

2. **Topping:** Beat together eggs, sugar, corn syrup and melted butter until blended. Stir in chocolate chips and nuts. Pour evenly over crust. Bake for 25 to 30 minutes longer or until set and golden. Cool completely, then cut into bars.

Variations

Try pecans or almonds for a nice flavor change. Peanut butter chips and peanuts are great, too!

Chocolate Almond Bars

These bars are delicious yet especially easy to make.

Makes about 2½ dozen bars

Preparation: 20 minutes

Baking: 45 minutes

Freezing: excellent

TIPS

You can substitute hard margarine, not soft margarine, for butter in most baking. However, in some baking, such as shortbread, you really need the flavor of butter — no substitute will do.

Use golden corn syrup, not white, for baking. White syrup is usually used in candy making.

If using a glass pan, decrease the oven temperature by 25°F (10°C).

- Preheat oven to 350°F (180°C)
- 9-inch (2.5 L) square cake pan, greased

Crust

1 cup	Robin Hood All-Purpose Flour	250 mL
¼ cup	granulated sugar	50 mL
⅓ cup	butter	75 mL

Topping

2	eggs	2
½ cup	granulated sugar	125 mL
½ cup	corn syrup	125 mL
2 tbsp	butter, melted	30 mL
1 cup	semi-sweet chocolate chips	250 mL
¾ cup	slivered almonds	175 mL

1. **Crust:** Combine flour and sugar. Using two knives, a pastry blender or your fingers, cut in butter until mixture resembles coarse crumbs. Press into prepared pan. Bake for 12 to 15 minutes or until light golden.

2. **Topping:** Beat eggs, sugar, corn syrup and melted butter until blended. Stir in chocolate chips and almonds. Pour evenly over warm crust. Bake for 25 to 30 minutes longer or until set and golden. Cool completely in pan on rack, then cut into bars.

Variation
Vary the kind of chips and nuts to suit your taste.

Chocolate and Almond Caramel Bars

A chewy caramel bar filled with creamy white chocolate and crunchy almonds on an oatmeal crust.

Makes about 5 dozen bars

Preparation: 15 minutes

Baking: 40 minutes

Freezing: excellent

TIP

These bars are delicious but rich. Cut into small pieces.

- Preheat oven to 350°F (180°C)
- 13- by 9-inch (3.5 L) cake pan, greased

Crust

2 cups	Robin Hood All-Purpose Flour	500 mL
2 cups	Robin Hood Oats	500 mL
1 cup	packed brown sugar	250 mL
1 tsp	baking soda	5 mL
1 cup	butter or margarine, melted	250 mL

Topping

1 1/2 cups	white chocolate chips	375 mL
1 cup	slivered almonds	250 mL
1 cup	toffee bits	250 mL
1 1/3 cups	caramel sundae sauce	325 mL
1/3 cup	Robin Hood All-Purpose Flour	75 mL

1. **Crust:** Combine flour, oats, brown sugar and baking soda in mixing bowl. Add melted butter. Mix well. Reserve 1 cup (250 mL) of the mixture for topping. Press remainder into prepared cake pan. Bake for 12 to 15 minutes or until light golden.

2. **Topping:** Combine chocolate chips, almonds and toffee bits. Sprinkle evenly over base. Mix together sundae sauce and flour until smooth. Pour evenly over crust. Sprinkle reserved oat mixture on top. Bake for 20 to 25 minutes longer or until golden. Cool completely, then cut into bars.

Butter Tart Squares

Here's a simplified version of the all-time Canadian favorite. It bakes in one pan and eliminates fussing with pastry.

Makes about 25 squares

Preparation: 20 minutes

Baking: 40 minutes

Freezing: excellent

TIPS

A food processor works well for shortbread-like crusts, but you can also make them by hand, in which case the butter should be at room temperature. Combine flour and icing sugar in a bowl. Using two knives, a pastry blender or your fingers, cut in butter until mixture resembles coarse crumbs. Then press into pan as directed.

These squares are foolproof compared to tarts, which have a tendency to overflow. They are a great choice for novice bakers.

If your raisins have become dry during storage, plump them in boiling water for a few minutes, then pat dry.

These bars are delicious served warm with ice cream.

- Preheat oven to 350°F (180°C)
- 9-inch (2.5 L) square cake pan, greased

Crust

1 cup	Robin Hood All-Purpose Flour	250 mL
2 tbsp	confectioner's (icing) sugar, sifted	30 mL
1/3 cup	cold butter, cut in chunks	75 mL

Topping

2	eggs	2
1 1/3 cups	lightly packed brown sugar	325 mL
1/4 cup	butter, melted	50 mL
1 tbsp	vinegar	15 mL
1 tsp	vanilla	5 mL
1 cup	raisins	250 mL

1. **Crust:** Combine flour, icing sugar and butter in a food processor fitted with a metal blade and process until crumbly, about 20 seconds. Press into prepared pan. Bake for 10 minutes or until light golden.

2. **Topping:** Combine eggs, brown sugar, butter, vinegar and vanilla in a mixing bowl. Beat just until blended. Stir in raisins. Pour over crust. Bake for 25 to 30 minutes longer or until set and browned. Cool completely in pan on rack, then cut into squares.

Variations

Replace all or half of the raisins with dried cranberries or chopped dried apricots.

Replace 1/4 cup (50 mL) raisins with chopped nuts.

Butterscotch Nut Bars

Try warm with ice cream for dessert.

Makes about 2 dozen bars

Preparation: 20 minutes
Baking: 48 minutes
Freezing: excellent

TIP

Store nuts in the freezer to keep fresh.

- *Preheat oven to 350°F (180°C)*
- *13- by 9-inch (3.5 L) cake pan, greased*

Crust

2 cups	Robin Hood All-Purpose Flour	500 mL
1/2 cup	granulated sugar	125 mL
3/4 cup	butter or margarine	175 mL

Topping

4	eggs	4
1 cup	granulated sugar	250 mL
1 cup	corn syrup	250 mL
1/4 cup	butter or margarine, melted	50 mL
1 3/4 cups	butterscotch chips	425 mL
1 1/3 cups	coarsely chopped pecans	325 mL

1. **Crust:** Combine flour, sugar and butter, mixing until crumbly. Press firmly into prepared pan. Bake for 15 to 18 minutes or until light golden.

2. **Topping:** Beat together eggs, sugar, corn syrup and butter until blended. Stir in butterscotch chips and pecans. Pour evenly over crust. Bake for about 30 minutes longer or until set and golden. Cool completely, then cut into bars.

Variation

Walnuts, almonds and hazelnuts are good choices, too.

Chocolate Butterscotch Ripple Squares

Two favorites — chocolate and butterscotch — in every bite.

Makes about 3 dozen squares

Preparation: 20 minutes

Baking: 35 minutes

Freezing: excellent

TIP

Cocoa powder can lump during storage. Sift before using for best results.

- Preheat oven to 350°F (180°C)
- 13- by 9-inch (3.5 L) cake pan, greased

1¾ cups	butterscotch chips	425 mL
1	can (10 oz/300 mL) sweetened condensed milk	1
2 tbsp	butter	30 mL
2¼ cups	packed brown sugar	550 mL
2	eggs	2
1 cup	butter, melted	250 mL
1½ tsp	vanilla	7 mL
1½ cups	Robin Hood All-Purpose Flour	375 mL
⅔ cup	Robin Hood Oats	150 mL
⅓ cup	cocoa powder	75 mL
1 cup	chopped walnuts	250 mL

1. Heat together butterscotch chips, sweetened condensed milk and 2 tbsp (30 mL) butter over low heat, stirring constantly, until melted and smooth. Set aside.

2. Mix together brown sugar, eggs, melted butter and vanilla until smooth. Stir in flour, oats, coconut and walnuts. Mix well. Spread half in prepared pan. Spread butterscotch mixture evenly over base. Dot spoonfuls of remaining batter on top. Spread lightly with knife to cover filling. Bake for 30 to 35 minutes or until set. Cool completely, then cut into squares.

Variations

Any nuts work fine. Pecans, hazelnuts and almonds are also favorites. Try peanut butter chips and peanuts as well.

Blondies

Blondies are blond brownies. They have a similar moist, slightly chewy texture but are flavored with butterscotch rather than chocolate.

Makes about 2 dozen squares

Preparation: 15 minutes
Baking: 45 minutes
Freezing: excellent

TIPS

Most bars and squares freeze well, which makes them ideal to have on hand for unexpected guests.

To freeze blondies, cool completely and cut into squares. Wrap individual servings in plastic wrap and freeze. When preparing to serve, remove the quantity required and let thaw. Cut in individual pieces, they thaw quickly, and you can remove just one for yourself or several for company. They actually taste great frozen, too.

These will rise during baking then collapse as they cool.

- Preheat oven to 325°F (160°C)
- 8-inch (2 L) square cake pan, greased

½ cup	butter, softened	125 mL
1¼ cups	packed brown sugar	300 mL
1	egg	1
1 tsp	vanilla	5 mL
1 cup	Robin Hood All-Purpose Flour	250 mL
1 tsp	baking powder	5 mL
¾ cup	white chocolate chips	175 mL
¾ cup	chopped hazelnuts	175 mL

1. Cream butter and brown sugar in a medium bowl until smooth and creamy. Add egg and vanilla, beating until smooth.
2. Combine flour and baking powder. Add to creamed mixture. Mix well. Stir in chips and nuts. Spread evenly in prepared pan.
3. Bake for 40 to 45 minutes or until just set and golden. Cool completely in pan on rack, then cut into squares.

Variation

Blondies are quite versatile. Make them with your favorite additions, such as nuts, chips, coconut, raisins or chopped dried apricots.

Crispy Peanut Butter Bars

A no-bake snack bar that's a perfect lunch-box or after-school treat.

Makes about 3 dozen bars

Preparation: 15 minutes
Refrigeration: 1 hour
Freezing: excellent

TIP

Mix thoroughly so all dry ingredients are moistened. Mixture will seem a bit crumbly before pressing into pan.

● *13- by 9-inch (3.5 L) cake pan, lined with foil and greased*

2½ cups	crisp rice cereal	625 mL
1¼ cups	Robin Hood Oats	300 mL
1 cup	chopped mixed dried fruit (apricots, dates, raisins, apples, cranberries, etc.)	250 mL
1 cup	chopped peanuts	250 mL
¾ cup	packed brown sugar	175 mL
¾ cup	creamy peanut butter	175 mL
¾ cup	liquid honey	175 mL
½ cup	cocoa powder	125 mL

1. Combine rice cereal, oats, dried fruit and peanuts in large bowl. Heat brown sugar, peanut butter and honey in small saucepan over low heat, stirring, until melted and smooth. Stir in cocoa powder. Pour over dry ingredients. Mix well. Press firmly into prepared pan. Refrigerate until set, about 1 hour. Remove from pan and peel off foil. Cut into bars.

Variation

Use a combination of fruits or one type only if you have a favorite.

Chocolate Peanut Butter Oat Bars

Swirls of chocolate and creamy peanut butter top a chewy oat cookie base.

Makes about 2 dozen bars

Preparation: 20 minutes

Baking: 30 minutes

Refrigeration: 15 minutes

Freezing: excellent

TIP

Swirl topping gently for a more attractive look.

- Preheat oven to 350°F (180°C)
- 8-inch (2 L) or 9-inch (2.5 L) square cake pan, greased

½ cup	butter or margarine, softened	125 mL
½ cup	packed brown sugar	125 mL
½ cup	corn syrup	125 mL
1 tsp	vanilla	5 mL
3 cups	Robin Hood Oats	750 mL
½ cup	semi-sweet chocolate chips	125 mL
¼ cup	creamy peanut butter	50 mL

1. Cream butter, brown sugar, corn syrup and vanilla in large bowl on medium speed of electric mixer until smooth. Stir in oats, mixing thoroughly. Press firmly into prepared pan. Bake for 25 to 30 minutes or until light golden and center is barely firm. Cool for 5 minutes. Sprinkle chocolate chips evenly on top. Drop small spoonfuls of peanut butter over chips. Let stand for 5 minutes to soften. Swirl chocolate and peanut butter together to marble. Cool completely, then refrigerate for 15 minutes to set topping. Cut into bars.

Variation
A sprinkling of chopped peanuts on top adds a nice touch.

Toffee Chocolate Bars

Layers of crunchy toffee bits, creamy caramel and chocolate top a crisp cookie base, making every bite a sheer delight.

Makes about 4 dozen bars

Preparation: 30 minutes
Cooking: 10 minutes
Baking: 42 minutes
Freezing: excellent

TIP

Pack brown sugar firmly in a dry measuring cup. It should hold its shape when turned out.

- Preheat oven to 350°F (180°C)
- 13- by 9-inch (3.5 L) cake pan, greased

Crust

¾ cup	butter or margarine, softened	175 mL
¾ cup	packed brown sugar	175 mL
1½ cups	Robin Hood All-Purpose Flour	375 mL

Filling

1	can (10 oz/300 mL) sweetened condensed milk	1
2 tbsp	butter or margarine	30 mL
1¾ cups	milk chocolate chips	425 mL
1⅓ cups	toffee bits	325 mL

1. **Crust:** Cream butter, brown sugar and flour until well blended and mixture comes together. Press evenly into prepared pan. Bake for 20 to 25 minutes or until light golden. Cool on wire rack while preparing filling.

2. **Filling:** Heat sweetened condensed milk and butter in heavy saucepan over medium heat, stirring constantly, for 5 to 10 minutes or until thickened. Spread over baked base. Bake for 12 to 15 minutes or until golden. Sprinkle chocolate chips evenly over top. Bake for 2 minutes longer or until chocolate is shiny and soft. Remove from oven. Spread chocolate evenly. Sprinkle toffee bits on top, pressing lightly into chocolate. Cool completely. If necessary, refrigerate just to set chocolate before cutting into bars. Store at room temperature.

Variation

Try semi-sweet or white chocolate chips for another taste sensation.

Apricot Raisin Meringue Squares

The cinnamon meringue is crumbly to cut, but this is quickly forgotten with the first taste.

Makes about 4 dozen squares

Preparation: 20 minutes

Baking: 50 minutes

Freezing: not recommended

TIP

Run knife under hot water before cutting meringue.

- *Preheat oven to 350°F (180°C)*
- *13- by 9-inch (3.5 L) cake pan, greased*

Crust

1 1/2 cups	Robin Hood All-Purpose Flour or 1 2/3 cups (400 mL) Robin Hood Best For Cake & Pastry Flour	375 mL
2 tbsp	granulated sugar	30 mL
1/4 tsp	salt	1 mL
1/3 cup	butter	75 mL
2	egg yolks, beaten	2
1/4 cup	sour cream	50 mL

Filling

1 1/4 cups	raisins	300 mL
3/4 cup	sour cream	175 mL
1/2 cup	apricot jam	125 mL
2	egg whites	2
1/2 cup	granulated sugar	125 mL
1/2 tsp	ground cinnamon	2 mL
1/3 cup	finely chopped walnuts or pecans	75 mL

1. **Crust:** Combine flour, sugar and salt in mixing bowl. Cut in butter until crumbly. Stir in egg yolks and sour cream. Mix well. Press into prepared pan. Bake for 15 to 20 minutes or until light golden.

2. **Filling:** Combine raisins, sour cream and jam. Spread evenly over crust. Beat egg whites to soft peaks. Gradually add sugar and cinnamon, beating to stiff peaks. Carefully spread meringue over raisin mixture. Sprinkle with nuts. Bake for 25 to 30 minutes or until light brown. Cool completely, then cut into squares.

Variation
Replace apricot jam with raspberry or strawberry.

Raisin Walnut Spice Bars

Old-time hermit cookies with a new twist.

Makes about
50 bars

Preparation: 15 minutes

Baking: 17 minutes

Freezing: excellent

TIP

Ground spices lose their flavor if not properly stored. Keep in airtight containers in a cool place for about six months. Buy in small amounts that you're likely to use in this time span.

- *Preheat oven to 375°F (190°C)*
- *Three baking sheets, greased*

1 cup	butter or margarine, softened	250 mL
2¼ cups	packed brown sugar	550 mL
3	eggs	3
⅓ cup	molasses	75 mL
4¼ cups	Robin Hood All-Purpose Flour	1.05 L
1½ tsp	baking powder	7 mL
1½ tsp	baking soda	7 mL
1½ tsp	ground cinnamon	7 mL
1 tsp	ground cloves	5 mL
1 tsp	ground nutmeg	5 mL
1 cup	raisins	250 mL
1 cup	chopped walnuts	250 mL
1	egg, lightly beaten	1

1. Cream butter and brown sugar in large bowl on medium speed of electric mixer until blended. Add eggs and molasses, beating until light and smooth.

2. Combine flour, baking powder, baking soda, cinnamon, cloves and nutmeg. Stir into creamed mixture thoroughly. Add raisins and walnuts, stirring just to blend. (Dough will be soft.)

3. Shape dough on baking sheets into six logs (14 inches long by 1½ inches wide by ½ inch high (35 cm by 4 cm by 1 cm). Put two logs on each sheet (they spread during baking). Brush with egg to glaze. Bake for 12 to 17 minutes or until golden. Underbaking will give a chewier texture. Bake longer for a firmer bar. Cool completely, then slice diagonally into bars. Store in airtight container.

BARS & SQUARES   137

Zucchini Raisin Bars

A hidden ingredient, zucchini, makes these bars wonderfully moist.

TIP

You can use carrots when zucchini is not in season.

- *Preheat oven to 350°F (180°C)*
- *9-inch (2.5 L) square cake pan, greased*

Bar

¼ cup	butter or shortening	50 mL
⅔ cup	packed brown sugar	150 mL
1	egg	1
1 tsp	vanilla	5 mL
1 cup	Robin Hood All-Purpose Flour	250 mL
1 tsp	baking soda	5 mL
½ tsp	cinnamon	2 mL
¼ tsp	ground cloves	1 mL
1 cup	shredded unpeeled zucchini	250 mL
½ cup	raisins	125 mL

Frosting

¼ cup	butter or shortening	50 mL
1½ cups	confectioner's (icing) sugar, sifted	375 mL
¼ tsp	cinnamon	1 mL
1 to 2 tbsp	milk	15 to 30 mL

1. **Bar:** Cream butter, brown sugar, egg and vanilla in large bowl on medium speed of electric mixer until light and creamy. Add flour, baking soda, cinnamon and cloves. Mix well. Stir in zucchini and raisins. Spread evenly in prepared pan. Bake for 25 to 30 minutes or until toothpick inserted in center comes out clean. Cool completely.

2. **Frosting:** Beat together butter, sugar, cinnamon and milk, adding enough milk to make a smooth spreadable consistency. Spread evenly over bars.

Variation
Replace ground cloves with ground ginger or nutmeg.

Apple Nut Bars

Moist, chewy and nutty, these flavorful bars are like a thin apple cake that needs no icing.

Makes about 2 dozen bars

Preparation: 15 minutes

Cooking: 5 minutes

Baking: 35 minutes

Freezing: excellent

TIPS

Use crisp tart apples for the best flavor. Granny Smiths, Northern Spys and Spartans are good choices.

Grate apples on a coarse grater just before using to prevent browning.

To enhance their flavor, toast the nuts on a baking sheet in a 350°F (180°C) oven for 5 to 10 minutes, stirring often.

If apples are very wet, increase the baking time by 5 to 10 minutes.

To turn these bars into a dessert, add a thin layer of Basic Cream Cheese Frosting (see recipe, page 200). You'll need about 1½ cups (375 mL), or half the recipe.

● *Preheat oven to 350°F (180°C)*
● *9-inch (2.5 L) square cake pan, greased*

6 tbsp	butter	90 mL
1 cup	packed brown sugar	250 mL
2	eggs	2
1 cup	Robin Hood All-Purpose Flour	250 mL
1 tsp	baking powder	5 mL
1 tsp	ground cinnamon	5 mL
¼ tsp	salt	1 mL
¼ tsp	ground nutmeg	1 mL
1 cup	chopped walnuts	250 mL
1	medium apple, peeled, cored and coarsely grated	1

1. Melt butter in a large saucepan. Stir in brown sugar. Bring mixture to a boil over medium heat, stirring often. Remove from heat; cool.

2. Beat eggs, one at a time, into cooled sugar mixture.

3. Combine flour, baking powder, cinnamon, salt and nutmeg. Add to saucepan, mixing until smooth. Stir in walnuts and apple. Mix well. Spread in prepared pan. Bake for 25 to 35 minutes or until toothpick inserted in center comes out clean. Cool completely in pan on rack, then cut into bars.

Variations

For a change, try using pears in this recipe. Their flavor is not as tart as apples.

Add dried cranberries or raisins to the batter.

Oatmeal Date Squares

The whole family loves this old-fashioned favorite, which is often called "Matrimonial Squares."

Makes about 2 dozen squares

Preparation: 20 minutes
Cooking: 10 minutes
Baking: 30 minutes
Freezing: excellent

TIPS

Loaded with dates and oats, these tasty squares are a great choice for a snack.

Dates are very sweet. Balancing them with a little lemon or orange juice cuts the sweetness while adding flavor.

Dried fruits, such as dates, raisins, figs and apricots, are packed with vitamins and fiber.

- Preheat oven to 375°F (190°C)
- 13- by 9-inch (3.5 L) cake pan, greased

Filling

3 cups	chopped pitted dates	750 mL
1 tbsp	grated orange zest	15 mL
1$\frac{1}{4}$ cups	orange juice	300 mL
$\frac{1}{2}$ cup	granulated sugar	125 mL

Base & Topping

1$\frac{3}{4}$ cups	Robin Hood Oats	425 mL
1$\frac{1}{3}$ cups	Robin Hood All-Purpose Flour	325 mL
1 cup	packed brown sugar	250 mL
1 tsp	baking soda	5 mL
$\frac{3}{4}$ cup	butter	175 mL

1. **Filling:** Combine dates, orange zest and juice, and sugar in a saucepan. Cook over medium heat, stirring often, until thick and smooth, about 10 minutes. Remove from heat and cool.

2. **Base & Topping:** Combine oats, flour, brown sugar and baking soda in a large bowl. Using two knives, a pastry blender or your fingers, cut in butter until mixture resembles coarse crumbs. Press half of the mixture (2$\frac{1}{2}$ cups/625 mL) into prepared pan. Spread filling over base. Sprinkle remaining oat mixture on top. Pat down lightly.

3. Bake for 25 to 30 minutes or until light golden. Cool completely in pan on rack, then cut into squares.

Variation

Replace the orange zest with lemon. Replace the orange juice with $\frac{1}{4}$ cup (50 mL) lemon juice plus 1 cup (250 mL) water.

Cranberry Orange Muffins (on plate)

Muffins

Cranberry Orange Muffins

Tart cranberries combine with orange in this refreshing muffin that is not too sweet.

Makes
1 dozen muffins

Preparation: 20 minutes

Baking: 25 minutes

**Freezing: excellent
(omit topping)**

TIPS

In addition to adding unique flavor to baked goods, honey keeps them moist.

Use liquid honey rather than the creamed variety in these muffins.

For easy cleanup, measure the melted butter before the honey. The slippery butter will coat the cup, and the honey won't stick to the sides.

When fresh cranberries aren't available, use partially thawed frozen ones. Don't thaw them completely or the batter will be pink.

- *Preheat oven to 400°F (200°C)*
- *12-cup muffin pan, greased or lined with paper liners*

Muffins

1	egg	1
1 1/4 cups	milk	300 mL
1/3 cup	butter, melted	75 mL
1/3 cup	liquid honey	75 mL
1 tbsp	grated orange zest	15 mL
2 1/2 cups	Robin Hood All-Purpose Flour	625 mL
1 tbsp	baking powder	15 mL
1/2 tsp	salt	2 mL
1 1/2 cups	fresh or frozen cranberries	375 mL

Topping

2 tbsp	granulated sugar	30 mL

1. **Muffins:** Beat egg, milk, butter, honey and orange zest in a large bowl until thoroughly blended.
2. Combine flour, baking powder and salt. Add to liquid ingredients all at once and stir just until moistened. Fold in cranberries. Spoon batter into prepared muffin pan.
3. **Topping:** Sprinkle sugar over top of muffins.
4. Bake for 20 to 25 minutes or until tops spring back when lightly touched.

Variation

Replace the orange zest with lemon zest and the cranberries with blueberries.

Cranberry Banana Oat Muffins

Sweet bananas and tart cranberries combine for a great taste sensation.

TIP

For an attractive finish, sprinkle some oats on top of the muffins before baking.

- Preheat oven to 375°F (190°C)
- 12-cup muffin pan, greased

1 1/4 cups	Robin Hood All-Purpose Flour	300 mL
1 cup	Robin Hood Oats	250 mL
2/3 cup	granulated sugar	150 mL
1 1/2 tsp	baking powder	7 mL
1 tsp	baking soda	5 mL
1/2 tsp	salt	2 mL
1	egg	1
1 3/4 cups	mashed ripe bananas (5 or 6 bananas)	425 mL
1/3 cup	butter or margarine, melted	75 mL
1 cup	cranberries	250 mL

1. Combine flour, oats, sugar, baking powder, baking soda and salt in mixing bowl. Mix well.
2. Beat together egg, bananas and melted butter until smooth. Add to dry ingredients. Stir to blend. Stir in cranberries just until combined. Spoon batter into prepared muffin pan, filling almost to top. Bake for 20 to 25 minutes or until tops spring back when lightly touched.

Variation
For a heartier muffin, use Robin Hood Whole Wheat Flour.

Apple Spice Muffins

A spicy crumble tops these oat-apple muffins. Freeze some to have on hand for a quick breakfast when you're on the run.

Makes
1 dozen muffins

Preparation: 20 minutes

Baking: 25 minutes

Freezing: excellent

TIPS

Grated apple adds moistness and flavor to muffins.

Grate the apple just before using to avoid browning.

Choose firm tart apples, such as Granny Smith.

This batter will be very stiff. The moisture is released from the apples during baking.

Buy spices in small amounts and store them in a cool place to keep them fresh.

- *Preheat oven to 400°F (200°C)*
- *12-cup muffin pan, greased or lined with paper liners*

2 cups	Robin Hood All-Purpose Flour	500 mL
1 cup	Robin Hood Oats	250 mL
¾ cup	packed brown sugar	175 mL
1 tbsp	baking powder	15 mL
½ tsp	salt	2 mL
½ cup	butter	125 mL
1 tsp	ground cinnamon	5 mL
¼ tsp	ground nutmeg	1 mL
2	eggs	2
1 cup	milk	250 mL
1 cup	grated peeled cored apple (about 2)	250 mL

1. Combine flour, oats, brown sugar, baking powder and salt in a mixing bowl. Using two knives, a pastry blender or your fingers, cut in butter until mixture resembles coarse crumbs. Set aside ½ cup (125 mL) for topping; stir cinnamon and nutmeg into reserved topping.

2. Beat eggs, milk and apple in a small bowl. Add to dry ingredients all at once, stirring just until moistened. Spoon batter into prepared muffin pan. Sprinkle topping evenly over batter; pat down gently.

3. Bake for 20 to 25 minutes or until tops spring back when lightly touched.

Variation
Replace apple with the same quantity of grated zucchini.

Apple Cranberry Muffins

Apples and cranberries are in season at the same time for a reason: they make a delectable combination.

Makes about 15 muffins

Preparation: 20 minutes

Baking: 30 minutes

Freezing: excellent

TIPS

These muffins are as good for breakfast as they are for dessert.

Grease the tops of the pans, as well as the bottoms and sides, so the topping won't stick and the muffins will be easy to remove.

Moist muffins freeze very well. It's nice to have extras on hand for days when there's no time to bake.

- *Preheat oven to 325°F (160°C)*
- *Two 12-cup muffin pans, greased or lined with paper liners*

Muffins

1 1/3 cups	packed brown sugar	325 mL
2/3 cup	vegetable oil	150 mL
1	egg	1
1 cup	buttermilk	250 mL
2 1/2 cups	Robin Hood All-Purpose Flour	625 mL
1 tsp	baking soda	5 mL
3/4 tsp	salt	3 mL
1/2 tsp	ground cinnamon	2 mL
1 1/2 cups	finely chopped peeled cored apple	375 mL
3/4 cup	fresh or frozen cranberries	175 mL

Topping

1/3 cup	granulated sugar	75 mL
1/2 tsp	ground cinnamon	2 mL
1 tbsp	butter, softened	15 mL

1. **Muffins:** Beat brown sugar, oil, egg and buttermilk in a large bowl until thoroughly blended.
2. Combine flour, baking soda, salt and cinnamon. Add to liquid ingredients, stirring just until blended. Fold in apple and cranberries. Spoon into prepared muffin pans.
3. **Topping:** Combine sugar, cinnamon and butter, mixing with a fork until crumbly. Sprinkle over muffins.
4. Bake for 25 to 30 minutes or until tops spring back when lightly touched.

Variation

Replace cranberries with the same quantity of fresh blueberries or dried cranberries.

Apple Cranberry Crumble Muffins

A crumbly almond streusel tops these huge, moist muffins.

**Makes
1 dozen muffins**

Preparation: 20 minutes

Baking: 30 minutes

Freezing: excellent

TIPS

Lightly toasting nuts before using brings out their flavor.

Grease top of pan as well as cups for easy removal.

- Preheat oven to 375°F (190°C)
- 12-cup muffin pan, greased

Muffins

2¼ cups	Robin Hood All-Purpose Flour	550 mL
1¼ cups	packed brown sugar	300 mL
1 tsp	baking soda	5 mL
½ tsp	salt	2 mL
1	egg	1
1 cup	plain yogurt	250 mL
½ cup	vegetable oil	125 mL
2 cups	diced peeled apples	500 mL
¾ cup	cranberries	175 mL

Topping

¼ cup	packed brown sugar	50 mL
¼ cup	chopped almonds	50 mL
3 tbsp	Robin Hood Oats	45 mL
½ tsp	cinnamon	2 mL
1 tbsp	butter or margarine, melted	15 mL

1. **Muffins:** Combine flour, brown sugar, baking soda and salt in large bowl.

2. Combine egg, yogurt and oil in small bowl. Add to dry ingredients, stirring just until moistened. Stir in apples and cranberries. Spoon batter into prepared muffin pan. (Cups will be very full.)

3. **Topping:** Combine all ingredients. Mix well and sprinkle over muffins. Bake for 25 to 30 minutes or until top springs back when lightly touched.

Variations

Replace cranberries with blueberries. Replace almonds with pecans.

Best-Ever Banana Muffins

Once you've tried this recipe, you'll always want to have ripe bananas on hand so you can whip up a batch of these delicious muffins.

Makes
1 dozen muffins

Preparation: 20 minutes

Baking: 25 minutes

Freezing: excellent

TIPS

The riper the bananas, the better the flavor.

One large banana should yield about ½ cup (125 mL) mashed banana.

To measure flour and other dry ingredients, spoon lightly into a dry measuring cup and level off with a spatula or the back of a knife.

The large quantity of bananas makes these muffins particularly flavourful and moist.

- Preheat oven to 375°F (190°C)
- 12-cup muffin pan, greased or lined with paper liners

1	egg	1
1½ cups	mashed banana (3 or 4 large)	375 mL
½ cup	butter, melted	125 mL
1½ cups	Robin Hood All-Purpose Flour	375 mL
¾ cup	granulated sugar	175 mL
1 tsp	baking powder	5 mL
1 tsp	baking soda	5 mL
½ tsp	salt	2 mL

1. Beat egg, mashed banana and melted butter in a large bowl until thoroughly blended.
2. Combine flour, sugar, baking powder, baking soda and salt. Add to banana mixture and stir just until moistened. Spoon batter into prepared muffin pan.
3. Bake for 20 to 25 minutes or until tops spring back when lightly touched.

Variations

Add 1 cup (250 mL) fresh or frozen cranberries or blueberries to the batter.

Add ¾ cup (175 mL) semi-sweet chocolate chips to the batter.

Banana Bran Muffins

Good-for-you bran muffins with a great banana taste.

**Makes
1 dozen muffins**

Preparation: 15 minutes

Baking: 20 minutes

Freezing: excellent

TIP

Use ripe bananas for the best flavor.

- *Preheat oven to 400°F (200°C)*
- *12-cup muffin pan, greased*

1 ½ cups	natural wheat bran	375 mL
1 cup	Robin Hood All-Purpose Flour	250 mL
½ cup	packed brown sugar	125 mL
1 ½ tsp	baking powder	7 mL
½ tsp	baking soda	2 mL
1 tsp	ground cinnamon	5 mL
¼ tsp	salt	1 mL
½ cup	chopped walnuts, optional	125 mL
2	eggs	2
1 cup	mashed ripe bananas (2 to 3 bananas)	250 mL
½ cup	milk	125 mL
½ cup	butter or margarine, melted	125 mL

1. Combine bran, flour, brown sugar, baking powder, baking soda, cinnamon and salt in large bowl. Stir in nuts, if using.

2. Beat together eggs, bananas, milk and butter in small bowl. Add to dry ingredients, stirring just until combined. Spoon batter into prepared muffin pan. Bake for 18 to 20 minutes or until tops spring back when lightly touched.

Variation

Omit cinnamon for a stronger banana taste.

Raspberry Muffins

These sweet, fruit-filled muffins are not typical breakfast fare. Enjoy them as a treat with coffee or as a simple dessert.

Makes 10 large or 12 medium muffins

Preparation: 15 minutes

Baking: 25 minutes

Freezing: excellent

TIPS

If using frozen raspberries, don't thaw them before adding to the batter. They won't hold their shape and will color the batter pink.

If you're making 10 large muffins, fill the empty muffin cups with water to ensure uniform baking.

- Preheat oven to 400°F (200°C)
- 12-cup muffin pan, greased or lined with paper liners

Muffins

1 cup	milk	250 mL
½ cup	butter, melted	125 mL
1	egg	1
2 cups	Robin Hood All-Purpose Flour	500 mL
⅓ cup	granulated sugar	75 mL
1 tbsp	baking powder	15 mL
½ tsp	salt	2 mL
1 cup	fresh or frozen raspberries	250 mL

Topping

2 tbsp	granulated sugar	30 mL

1. **Muffins:** Beat milk, melted butter and egg thoroughly in a large mixing bowl.
2. Combine flour, sugar, baking powder and salt. Stir into liquid ingredients just until combined. Fold in raspberries. Spoon into prepared muffin pan.
3. **Topping:** Sprinkle sugar over top of muffins.
4. Bake for 20 to 25 minutes or until tops spring back when lightly touched.

Variation

For a decadent touch, stir ⅔ cup (150 mL) white or semi-sweet chocolate chips into the batter. After the muffins have baked, drizzle tops with the same kind of melted chocolate.

Blueberry Oat Muffins

Try cranberries, raisins or chocolate chips for another muffin treat.

Makes about 1 dozen muffins

Preparation: 15 minutes

Baking: 25 minutes

Freezing: excellent

TIP

If wild blueberries are available, choose them for a wonderful flavor.

- Preheat oven to 375°F (190°C)
- 12-cup muffin pan, greased

1 cup	Robin Hood Oats	250 mL
1 cup	buttermilk or soured milk	250 mL
1 cup	Robin Hood All-Purpose Flour	250 mL
¾ cup	packed brown sugar	175 mL
1 tsp	baking powder	5 mL
½ tsp	baking soda	2 mL
½ tsp	salt	2 mL
1	egg	1
¼ cup	butter or margarine, melted	50 mL
1 cup	blueberries	250 mL

1. Combine oats and buttermilk. Let stand for 10 minutes.
2. Combine flour, brown sugar, baking powder, baking soda and salt in large mixing bowl. Stir well to blend. Add egg and melted butter to oat mixture. Mix well. Add to dry ingredients, stirring just until moistened. Gently fold in blueberries. Spoon batter into prepared muffin pan. Bake for 20 to 25 minutes or until tops spring back when lightly touched.

Blueberry Orange Muffins

Although these muffins are especially delicious made with fresh blueberries, in season, you can enjoy them year-round made with frozen fruit.

Makes
1 dozen muffins

Preparation: 20 minutes

Baking: 23 minutes

Freezing: excellent

TIPS

Make these with wild blueberries, if available. The flavor is intense and, because they are smaller, there is more luscious fruit in every bite.

Sprinkle coarse sugar over the top just before baking for a glistening top.

- *Preheat oven to 400°F (200°C)*
- *12-cup muffin pan, greased or lined with paper liners*

$\frac{1}{2}$ cup	butter, softened	125 mL
1 cup	granulated sugar	250 mL
2	eggs	2
$\frac{1}{2}$ cup	sour cream	125 mL
1 tbsp	grated orange zest	15 mL
$\frac{1}{2}$ cup	orange juice	125 mL
2 cups	Robin Hood All-Purpose Flour	500 mL
1 tsp	baking powder	5 mL
$\frac{1}{2}$ tsp	baking soda	2 mL
$\frac{1}{4}$ tsp	salt	1 mL
1 cup	blueberries	250 mL

1. Cream butter and sugar in a large bowl until light and creamy. Add eggs, one at a time, beating lightly after each addition. Add sour cream, and orange zest and juice. Mix well.

2. Combine flour, baking powder, baking soda and salt. Stir into creamed mixture just until blended. Gently fold in berries. Spoon batter into prepared muffin pan.

3. Bake for 18 to 23 minutes or until tops spring back when lightly touched.

Variation
Replace blueberries with cranberries.

Cranberry Lemon Muffins

Tangy lemon and tart cranberries pair up for a refreshingly tasty muffin.

Makes 1 dozen muffins

Preparation: 20 minutes

Baking: 25 minutes

Freezing: excellent, not glazed

TIP

For a crunchy topping, sprinkle batter with a mixture of 1/3 cup (75 mL) chopped almonds and 2 tbsp (30 mL) granulated sugar before baking.

- Preheat oven to 400°F (200°C)
- 12-cup muffin pan, greased

Muffins

2 1/2 cups	Robin Hood All-Purpose Flour	625 mL
1 tbsp	baking powder	15 mL
1/2 tsp	salt	2 mL
1/2 tsp	ground cinnamon	2 mL
1	egg	1
1 1/4 cups	milk	300 mL
1/3 cup	vegetable oil	75 mL
1/3 cup	liquid honey	75 mL
2 tsp	grated lemon zest	10 mL
1 1/2 cups	fresh or frozen cranberries	375 mL

Glaze (optional)

2/3 cup	confectioner's (icing) sugar, sifted	150 mL
1 tsp	grated lemon zest	5 mL
3 to 4 tsp	lemon juice	15 to 20 mL

1. **Muffins:** Combine flour, baking powder, salt and cinnamon in a bowl.
2. Combine egg, milk, oil, honey and lemon zest in large bowl. Add dry ingredients. Stir just until dry ingredients are moistened. Fold in cranberries. Spoon batter into prepared muffin pan. Bake for 20 to 25 minutes or until tops spring back when lightly touched.
3. **Glaze (optional):** Combine confectioner's sugar, lemon zest and enough juice to make smooth, spreadable consistency. Spread on warm muffins.

Variation

Replace lemon zest and juice with orange.

Morning Muffin Magic

A nutritious and delicious way to start your day (see photo, page 157).

(see photo, page 157).

Makes 12 large or 16 regular muffins

Preparation: 15 minutes

Baking: 27 minutes

Freezing: excellent

TIPS

Be sure to peel the carrots. The reaction of peel in the batter can form green specks.

For large muffins, grease top of pan as well as cups.

- Preheat oven to 350°F (180°C)
- Two 12-cup muffin pans, greased

2 cups	Robin Hood All-Purpose Flour	500 mL
1¼ cups	granulated sugar	300 mL
2 tsp	baking soda	10 mL
2 tsp	ground cinnamon	10 mL
½ tsp	salt	2 mL
½ cup	raisins	125 mL
½ cup	chopped nuts	125 mL
½ cup	flaked coconut	125 mL
3	eggs	3
¾ cup	vegetable oil	175 mL
1 tsp	vanilla	5 mL
2 cups	grated peeled carrots	500 mL
1	grated peeled apple	1

1. Combine flour, sugar, baking soda, cinnamon and salt in large bowl. Stir in raisins, nuts and coconuts to blend.

2. Beat together eggs, oil, vanilla, carrots and apple in medium bowl. Add to dry ingredients, stirring just until moistened. Spoon batter into prepared muffin pans, filling three-quarters full for regular size or full for large size. Bake for 20 to 27 minutes or until tops spring back when lightly touched.

Variation
Replace carrot with zucchini.

Cranberry Breakfast Muffins

Red River Cereal and oats combine with fresh cranberries in this hearty, healthy muffin.

Makes
1 dozen muffins

Preparation: 15 minutes

Standing time: 40 minutes

Baking: 25 minutes

Freezing: excellent

TIP

Keep a few bags of cranberries in your freezer to enjoy these muffins year-round.

- *Preheat oven to 375°F (190°C)*
- *12-cup muffin pan, greased*

¾ cup	Robin Hood Oats	175 mL
½ cup	Red River Cereal	125 mL
1 cup	buttermilk or soured milk	250 mL
1 cup	Robin Hood All-Purpose Flour	250 mL
¾ cup	packed brown sugar	175 mL
1 tsp	baking powder	5 mL
¾ tsp	baking soda	3 mL
½ tsp	salt	2 mL
1	egg	1
⅓ cup	butter, melted	75 mL
1 cup	fresh or frozen cranberries	250 mL

1. Combine oats, Red River Cereal and buttermilk in large bowl. Let stand for 40 minutes. Combine flour, sugar, baking powder, baking soda and salt. Add egg and melted butter to cereal mixture. Add dry ingredients. Mix well. Stir in cranberries. Spoon batter into prepared muffin pan. Bake for 20 to 25 minutes or until tops spring back when lightly touched.

Variation
Replace cranberries with blueberries.

Cocoa Oatmeal Muffins

Add cocoa powder to oatmeal muffins for a taste that's worth waking up to. A creamy honey spread adds the crowning touch.

Makes
1 dozen muffins

Preparation: 15 minutes

Baking: 20 minutes

Freezing: excellent

TIPS

Sprinkle top of muffin batter with oats before baking, if desired.

Add chocolate chips for a more chocolatey taste.

- *Preheat oven to 400°F (200°C)*
- *12-cup muffin pan, greased*

Muffins

1 ¼ cups	Robin Hood All-Purpose Flour	300 mL
1 cup	granulated sugar	250 mL
¾ cup	Robin Hood Oats	175 mL
⅓ cup	cocoa powder	75 mL
1 tbsp	baking powder	15 mL
1 tsp	salt	5 mL
2	eggs	2
1 cup	milk	250 mL
½ cup	butter or margarine, melted	125 mL
1 tsp	vanilla	5 mL
1 cup	chopped walnuts	250 mL

Honey Spread

½ cup	butter or margarine, softened	125 mL
⅓ cup	liquid honey	75 mL

1. **Muffins:** Combine flour, sugar, oats, cocoa powder, baking powder and salt in large bowl. Mix well.

2. Beat together eggs, milk, melted butter and vanilla in small bowl. Add milk mixture and nuts all at once to dry ingredients, stirring just until moistened. Spoon batter into prepared muffin pan. Bake for 15 to 20 minutes or until tops spring back when lightly touched.

3. **Honey Spread:** Beat together butter and honey until smooth. Spread on warm muffins.

Date 'n' Orange Muffins

A double hit of orange combined with soft, sweet dates make these muffins a real delight. Enjoy them plain, with a drizzle of honey or spread with cream cheese.

Makes
1 dozen muffins

Preparation: 20 minutes

Baking: 20 minutes

Freezing: excellent
(without topping)

TIPS

Be sure to use soft dates in this recipe. Dates dry out as they age. If yours are dry, cover them with boiling water to soften before using. Drain off the water before using.

When cutting dates, spray your knife or scissors with cooking spray or brush lightly with oil to prevent them from sticking.

Use freshly squeezed juice for optimum flavor.

Use a soft toothbrush to clean a citrus grater easily.

- Preheat oven to 375°F (190°C)
- 12-cup muffin pan, greased or lined with paper liners

Muffins

2 cups	Robin Hood All-Purpose Flour	500 mL
1/2 cup	granulated sugar	125 mL
1 tbsp	grated orange zest	15 mL
2 tsp	baking powder	10 mL
1 tsp	baking soda	5 mL
1/2 tsp	salt	2 mL
1	egg	1
1 cup	chopped pitted dates	250 mL
1/2 cup	orange juice	125 mL
1/2 cup	milk	125 mL
1/4 cup	vegetable oil	50 mL

Topping, optional

1/4 cup	granulated sugar	50 mL
1 tbsp	grated orange zest	15 mL

1. **Muffins:** Combine flour, sugar, orange zest, baking powder, baking soda and salt in a large bowl.
2. Beat egg, dates, orange juice, milk and oil in a small bowl. Add to dry ingredients, stirring just until moistened. Spoon into prepared muffin pan.
3. **Topping (optional):** Mix sugar with orange zest. Sprinkle 1 tsp (5 mL) over each muffin.
4. Bake for 15 to 20 minutes or until tops spring back when lightly touched.

Variation
Replace dates with raisins or dried cranberries.

Luscious Date Bran Muffins

High in flavor and fiber but low in fat, these muffins are a tasty choice.

Makes
1 dozen muffins
Preparation: 20 minutes
Baking: 25 minutes
Freezing: excellent

TIPS

Because the dates are cooked to a purée, they add flavor and moistness throughout the muffin.

For use in this recipe, be sure to buy natural bran, which should not be confused with cold-cereal bran products. Natural bran, which is also found in the cereal section of the supermarket, is small dry flakes that look like wheat germ.

- *Preheat oven to 375°F (190°C)*
- *12-cup muffin pan, greased or lined with paper liners*

Filling

1 cup	chopped pitted dates	250 mL
1 cup	hot water	250 mL
½ cup	packed brown sugar	125 mL
1 tbsp	lemon juice	15 mL

Muffins

1½ cups	natural bran	375 mL
1 cup	Robin Hood All-Purpose Flour	250 mL
1 tsp	baking soda	5 mL
1 tsp	salt	5 mL
½ tsp	baking powder	2 mL
1	egg	1
1 cup	buttermilk	250 mL
½ cup	packed brown sugar	125 mL
1 tbsp	vegetable oil	15 mL

1. **Filling:** Mix dates, water, brown sugar and lemon juice in a saucepan. Simmer over medium heat until thickened. Set aside to cool.
2. **Muffins:** Combine bran, flour, baking soda, salt and baking powder in a mixing bowl.
3. In a separate bowl, beat egg, buttermilk, brown sugar and oil until thoroughly blended. Add all at once to dry ingredients. Stir just until moistened. Stir in date filling. Mix well. Spoon batter into prepared muffin pan.
4. Bake for 20 to 25 minutes or until tops spring back when lightly touched.

Variation
Add 1 tbsp (15 mL) grated orange zest to the filling.

Spicy Carrot Muffins

These flavorful muffins are wholesome and delicious.

Makes 1 dozen large or 16 regular muffins

Preparation: 15 minutes

Baking: 27 minutes

Freezing: excellent

TIPS

For added fiber, use Robin Hood Whole Wheat Flour in place of all or part of the Robin Hood All-Purpose Flour.

Be sure to peel the carrots. The reaction of the peel in the batter to the leavening can form green specks.

If you're making large muffins, grease the top of the pan. Cut the parts of the tops that have overflowed and run into each other into squares, then remove from the pan.

- *Preheat oven to 350°F (180°C)*
- *One or two 12-cup muffin pans, greased or lined with paper liners*

2 cups	Robin Hood All-Purpose Flour	500 mL
1 1/4 cups	granulated sugar	300 mL
3/4 cup	raisins	175 mL
1/2 cup	chopped walnuts	125 mL
2 tsp	baking soda	10 mL
1 1/2 tsp	ground cinnamon	7 mL
1/2 tsp	ground nutmeg	2 mL
1/2 tsp	salt	2 mL
2 1/2 cups	grated peeled carrots	625 mL
3	eggs	3
3/4 cup	vegetable oil	175 mL

1. Combine flour, sugar, raisins, walnuts, baking soda, cinnamon, nutmeg and salt in a large bowl. Stir well.

2. Beat carrots, eggs and oil. Add to dry ingredients all at once, stirring just until moistened. Spoon batter into prepared muffin pans, filling three-quarters full for regular-size or full for large-size muffins.

3. Bake for 20 minutes for regular muffins or 27 minutes for large muffins or until tops spring back when lightly touched.

Variations

Omit nuts, if desired.

Replace the carrots with shredded zucchini.

Replace raisins with dried cranberries or dried cherries.

Strawberry Rhubarb Muffins

The top half is amazing, and the bottom is just as good.

Makes 18 muffins

Preparation: 20 minutes
Baking: 30 minutes
Freezing: excellent

TIP

Reheat previously frozen baked muffins in oven to crisp tops.

- *Preheat oven to 350°F (180°C)*
- *Two 12-cup muffin pans, greased*

Muffins

2¾ cups	Robin Hood All-Purpose Flour	675 mL
1¼ cups	packed brown sugar	300 mL
1¼ tsp	baking soda	6 mL
½ tsp	salt	2 mL
½ cup	butter or margarine, melted	125 mL
1	egg	1
1 cup	buttermilk or soured milk	250 mL
1¼ cups	chopped rhubarb	300 mL
¾ cup	chopped strawberries	175 mL

Topping

½ cup	packed brown sugar	125 mL
½ tsp	cinnamon	2 mL

1. **Muffins:** Combine flour, brown sugar, baking soda and salt in a large bowl. Mix well.
2. Combine melted butter, egg, buttermilk, rhubarb and strawberries in large mixing bowl. Add dry ingredients. Mix thoroughly until dry ingredients are moistened. Spoon batter into prepared muffin pans.
3. **Topping:** Combine brown sugar and cinnamon. Sprinkle evenly on muffins. Bake for 25 to 30 minutes or until tops spring back when lightly touched.

Variation
Replace strawberries with raspberries or additional rhubarb.

Peach Shortcake Muffins

Serve as a morning muffin or warm with whipped cream as a dessert.

**Makes
1 dozen muffins**

Preparation: 20 minutes
Baking: 25 minutes
Freezing: excellent

TIP

To peel peaches easily, first dip in boiling water, then cold water.

- *Preheat oven to 400°F (200°C)*
- *12-cup muffin pan, greased*

Muffin

1²/₃ cups	Robin Hood All-Purpose Flour	400 mL
¹/₂ cup	granulated sugar	125 mL
2¹/₂ tsp	baking powder	12 mL
¹/₂ tsp	ground ginger	2 mL
¹/₄ tsp	salt	1 mL
6 tbsp	butter or margarine	90 mL
1 cup	milk	250 mL
1²/₃ cups	coarsely chopped fresh or canned peaches	400 mL

Topping

2 tbsp	granulated sugar	30 mL
¹/₂ tsp	cinnamon	2 mL

1. **Muffins:** Combine flour, sugar, baking powder, ginger and salt in large bowl. Cut in butter with pastry blender until crumbly. Add milk and peaches, stirring just until blended. Spoon batter into prepared muffin pan.

2. **Topping:** Combine sugar and cinnamon. Sprinkle over muffins. Bake for 20 to 25 minutes or until tops spring back when lightly touched.

Variation
Replace peaches with fresh strawberries.

Cheddar, Bacon and Corn Muffins

Enjoy traditional breakfast foods all in one savory muffin.

Makes
1 dozen muffins

Preparation: 20 minutes

Baking: 20 minutes

Freezing: excellent

TIPS

Savory muffins are at their most flavorful when served warm. Enjoy these with soup or a salad for lunch or with a hearty stew or chili for dinner.

For another taste sensation, try splitting baked muffins and grilling them under the broiler or on the barbecue.

Cook bacon until very crisp. Cool, then crumble. If you are cooking it ahead of time, and the reserved bacon drippings have solidified, be sure to melt them before adding to the batter.

- Preheat oven to 375°F (190°C)
- 12-cup muffin pan, greased or lined with paper liners

8	slices bacon	8
1 cup	Robin Hood All-Purpose Flour	250 mL
1 cup	cornmeal	250 mL
2 tbsp	granulated sugar	30 mL
1 tbsp	baking powder	15 mL
$\frac{1}{4}$ tsp	salt	1 mL
1	egg, beaten	1
1	can (10 oz/284 mL) creamed corn	1
1 cup	grated Cheddar cheese	250 mL
$\frac{1}{2}$ cup	milk	125 mL
$\frac{1}{4}$ cup	bacon drippings	50 mL

1. Cook bacon in a skillet over medium heat until very crisp. Drain on paper towels. Crumble and set aside. Reserve $\frac{1}{4}$ cup (50 mL) of the drippings.

2. Combine flour, cornmeal, sugar, baking powder, salt and bacon in a mixing bowl. In a separate bowl, beat egg, corn, cheese, milk and reserved bacon drippings until thoroughly blended. Add all at once to dry ingredients. Stir just until moistened. Spoon batter into prepared muffin pan.

3. Bake for 15 to 20 minutes or until tops spring back when lightly touched. Serve warm.

Variation

You can replace the bacon drippings with vegetable oil or melted butter; but the bacon flavor will not be as prominent.

Oat and Honey Bran Muffins

A tasty way to add nutrition to your diet!

Makes 18 muffins

Preparation: 15 minutes

Baking: 25 minutes

Freezing: excellent

TIP

If you don't have buttermilk, pour 1 tbsp (15 mL) lemon juice in measuring cup. Add milk to make 1 cup (250 mL). Let stand for 5 minutes; stir.

- Preheat oven to 375°F (190°C)
- Two 12-cup muffin pans, greased

1 cup	Robin Hood Oats	250 mL
¾ cup	wheat germ	175 mL
½ cup	natural wheat bran	125 mL
½ tsp	salt	2 mL
½ tsp	cinnamon	2 mL
1 cup	buttermilk or soured milk	250 mL
¾ cup	liquid honey	175 mL
2	eggs, beaten	2
½ cup	vegetable oil	125 mL
1 cup	Robin Hood Whole Wheat Flour or All-Purpose Flour	250 mL
2 tsp	baking powder	10 mL
1 tsp	baking soda	5 mL
½ cup	raisins	125 mL

1. Combine oats, wheat germ, bran, salt, cinnamon and buttermilk. Mix well and let stand for 15 minutes. Add honey, eggs and oil. Mix well.

2. Combine flour, baking powder and baking soda. Add to oat mixture. Stir just until moistened. Stir in raisins. Spoon batter into prepared muffin pans, filling three-quarters full. Bake for 20 to 25 minutes or until tops spring back when lightly touched. Loosen edges and turn out onto racks to cool.

Variation

Dried cranberries or chopped apricots are also great.

Chocolate Zucchini Muffins

Chocolate fans will especially appreciate these moist, tasty muffins.

Makes 16 muffins

Preparation: 20 minutes
Baking: 25 minutes
Freezing: excellent

TIPS

Don't peel the zucchini before shredding. The green flecks add color and texture.

Shred zucchini just before using. Let stand, it releases a fair amount of moisture.

Because cocoa tends to clump when stored, it needs to be sifted before it is added to a recipe. Measure, then sift before using.

- *Preheat oven to 375°F (190°C)*
- *Two 12-cup muffin pans, greased or lined with paper liners*

¾ cup	butter, softened	175 mL
2 cups	granulated sugar	500 mL
3	eggs	3
2½ cups	Robin Hood All-Purpose Flour	625 mL
½ cup	unsweetened cocoa powder, sifted	125 mL
2½ tsp	baking powder	12 mL
1½ tsp	baking soda	7 mL
½ tsp	salt	2 mL
½ tsp	ground cinnamon	2 mL
2 cups	shredded zucchini	500 mL
½ cup	milk	125 mL
1 cup	semi-sweet chocolate chips	250 mL

1. Cream butter and sugar in a large bowl until light and creamy. Add eggs, one at a time, beating lightly after each addition.
2. Combine flour, cocoa, baking powder, baking soda, salt and cinnamon. Add to creamed mixture alternately with zucchini and milk, making two additions of each. Mix well. Fold in chocolate chips. Spoon batter into prepared muffin pan.
3. Bake for 20 to 25 minutes or until tops spring back when lightly touched.

Variations

Replace chocolate chips with any kind of nut.

Replace zucchini with shredded peeled carrot.

Chocolate Raspberry Torte

Cakes & Frostings

Chocolate Raspberry Torte

The combination of chocolate, fresh raspberries and whipped cream is always a winner. You can also make this using strawberry jam and fresh strawberries.

Makes about 12 servings

Preparation: 35 minutes

Baking: 40 minutes

Chilling: 30 minutes

Freezing: excellent

TIPS

To make chocolate curls, use milk chocolate bars at room temperature. Draw a vegetable peeler across the bar. For smaller curls, use the narrow edge of the bar; for large curls, use the wide side.

When spreading a cream filling between cake layers, leave a small border around the edge so the cream doesn't spread into the frosting on the side of the cake.

Because it is soft, the chocolate-sour cream frosting spreads beautifully. It firms up as it cools.

- Preheat oven to 350°F (180°C)
- Two 9-inch (1.5 L) round cake pans, greased and floured

Cake

2 cups	Robin Hood All-Purpose Flour	500 mL
2 cups	granulated sugar	500 mL
¾ cup	unsweetened cocoa powder	175 mL
1½ tsp	baking powder	7 mL
1½ tsp	baking soda	7 mL
1 tsp	salt	5 mL
2	eggs	2
1 cup	milk	250 mL
½ cup	vegetable oil	125 mL
2 tsp	vanilla	10 mL
1 cup	boiling water	250 mL

Filling

2 cups	whipping (35%) cream	500 mL
¼ cup	confectioner's (icing) sugar, sifted	50 mL
1 cup	raspberry jam	250 mL

Frosting

1½ cups	semi-sweet chocolate chips	375 mL
¾ cup	sour cream	175 mL
	Chocolate curls, optional	
	Fresh raspberries, optional	

1. **Cake:** Sift flour, sugar, cocoa, baking powder, baking soda and salt into a large mixer bowl. Add eggs, milk, oil and vanilla. Beat on medium speed of electric mixer for 2 minutes. Stir in boiling water until smooth. (Batter will be thin.) Pour into prepared pans.

2. Bake for 35 to 40 minutes or until a toothpick inserted in center comes out clean. Cool for 10 minutes in pans on rack, then remove layers and cool completely. Cut each in half horizontally to make four layers.

3. **Filling:** Beat whipping cream and icing sugar until stiff peaks form.

4. **Frosting:** In a small saucepan over low heat, melt chocolate chips (or microwave on Medium (50 %) for 2 minutes). Stir until smooth. Stir in sour cream.

5. **Assembly:** Place one halved cake layer cut-side up on serving plate. Spread with ⅓ cup (75 mL) jam and one-third of the cream mixture. Repeat layering, ending with top cake layer cut-side down. Frost top and sides of cake with frosting. Decorate with chocolate curls and fresh raspberries, if using. Chill until ready to serve and chocolate has set, about 30 minutes.

Rhubarb Cake

Fresh, rosy rhubarb adds its refreshing flavor to this delicious cake — a wonderful way to use up any surplus rhubarb from the garden.

Makes about 12 servings

Preparation: 20 minutes

Baking: 50 minutes

Freezing: not recommended

TIPS

Use only fresh rhubarb in this recipe. The cake is very moist, and frozen rhubarb would make the texture too soggy. Choose stalks of uniform thickness and cut into similar-size pieces to ensure that they cook evenly.

Stalks that are fairly thin and pink to red, rather than green, are the most flavorful and tender.

One stalk should give you about ½ cup (125 mL) chopped rhubarb.

Baked goods containing rhubarb go well with custard sauce, vanilla ice cream or whipped cream.

- Preheat oven to 350°F (180°C)
- 9-inch (2.5 L) square cake pan, greased

Cake

½ cup	butter, softened	125 mL
1⅓ cups	packed brown sugar	325 mL
1	egg	1
1 tsp	vanilla	5 mL
1 cup	buttermilk	250 mL
2 cups	Robin Hood All-Purpose Flour	500 mL
1 tsp	baking soda	5 mL
½ tsp	salt	2 mL
2 cups	chopped fresh rhubarb	500 mL

Topping

⅓ cup	packed brown sugar	75 mL
1 tsp	ground cinnamon	5 mL

1. **Cake:** Beat butter, brown sugar, egg and vanilla in a large mixer bowl on medium speed of electric mixer until smooth and blended. Add buttermilk; mix well.
2. Combine flour, baking soda and salt. Add to buttermilk mixture, beating just until smooth. Fold in rhubarb. Spread batter evenly in prepared pan.
3. **Topping:** Combine brown sugar and cinnamon. Sprinkle evenly over batter.
4. Bake for 45 to 50 minutes or until toothpick inserted in center comes out clean. Cool in pan on rack.

Variation
Replace half of the rhubarb with strawberries or raspberries.

Pineapple Upside-Down Cake

Though simple to make, this dessert always looks and tastes fabulous. Keep a can of pineapple rings in your pantry so you'll be able to prepare this anytime.

Makes about 9 servings

Preparation: 20 minutes

Baking: 75 minutes

Freezing: not recommended

TIPS

To add color and eye appeal, place a maraschino cherry in the center of each pineapple ring. Candied cherries also work well.

A 19 oz (540 mL) can of pineapple rings will give you the right number of rings. There may be one left over for the cook to eat.

You can prepare the brown sugar topping right in the pan, so there won't be an extra pan to clean. To melt the butter, place the pan, with the butter, in the preheated oven or on the stove top over low heat.

- Preheat oven to 350°F (180°C)
- 9-inch (2.5 L) square cake pan, ungreased

Topping

1/3 cup	butter	75 mL
1 cup	packed brown sugar	250 mL
9	slices canned pineapple, drained	9
9	maraschino cherries, drained, optional	9

Cake

1/2 cup	butter, softened	125 mL
1 cup	granulated sugar	250 mL
2	eggs	2
1 tsp	vanilla	5 mL
1 3/4 cups	Robin Hood All-Purpose Flour	425 mL
1 tbsp	baking powder	15 mL
1/2 tsp	salt	2 mL
3/4 cup	milk	175 mL

1. **Topping:** Melt butter in cake pan (see Tips, left). Stir in brown sugar; mix well and spread evenly over bottom of pan. Place pineapple on top and a cherry in the center of each ring, if using. Set aside.

2. **Cake:** Cream butter, sugar, eggs and vanilla in a large bowl on medium speed of electric mixer until light and creamy. Combine flour, baking powder and salt. Add to creamed mixture alternately with milk, making three dry and two liquid additions and beating lightly after each addition. Spread batter evenly over pineapple.

3. Bake for 65 to 75 minutes or until toothpick inserted in center comes out clean. Cool for 10 minutes in pan on rack, then loosen cake around edges and invert onto a serving plate. Serve warm or cool.

Variation

Replace pineapple with enough peach slices to cover the bottom of the pan in a single layer. If using canned, drain first.

Cranberry Kuchen

This cranberry kuchen is a moist and delicious coffee cake.

Makes about 12 servings

Preparation: 20 minutes
Baking: 55 minutes
Freezing: excellent

TIP

Too little greasing or leaving cakes in pans too long can cause sticking. To prevent sticking, grease pans generously with shortening (not butter) and remove cake after cooling for 10 minutes.

- Preheat oven to 350°F (180°C)
- 10-inch (25 cm) springform pan, greased

Cake

$\frac{1}{2}$ cup	butter or margarine	125 mL
$1\frac{1}{4}$ cups	granulated sugar, divided	300 mL
1 tsp	vanilla	5 mL
3	eggs	3
2 cups	Robin Hood All-Purpose Flour or $2\frac{1}{4}$ cups (550 mL) Robin Hood Best For Cake & Pastry Flour	500 mL
2 tsp	baking powder	10 mL
$\frac{1}{2}$ tsp	baking soda	2 mL
$\frac{1}{2}$ tsp	salt	2 mL
$1\frac{1}{4}$ cups	sour cream	300 mL
2 cups	chopped cranberries	500 mL

Topping

$\frac{1}{4}$ cup	packed brown sugar	50 mL
2 tbsp	Robin Hood All-Purpose or Best For Cake & Pastry Flour	30 mL
2 tbsp	chopped almonds	30 mL
1 tbsp	butter or margarine, softened	15 mL
$\frac{1}{2}$ tsp	ground cinnamon	2 mL

1. **Cake:** Cream together butter, 1 cup (250 mL) sugar and vanilla in large bowl with electric mixer. Add eggs, one at a time, beating until light and fluffy. Combine flour, baking powder, baking soda and salt. Alternately add dry ingredients and sour cream to creamed mixture, ending with dry ingredients. (Batter will be fairly thick.) Combine cranberries and remaining $\frac{1}{4}$ cup (50 mL) sugar. Spread half of the batter in prepared pan and sprinkle with cranberry mixture. Top with remaining batter.

2. **Topping:** Combine brown sugar, flour, almonds, butter and cinnamon; sprinkle over batter. Bake for 50 to 55 minutes or until toothpick inserted in center comes out clean.

Variation

Add 1 tbsp (15 mL) grated orange zest to batter.

Tropical Treat Cake

Several fruits combine in a wonderfully moist cake that needs no frosting. It's a nice snack or lunch-box cake or a pleasing dessert served with a dollop of whipped cream.

Makes about 8 servings

Preparation: 15 minutes
Baking: 55 minutes
Freezing: excellent

TIP

Use a ripe banana for the best flavor.

- Preheat oven to 350°F (180°C)
- 9-inch (2.5 L) square cake pan, greased

1	large orange	1
1	medium banana	1
1 cup	raisins	250 mL
1¾ cups	Robin Hood All-Purpose Flour	425 mL
1 tsp	baking soda	5 mL
½ tsp	ground cinnamon	2 mL
¼ tsp	salt	1 mL
½ cup	shortening	125 mL
1 cup	granulated sugar	250 mL
2	eggs	2
½ cup	buttermilk or soured milk	125 mL
1 tsp	vanilla	5 mL

1. Peel and cut orange into pieces; remove seeds. Combine orange, banana and raisins in food processor and chop coarsely. Combine flour, baking soda, cinnamon and salt.

2. Cream together shortening, sugar and eggs in large bowl on high speed of electric mixer until light and creamy. Add fruit mixture. Add dry ingredients alternately with buttermilk and vanilla, mixing lightly after each addition. Spread batter evenly in prepared pan. Bake for 50 to 55 minutes or until toothpick inserted in center comes out clean.

Sunny Citrus Pound Cake

Plain and simple is often the most delicious. Serve unadorned with coffee for an afternoon treat or as dessert with fresh fruit.

Makes about 16 servings

Preparation: 25 minutes

Baking:
1 hour 15 minutes

Freezing: excellent, not glazed

TIP

Expect a crack on top. This is typical of most pound cakes.

- Preheat oven to 350°F (180°C)
- 10-inch (3 L) Bundt or 10-inch (4 L) tube pan, greased and floured

Cake

3 cups	Robin Hood All-Purpose Flour	750 mL
¾ tsp	salt	3 mL
½ tsp	baking powder	2 mL
½ tsp	baking soda	2 mL
1 cup	unsalted butter, softened	250 mL
2¼ cups	granulated sugar	550 mL
4	eggs	4
1 tbsp	grated orange zest	15 mL
2 tsp	grated lemon zest	10 mL
¾ cup	plain yogurt	175 mL
⅓ cup	orange juice	75 mL

Glaze (optional)

⅓ cup	granulated sugar	75 mL
¼ cup	lemon juice	50 mL

1. **Cake:** Combine flour, salt, baking powder and baking soda; set aside. Cream butter and sugar in large mixer bowl on medium speed of electric mixer until well blended. Add eggs, one at a time, beating lightly after each until smooth, then beat on high speed until thick and creamy, about 5 minutes. Add zests. Add dry ingredients alternately with yogurt and orange juice, beating on low speed until blended. Spread batter in prepared pan. Bake for 65 to 75 minutes or until toothpick inserted in center comes out clean. Cool for 10 minutes in pan, then remove to wire rack.

2. **Glaze (optional):** Heat together sugar and juice, stirring to dissolve sugar. Poke holes with toothpick, skewer or fork in surface of warm cake. Brush glaze over cake, letting it soak in. Cool cake completely before slicing.

Variation

For an orange cake, omit lemon zest in cake and use orange juice in the glaze.

Orange Cake

A real family favorite. The fabulous flavors and texture come from grinding the whole orange with raisins and nuts.

Makes about 12 servings

Preparation: 25 minutes
Baking: 40 minutes
Freezing: excellent

TIP

Submerging an orange in hot water for 15 minutes before squeezing will yield almost twice the amount of juice.

- Preheat oven to 350°F (180°C)
- 13- by 9-inch (3.5 L) cake pan, greased

Cake

1	large orange	1
1 cup	raisins	250 mL
$\frac{1}{2}$ cup	walnuts	125 mL
2 cups	Robin Hood All-Purpose Flour or 2$\frac{1}{4}$ cups (550 mL) Robin Hood Best For Cake & Pastry Flour	500 mL
1 cup	granulated sugar	250 mL
1 tsp	baking soda	5 mL
1 tsp	salt	5 mL
1 cup	milk	250 mL
$\frac{1}{2}$ cup	shortening	125 mL
2	eggs	2

Frosting

$\frac{1}{2}$ cup	butter, softened	125 mL
3 cups	confectioner's (icing) sugar, sifted	750 mL
1 tbsp	grated orange zest	15 mL
$\frac{1}{3}$ cup	orange juice	75 mL

1. **Cake:** Squeeze orange; reserve juice for frosting. Grind together or finely chop in food processor orange rind and pulp, raisins and nuts. Set aside. Combine flour, sugar, baking soda, salt, milk, shortening and eggs in large mixer bowl. Beat on low speed just until blended, then on medium speed for 3 minutes. Stir in orange raisin mixture. Spread batter evenly in prepared pan. Bake for 35 to 40 minutes. Cool completely.

2. **Frosting:** Beat together butter, sugar and orange zest and juice until smooth and creamy. Spread over cake.

Variation
Use dates in place of raisins.

Lemon Poppy Seed Layer Cake

The lemon lover's dream dessert. The crunch of poppy seeds adds an interesting texture to cakes.

Makes about 12 servings

Preparation: 40 minutes

Baking: 40 minutes

Freezing: excellent

TIPS

You can also use $2\frac{1}{4}$ cups (550 mL) Robin Hood Best For Cake & Pastry Flour

Use shortening, not butter to grease pans. Cooking spray works well, too.

Prepare entire cake a day ahead to let flavors mellow.

- Preheat oven to 350°F (180°C)
- Two 9-inch (1.5 L) round cake pans, greased and floured

Cake

2 cups	Robin Hood All-Purpose Flour	500 mL
1 tbsp	baking powder	15 mL
$\frac{3}{4}$ tsp	salt	3 mL
$1\frac{1}{3}$ cups	butter, softened	325 mL
$1\frac{1}{3}$ cups	granulated sugar	325 mL
$1\frac{1}{2}$ tsp	vanilla	7 mL
4	eggs	4
$\frac{1}{2}$ cup	milk	125 mL
$\frac{1}{4}$ cup	poppy seeds	50 mL

Filling

2	eggs	2
2 tbsp	grated lemon zest	30 mL
6 tbsp	fresh lemon juice	90 mL
1 cup	granulated sugar	250 mL
$\frac{1}{4}$ cup	butter, softened	50 mL

Frosting

$\frac{1}{2}$ cup	butter, softened	125 mL
4 cups	confectioner's (icing) sugar, sifted	1 L
1 tbsp	grated lemon zest	15 mL
2 tbsp	fresh lemon juice	30 mL
$\frac{1}{4}$ cup	light (10%) cream	50 mL

1. **Cake:** Combine flour, baking powder and salt. Cream butter in large bowl on medium speed of electric mixer until creamy. Gradually add sugar and vanilla, beating until light and fluffy. Add eggs, one at a time, beating well after each addition. Add dry ingredients alternately with milk, mixing lightly just to blend. Fold in poppy seeds. (Batter will be quite stiff.) Spread batter evenly in prepared pans. Bake for 35 to 40 minutes or until toothpick inserted in center comes out clean. Cool for 10 minutes, then remove from pans and cool completely.

2. **Filling:** Beat together eggs, lemon zest, juice and sugar in small saucepan. Add butter. Cook over low heat, stirring constantly, until thickened. Cool completely. Mixture will thicken on cooling. Prepare several days ahead, if desired. Refrigerate until using.

3. **Frosting:** Beat together all ingredients until smooth and creamy.

4. **Assembly:** Cut cake layers in half horizontally to make four layers. Place one layer on plate. Spread half of filling on top. Place second cake layer over filling and spread with some of the frosting. Top with another cake layer, remaining filling and last cake layer. Cover sides and top of cake with remaining frosting.

Raspberry Streusel Coffee Cake

Enjoy this luscious cake warm for breakfast or brunch.

Makes about 16 servings

Preparation: 20 minutes

Baking: 45 minutes

Freezing: excellent

TIPS

This cake freezes well, so take advantage of fresh raspberries in season and make a few extra.

Thawed frozen raspberries work well in this recipe. Be aware that they will slightly color the batter.

For easy snacking and packing in lunch boxes, cut, wrap and freeze individual pieces of this cake. Simply remove the number required and let them thaw in their wrappers.

- Preheat oven to 375°F (190°C)
- 9-inch (2.5 L) square cake pan, greased

Topping

¼ cup	butter, softened	50 mL
⅓ cup	Robin Hood All-Purpose Flour	75 mL
⅓ cup	lightly packed brown sugar	75 mL
1 tsp	ground cinnamon	5 mL

Cake

¼ cup	butter, softened	50 mL
¾ cup	granulated sugar	175 mL
1	egg	1
1 tsp	vanilla	5 mL
¾ cup	milk	175 mL
1¾ cups	Robin Hood All-Purpose Flour	425 mL
1 tbsp	baking powder	15 mL
½ tsp	salt	2 mL
1½ cups	fresh or frozen raspberries, thawed and drained	375 mL

1. **Topping:** Combine butter, flour, sugar and cinnamon, mixing until crumbly. Set aside.
2. **Cake:** Cream butter, sugar, egg and vanilla until thoroughly blended. Add milk, blending well. Combine flour, baking powder and salt; stir well. Add to creamed mixture all at once and stir just until moistened. Spread half of the batter in prepared pan. Spoon raspberries over batter. Spread remaining batter over berries.
3. Sprinkle topping evenly over batter. Press in lightly.
4. Bake for 40 to 45 minutes or until toothpick inserted in center comes out clean. Serve warm.

Variation

Replace raspberries with blueberries.

Lemon Almond Cake

A light and refreshing cake that needs no frosting.

TIP

A nice cake to prepare a day ahead, allowing the glaze to soak into the cake.

- Preheat oven to 350°F (180°C)
- 10-inch (3 L) Bundt or 10-inch (4 L) tube pan, greased and floured

Cake

3 cups	Robin Hood All-Purpose Flour	750 mL
1 tbsp	baking powder	15 mL
1 tsp	salt	5 mL
¾ cup	butter, softened	175 mL
2 cups	granulated sugar	500 mL
4	eggs	4
1 cup	milk	250 mL
1 cup	ground almonds	250 mL
2 tbsp	grated lemon zest	30 mL

Glaze

¾ cup	granulated sugar	175 mL
⅓ cup	lemon juice	75 mL

1. **Cake:** Combine flour, baking powder and salt. Cream butter and sugar in large bowl on medium speed of electric mixer until light. Add eggs, one at a time, beating until light and fluffy. On low speed, add dry ingredients to creamed mixture alternately with milk, mixing lightly after each addition. Stir in almonds and lemon zest.

2. Spread batter evenly in prepared pan. Bake for 60 to 65 minutes or until toothpick inserted in center comes out clean. Cool in pan for 20 minutes. Remove from pan and place on cake plate.

3. **Glaze:** Heat sugar and lemon juice together in small saucepan until sugar is dissolved. Prick surface of cake with fork, toothpick or skewer. Brush warm cake with glaze. Repeat brushing until all glaze is used.

Jelly Roll

Try this once and you'll realize that making a jelly roll is not as hard as it looks. The hard part is choosing a filling, there are so many options.

Makes about 10 servings

Preparation: 25 minutes

Baking: 15 minutes

Freezing: excellent

TIPS

A jelly roll pan is a cookie sheet with ½-inch (1 cm) sides. Although 15- by 10-inch (2 L) is the most common size, they also come in a larger version. All our recipes have been made in the smaller pan. Check to make sure you have the right size or your cake will not cook properly.

An endless variety of fillings work well in a plain jelly roll. You can use jam or jelly, pie filling, frosting, ice cream, or plain or flavored whipped cream, among others.

Complete the roll with a dusting of confectioner's (icing) sugar, whipped cream or a frosting that suits the filling.

For decorations, use chopped nuts, shaved chocolate or small candies. Add a row of candles for a birthday.

- Preheat oven to 375°F (190°C)
- 15- by 10-inch (2 L) jelly roll pan, greased and lined with waxed paper

4	eggs, separated	4
⅓ cup	granulated sugar	75 mL
½ cup	granulated sugar	125 mL
1 tsp	vanilla	5 mL
¾ cup	Robin Hood All-Purpose Flour	175 mL
1 tsp	baking powder	5 mL
½ tsp	salt	2 mL
⅔ cup	confectioner's (icing) sugar	150 mL
1½ cups	jam	375 mL

1. Beat egg whites in a small bowl on high speed of electric mixer until soft peaks form. Gradually add ⅓ cup (75 mL) sugar, beating until stiff peaks form. Set aside.

2. Beat egg yolks in a separate small bowl on high speed of electric mixer until creamy. (Although it uses extra dishes, it is important to beat both the egg whites and the yolks in separate small bowls to get the necessary volume.) Gradually add ½ cup (125 mL) sugar and vanilla, beating on high speed until thick, about 5 minutes. Transfer to a large bowl.

3. Combine flour, baking powder and salt. Sprinkle over egg yolk mixture. Add beaten egg white mixture and gently fold to blend thoroughly. Spread batter evenly in prepared pan.

4. Bake for 12 to 15 minutes or until the top is golden and springs back when lightly touched.

5. Sprinkle a large tea towel with ⅓ cup (75 mL) of the icing sugar. Immediately invert hot cake onto towel. Carefully remove waxed paper. Trim any crisp cake edges, if necessary. Roll warm cake up in towel, starting from one narrow end. Cool cake completely in towel on rack.

6. Unroll cake and spread with jam. Reroll tightly without towel. Sprinkle with remaining ⅓ cup (75 mL) icing sugar.

Cherry Almond Coffee Cake

An easy-to-make cake for dessert or a coffee-time treat.

Preparation: 15 minutes

Baking: 1 hour
or 1 hour 15 minutes

Freezing: excellent

TIP

Always put a piece of aluminum foil under springform pans while baking. Often they can leak a little, so this will keep your oven clean.

- *Preheat oven to 350°F (180°C)*
- *8½-inch (21 cm) or 9-inch (23 cm) springform pan, greased*

2¼ cups	Robin Hood All-Purpose Flour	550 mL
¾ cup	granulated sugar	175 mL
¾ cup	butter or margarine	175 mL
½ tsp	baking powder	2 mL
½ tsp	baking soda	2 mL
1	egg	1
¾ cup	buttermilk or soured milk	175 mL
1 tsp	almond extract	5 mL
1	can (19 oz/540 mL) cherry pie filling	1
⅓ cup	sliced almonds	75 mL

1. Combine flour and sugar in large bowl. Cut in butter with pastry blender until mixture is crumbly. Set aside ½ cup (125 mL) for topping. Add baking powder and baking soda to remainder. Beat together egg, buttermilk and almond extract. Add to dry ingredients, stirring just until moistened.

2. Spread two-thirds of the batter over bottom and partway up side of prepared pan. Spoon pie filling evenly over batter. Drop small spoonfuls of remaining batter over filling. Stir almonds into reserved crumbled mixture. Sprinkle over batter.

3. Bake for 65 to 75 minutes for 8½-inch (21 cm) pan or 50 to 60 minutes for 9-inch (23 cm) pan or until toothpick inserted in center comes out clean. Cover with foil if top is becoming too brown.

Variation

Try apple, mixed berry or blueberry pie filling for another new taste.

Sour Cream Coffee Cake

This not-too-sweet cake is a coffee-time favorite.

Makes about 8 servings

Preparation: 20 minutes
Baking: 60 minutes
Freezing: excellent

TIPS

Always have your ingredients at room temperature before you start to bake.

Don't substitute margarine for butter — the flavor just won't be the same.

When adding dry ingredients to sour cream, beat just enough to blend. Overbeating at this stage will toughen the cake and give it a coarser texture.

Press nuts lightly into batter on top of cake before baking to help them stick.

- Preheat oven to 350°F (180°C)
- 8-inch (20 cm) springform pan, greased

Cake
1 cup	sour cream	250 mL
1 tsp	baking soda	5 mL
½ cup	butter, softened	125 mL
1 cup	granulated sugar	250 mL
2	eggs	2
1 tsp	vanilla	5 mL
1¾ cups	Robin Hood All-Purpose Flour	425 mL
1 tsp	baking powder	5 mL
½ tsp	salt	2 mL

Topping
½ cup	packed brown sugar	125 mL
¼ cup	chopped pecans	50 mL
1 tsp	ground cinnamon	5 mL

1. **Cake:** Combine sour cream and baking soda in a small bowl; set aside.

2. Cream butter and sugar in a large mixer bowl on medium speed of electric mixer until light and fluffy. Add eggs, one at a time, beating thoroughly after each addition. Stir in vanilla.

3. Combine flour, baking powder and salt. Add to creamed mixture alternately with sour cream mixture, making three dry and two liquid additions on low speed, mixing lightly after each addition. Spread half of the batter in prepared pan.

4. **Topping:** Combine brown sugar, pecans and cinnamon. Sprinkle half over batter. Cover with remaining batter, then remaining topping. Press topping lightly into batter.

5. Bake for 50 to 60 minutes or until toothpick inserted in center comes out clean. Cover with aluminum foil if top is browning too quickly. Cool completely in pan on rack. Loosen edge of cake with a knife, then remove pan rim.

Variation
Replace pecans with walnuts, almonds, hazelnuts or cashews.

Glazed Apple Pinwheel Cake

This showstopper fruit cake looks much harder to make than it actually is. It's an easy way to impress your guests.

Makes about 16 servings

Preparation: 25 minutes

Baking: 55 minutes

Freezing: not recommended

TIPS

Use firm apples, such as Golden Delicious, which will hold their shape during baking.

Select apples that are the same size.

Brush cut fruit such as apples, pears, peaches and bananas with lemon juice to prevent it from turning brown.

Heat jam or jelly slightly to soften, if necessary.

- Preheat oven to 350°F (180°C)
- 10-inch (25 cm) springform pan, greased

4 or 5	Golden Delicious apples, peeled, cored and quartered	4 or 5
1 tbsp	lemon juice	15 mL
½ cup	butter, softened	125 mL
¾ cup	granulated sugar	175 mL
2	eggs	2
1 tsp	lemon extract	5 mL
1¾ cups	Robin Hood All-Purpose Flour	425 mL
1½ tsp	baking powder	7 mL
½ tsp	salt	2 mL
½ cup	milk	125 mL
¾ cup	strained apricot jam	175 mL

1. Cut several deep slashes lengthwise in each apple quarter. Brush cut apples with lemon juice; set aside.
2. Beat butter, sugar, eggs and lemon extract in a large bowl on medium speed of electric mixer until light and creamy.
3. Combine flour, baking powder and salt. Add to creamed mixture alternately with milk, making three dry and two liquid additions on low speed, mixing well. Spread batter in prepared pan. Arrange apple quarters, slashed side up, on top of batter.
4. Bake for 50 to 55 minutes or until toothpick inserted in center comes out clean. Cool completely in pan on rack. Brush apricot jam over cooled cake.

Variation

Use apple jelly instead of apricot jam to glaze this cake. It works well for many cakes. If you're using red fruits, use red currant jelly.

Best-Ever Banana Cake

Light, moist and big on banana flavor — make this your next birthday cake.

Makes about 12 servings

Preparation: 20 minutes

Baking: 40 minutes

Freezing: excellent

TIPS

This cake can also be prepared in a 13- by 9-inch (3.5 L) cake pan — just increase the baking time by 5 minutes.

If you don't have buttermilk, put 1½ tsp (7 mL) vinegar or lemon juice in a measuring cup and fill with milk to make ½ cup (125 mL). Let stand for 5 minutes, then stir.

The riper the bananas, the better the flavor. Ripe bananas also give a nice texture and appearance to baked goods. The dark flecks scattered throughout are very attractive.

This is an easy-to-make, one-bowl cake in which everything is beaten together. The conventional method adds liquid and dry ingredients alternately, in stages.

Try garnishing this cake with dried banana chips.

- Preheat oven to 350°F (180°C)
- Two 8-inch (1.2 L) round cake pans, greased and floured

2 cups	Robin Hood All-Purpose Flour	500 mL
1¾ tsp	baking powder	8 mL
1 tsp	baking soda	5 mL
½ tsp	salt	2 mL
1¼ cups	granulated sugar	300 mL
1 cup	mashed ripe banana (2 large)	250 mL
½ cup	butter, softened	125 mL
½ cup	buttermilk	125 mL
2	eggs	2
1 tsp	vanilla	5 mL

1. Combine flour, baking powder, baking soda and salt in a large mixer bowl. Add sugar, banana, butter and buttermilk. Beat at medium speed of electric mixer for 2 minutes. Add eggs and vanilla. Beat at medium speed for 1 minute. Spread batter evenly in prepared pans.

2. Bake for 35 to 40 minutes or until toothpick inserted in center comes out clean. Cool for 10 minutes in pans on rack, then remove from pans and transfer to rack to cool completely. Frost with Banana Butter Frosting (see recipe, below.)

Variations

Frost with Cocoa Butter Frosting (see recipe, page 216) Peanut Butter Frosting (see recipe, page 58) or Chocolate Whipped Cream (see recipe, page 218).

If you will finish eating the cake the same day it is baked, add a layer of sliced bananas between the cake layers.

Banana Butter Frosting

- Makes about 3 cups (750 mL) frosting
- Enough to fill and frost a 9-inch (23 cm) 2-layer cake

½ cup	butter, softened	125 mL
½ cup	mashed ripe banana (about 1 large)	125 mL
4 cups	icing sugar, sifted	1 L
1 tbsp	half-and-half (10%) cream	15 mL

1. In a large mixer bowl, cream butter, mashed banana and half of the icing sugar on medium speed of electric mixer until creamy. Add cream. Add remaining icing sugar gradually, beating until smooth and creamy.

Crunchy Top Banana Cake

Cut into small squares, these "banana bites" make a terrific after-school treat.

Makes about 20 servings

Preparation: 15 minutes

Baking: 43 minutes

Freezing: excellent

TIP

Watch topping closely when broiling. It will burn very quickly.

- Preheat oven to 350°F (180°C)
- 13- by 9-inch (3.5 L) cake pan, greased

Cake

2 cups	Robin Hood All-Purpose Flour or 2$\frac{1}{4}$ cups (550 mL) Robin Hood Best For Cake & Pastry Flour	500 mL
1$\frac{1}{2}$ tsp	baking powder	7 mL
1 tsp	baking soda	5 mL
$\frac{1}{2}$ tsp	salt	2 mL
1$\frac{1}{2}$ cups	granulated sugar	375 mL
$\frac{1}{2}$ cup	shortening	125 mL
$\frac{1}{2}$ cup	buttermilk or soured milk, divided	125 mL
1 cup	mashed ripe bananas (3 to 4 bananas)	250 mL
2	eggs	2
1 tsp	vanilla	5 mL

Topping

$\frac{1}{3}$ cup	butter	75 mL
$\frac{3}{4}$ cup	packed brown sugar	175 mL
3 tbsp	light (10%) cream	45 mL
1 cup	flaked coconut	250 mL
$\frac{3}{4}$ cup	chopped nuts	175 mL

1. **Cake:** Combine flour, baking powder, baking soda and salt in large bowl. Add sugar, shortening, $\frac{1}{4}$ cup (50 mL) buttermilk and bananas. Beat on medium speed of electric mixer for 2 minutes. Add eggs, vanilla and remaining $\frac{1}{4}$ cup (50 mL) buttermilk. Beat on medium speed for 1 minute. Spread batter evenly in prepared pan. Bake for 30 to 40 minutes or until toothpick inserted in center comes out clean.

2. **Topping:** While cake is baking, prepare topping. Melt butter in small saucepan. Stir in brown sugar, cream, coconut and nuts thoroughly. Remove cake from oven and immediately spread topping evenly over cake. Broil 6 inches (15 cm) below element for 2 to 3 minutes or until bubbly and golden.

Queen Elizabeth Cake

A broiled topping works well on almost any cake, and on this moist, old-fashioned date cake, it's a real winner.

Makes about 12 servings

Preparation: 25 minutes

Baking: 45 minutes

Cooking: 3 minutes

Broiling: 3 minutes

Freezing: excellent

TIPS

Broiled toppings brown very quickly. Place them about 6 inches (15 cm) below the element and watch carefully.

In this recipe, flaked coconut works better than shredded, which tends to burn under the broiler.

- Preheat oven to 350°F (180°C)
- 9-inch (2.5 L) square cake pan, greased

Cake

1 cup	boiling water	250 mL
1 cup	chopped pitted dates	250 mL
1 tsp	baking soda	5 mL
1/4 cup	butter, softened	50 mL
1 cup	granulated sugar	250 mL
1	egg	1
1 tsp	vanilla	5 mL
1 1/2 cups	Robin Hood All-Purpose Flour	375 mL
1 tsp	baking powder	5 mL
1/2 tsp	salt	2 mL

Topping

1 cup	flaked coconut	250 mL
1/2 cup	packed brown sugar	125 mL
1/4 cup	butter	50 mL
1/4 cup	half-and-half (10%) cream	50 mL

1. **Cake:** Pour boiling water over dates and baking soda in a small bowl; mix and let stand until lukewarm.
2. Cream butter and sugar in a medium bowl until light and creamy. Beat in egg and vanilla. Combine flour, baking powder and salt. Add to creamed mixture alternately with date mixture, making three dry and two liquid additions. Mix well. Spread evenly in prepared pan.
3. Bake for 40 to 45 minutes or until toothpick inserted in center comes out clean.
4. **Topping:** While cake is baking, combine flaked coconut, brown sugar, butter and cream in a saucepan. Bring to a boil over medium heat and boil for 1 minute, stirring often. Spread over cake as soon as it comes out of the oven.
5. Broil 6 inches (15 cm) from element for 2 to 3 minutes or until bubbly and golden. Cool completely in pan on rack.

Variation
Substitute chopped nuts for half of the coconut in the topping.

Cranberry Apple Cake

This cake is nice frosted, plain or simply sprinkled with confectioner's sugar.

Makes about 12 servings

Preparation: 15 minutes

Baking: 1½ hours

Freezing: excellent

TIP

Store dried cranberries in the freezer to retain their soft, moist texture.

- Preheat oven to 325°F (160°C)
- 10-inch (4 L) tube pan, greased and floured

Cake

1¼ cups	vegetable oil	300 mL
1¼ cups	granulated sugar	300 mL
½ cup	packed brown sugar	125 mL
4	eggs	4
3 cups	Robin Hood All-Purpose Flour	750 mL
2 tsp	ground cinnamon	10 mL
1 tsp	baking soda	5 mL
1 tsp	baking powder	5 mL
¾ tsp	salt	3 mL
½ tsp	nutmeg	2 mL
3½ cups	diced peeled apples	875 mL
6 oz	dried cranberries (1 cup/250 mL)	170 g

Frosting

¼ cup	packed brown sugar	50 mL
2½ tbsp	light (10%) cream	37 mL
2 tbsp	butter	30 mL
⅔ cup	confectioner's (icing) sugar (approx)	150 mL

1. **Cake:** Beat oil, granulated and brown sugars and eggs in large mixing bowl. Combine flour, cinnamon, baking soda, baking powder, salt and nutmeg. Add to batter along with apples and cranberries, stirring until moistened. Spread in prepared pan. Bake for about 1½ hours or until toothpick inserted in center comes out clean. Cool for 20 minutes in pan, then transfer to wire rack and cool completely.

2. **Frosting:** Heat brown sugar, cream and butter in saucepan over medium heat, stirring until sugar is dissolved and mixture comes to a boil. Cool to room temperature. Add enough confectioner's sugar to make a drizzling consistency, beating until smooth. Drizzle over cake. Decorate as desired.

Apple-Filled Cake

An abundance of cinnamon-coated apples make this simple cake moist and not too sweet.

Makes about 16 servings

Preparation: 20 minutes

Baking: 55 minutes

Freezing: excellent

TIPS

Use a tart, firm apple, such as Granny Smith.

Slice apples thinly for even cooking.

Keep apples on hand for this and other quick fruit desserts, such as apple crisp.

One apple should make almost 1 cup (250 mL) sliced. Always have one more apple on hand than you think you'll need.

- *Preheat oven to 350°F (180°C)*
- *9-inch (2.5 L) square cake pan, greased*

2	eggs	2
1 cup	granulated sugar	250 mL
1/2 cup	vegetable oil	125 mL
3 tbsp	apple juice	45 mL
1 1/2 cups	Robin Hood All-Purpose Flour	375 mL
2 tsp	baking powder	10 mL
1/4 tsp	salt	1 mL
4 cups	thinly sliced peeled cored apples (about 5)	1 L
1/2 cup	packed brown sugar	125 mL
2 tsp	ground cinnamon	10 mL

1. Beat eggs and granulated sugar in a large bowl until thoroughly blended. Beat in oil and apple juice.
2. Combine flour, baking powder and salt. Stir into egg mixture, beating just until smooth. Spread half of the batter in prepared pan.
3. Combine apples, brown sugar and cinnamon. Toss lightly to coat. Spread over batter in pan. Cover with remaining batter.
4. Bake for 50 to 55 minutes or until toothpick inserted in center comes out clean. Cool completely in pan on rack.

Toffee Apple Cake

No need for a frosting — the topping bakes right on the cake.

Makes about 15 servings

Preparation: 20 minutes

Baking: 40 minutes

Freezing: excellent

TIPS

An ideal cake for lunch boxes. Wrap individual pieces and freeze, then pack them when making lunches in the morning. They will be perfectly thawed by noon.

Toffee bits are sold in packages like chocolate chips.

- Preheat oven to 350°F (180°C)
- 13- by 9-inch (3.5 L) cake pan, greased

Cake

¹⁄₂ cup	butter, softened	125 mL
1 cup	granulated sugar	250 mL
2	eggs	2
1 tsp	vanilla	5 mL
2 cups	Robin Hood All-Purpose Flour	500 mL
1 tsp	baking powder	5 mL
1 tsp	baking soda	5 mL
¹⁄₄ tsp	salt	1 mL
1 cup	sour cream	250 mL
2 cups	diced peeled apples	500 mL
³⁄₄ cup	toffee bits	175 mL

Topping

¹⁄₃ cup	Robin Hood All-Purpose Flour	75 mL
2 tbsp	packed brown sugar	30 mL
¹⁄₄ cup	butter	50 mL
³⁄₄ cup	toffee bits	175 mL

1. **Cake:** Cream butter, sugar, eggs and vanilla in large bowl on medium speed of electric mixer until light and fluffy. Combine flour, baking powder, baking soda and salt. Add to creamed mixture alternately with sour cream, making three additions of dry ingredients and two of sour cream. Fold in apples and toffee bits. Spread batter evenly in prepared pan.

2. **Topping:** Combine flour, brown sugar, butter and toffee bits, mixing until crumbly. Sprinkle evenly over batter.

3. Bake for 35 to 40 minutes or until toothpick inserted in center comes out clean.

Pineapple Walnut Carrot Cake

Crushed pineapple adds color, flavor and moistness to a traditional favorite.

Makes about 12 servings

Preparation: 20 minutes

Baking: 70 minutes

Freezing: excellent

TIPS

Drain pineapple well. Carrot cake is moist, and excess liquid will cause it to fall.

Don't worry if the batter seems very stiff. During baking, the carrots release moisture.

Always peel carrots before shredding them.

Instead of the Cream Cheese Frosting, drizzle this cake with an Orange Glaze (see recipe, page 219) or finish simply with a dusting of confectioner's (icing) sugar.

Don't limit the use of this delicious frosting to carrot cake. It's very versatile. Try it on spice cake and chocolate cake, too.

When you package frosted pieces of cake for lunch boxes, lightly grease the area of the wrapping that will come into contact with the frosting. When the cake is unwrapped, the frosting will stay on the cake, not the wrapping.

- Preheat oven to 350°F (180°C)
- 10-inch (4 L) tube pan, greased and floured

1 cup	vegetable oil	250 mL
1½ cups	granulated sugar	375 mL
4	eggs	4
2 cups	Robin Hood All-Purpose Flour	500 mL
2 tsp	baking powder	10 mL
2 tsp	ground cinnamon	10 mL
1½ tsp	baking soda	7 mL
1 tsp	salt	5 mL
2 cups	shredded peeled carrots	500 mL
¾ cup	crushed pineapple, drained	175 mL
¾ cup	chopped walnuts, optional	175 mL

1. Pour vegetable oil into a large mixer bowl. Add sugar gradually, beating on medium speed of electric mixer until well blended. Add eggs, one at a time, beating after each addition. Continue beating until mixture is light.

2. Combine flour, baking powder, cinnamon, baking soda and salt. Add to sugar mixture, beating on medium speed until combined. Stir in remaining ingredients. Pour batter into prepared pan.

3. Bake for 60 to 70 minutes or until toothpick inserted in center comes out clean. Cool for 20 minutes in pan on rack, then remove from pan and transfer to rack to cool completely.

Basic Cream Cheese Frosting

- *Makes about 3 cups (750 mL) frosting*
- *Enough to fill and frost a 9-inch (23 cm) 2-layer cake*

1	package (8 oz/250 g) cream cheese, softened	1
½ cup	butter, softened	125 mL
1 tsp	vanilla	5 mL
3 to 3½ cups	confectioner's (icing) sugar, sifted	750 to 875 mL

1. Beat cream cheese, butter and vanilla in a large mixer bowl on medium speed of electric mixer until fluffy. Gradually add icing sugar, beating until light and creamy. If necessary, add icing sugar, 1 tbsp (15 mL), at a time to stiffen.

Orange Cream Cheese Frosting: Omit vanilla. Add 1 tbsp (15 mL) grated orange zest and 2 tbsp (30 mL) orange juice to cheese mixture, alternately with icing sugar.

Pecan Cream Cheese Frosting: Fold 1 cup (250 mL) finely chopped pecans into frosting.

Moist and Chewy Caramel Apple Cake

An ideal company or family dessert. Nuts and coconut on top are covered with a caramel topping that soaks into the cake for a great finish.

Makes about 12 servings

Preparation: 20 minutes

Baking: 45 minutes

Freezing: excellent

TIP

Flaked coconut is best. The shredded variety seems a bit too stringy.

- *Preheat oven to 350°F (180°C)*
- *13- by 9-inch (3.5 L) cake pan, greased*

2½ cups	Robin Hood All-Purpose Flour	625 mL
2 cups	granulated sugar	500 mL
2 tsp	salt	10 mL
1½ tsp	baking soda	7 mL
½ tsp	baking powder	2 mL
1¼ cups	undiluted evaporated milk, divided	300 mL
⅓ cup	water	75 mL
2	eggs, lightly beaten	2
2 cups	chopped peeled apples	500 mL
⅓ cup	packed brown sugar	75 mL
1 cup	flaked coconut	250 mL
½ cup	chopped nuts	125 mL
20	individual vanilla caramels	20

1. Combine flour, sugar, salt, baking soda and baking powder in large bowl. Combine ½ cup (125 mL) evaporated milk, water, eggs and apples in medium bowl. Stir into dry ingredients. Mix well. Spread batter evenly in prepared pan. Sprinkle with brown sugar, then coconut and nuts. Bake for 40 to 45 minutes or until top springs back when lightly touched. Cover loosely with foil if topping is becoming too brown.

2. Meanwhile, combine remaining ¾ cup (175 mL) evaporated milk and caramels in small saucepan. Cook, stirring, over low heat until mixture is smooth. Pour evenly over hot cake. Cool completely before serving.

Variation
Pecans, walnuts and almonds all work well.

Strawberry Cream Torte

A buttery cake shell holds a creamy cheese filling with strawberry jam inside. There's no need for icing, but an icing drizzle or dusting of confectioner's (icing) sugar adds an appealing finishing touch.

Makes about 12 servings

Preparation: 25 minutes

Baking: 55 minutes

Freezing: excellent

TIPS

Place pan on a piece of aluminum foil in the oven to catch any drips that may leak out.

Make sure the cream cheese is at room temperature so it will blend smoothly with the other ingredients.

If there are large pieces of fruit in the jam, chop them a bit for an even consistency.

Stir jam to soften before spooning it over the filling.

- *Preheat oven to 350°F (180°C)*
- *10-inch (25 cm) springform pan, greased*

Crust

¾ cup	butter, softened	175 mL
1¾ cups	Robin Hood All-Purpose Flour	425 mL
½ cup	granulated sugar	125 mL
1 tsp	vanilla	5 mL
½ tsp	baking powder	2 mL
½ tsp	baking soda	2 mL
¼ tsp	salt	1 mL
2	eggs	2

Filling

1	package (8 oz/250 g) cream cheese, softened	1
1	egg	1
¼ cup	granulated sugar	50 mL
1 tsp	vanilla	5 mL
1 tsp	lemon juice	5 mL
1 cup	strawberry jam	250 mL

1. Crust: Combine butter, flour, sugar, vanilla, baking powder, baking soda, salt and eggs in a large mixer bowl. Beat at medium speed of electric mixer for about 2 minutes or until smooth. Spread over bottom and 2 inches (5 cm) up side of prepared pan. Set aside.

2. Filling: Beat cream cheese, egg, sugar, vanilla and lemon juice in a small bowl on medium speed of electric mixer until smooth and creamy. Spread ¼ cup (50 mL) of the jam over prepared crust. Pour cheese mixture evenly over top. Spoon remaining jam evenly over cheese mixture.

3. Bake for 45 to 55 minutes or until set and light golden. Serve slightly warm or cool.

Variations

Replace strawberry jam with your favorite kind. Apricot, peach, raspberry, plum, pineapple and mixed berry all work well in this recipe.

Decorate the plate with fresh berries for a pretty presentation.

Triple Chocolate Fudge Cake

How can you go wrong with a combination of chocolate cake, filling and glaze?

Makes about 12 servings

Preparation: 30 minutes

Baking: 35 minutes

Refrigeration: 30 minutes

Freezing: excellent

TIP

Don't be surprised that the batter is quite thin.

- Preheat oven to 350°F (180°C)
- Two 9-inch (1.5 L) round cake pans, greased and floured

Cake

2¼ cups	Robin Hood Best For Cake & Pastry Flour or 2 cups (500 mL) Robin Hood All-Purpose Flour	550 mL
2 tsp	baking soda	10 mL
½ tsp	salt	2 mL
½ cup	butter, softened	125 mL
2¼ cups	packed brown sugar	550 mL
3	eggs	3
1½ tsp	vanilla	7 mL
3	squares (each 1 oz/28 g) unsweetened chocolate, melted and cooled	3
1 cup	sour cream	250 mL
1 cup	boiling water	250 mL

Filling

½ cup	butter, softened	125 mL
3 to 3½ cups	confectioner's (icing) sugar, sifted	750 to 875 mL
⅓ cup	light (10%) cream	75 mL
2	squares (each 1 oz/28 g) unsweetened chocolate, melted and cooled	2

Glaze

4	squares (each 1 oz/28 g) unsweetened chocolate	4
2 tbsp	strong brewed coffee, optional	30 mL
3 tbsp	butter, softened	45 mL

1. **Cake:** Combine flour, baking soda and salt. Beat butter, sugar and eggs on medium speed of electric mixer until light, 5 minutes. Beat in vanilla and chocolate. Add dry ingredients alternately with sour cream, mixing lightly until smooth. Stir in boiling water. Pour into pans. Bake for 30 to 35 minutes or until toothpick inserted in center comes out clean. Cool for 10 minutes, then remove from pans and cool completely.

2. **Filling:** Beat together all ingredients with electric mixer until light and fluffy. If necessary, add a little more confectioner's sugar or cream to make a spreadable consistency. Spread some of the filling between cake layers. Spread sides of cake with remaining filling. Refrigerate for 30 minutes.

3. **Glaze:** Melt chocolate in coffee over low heat, stirring until smooth. Remove from heat. Gradually add butter, blending until smooth. Spread glaze over top of cake, letting it drizzle down sides. Let glaze set before cutting.

Apricot Walnut Torte

This is a melt-in-your-mouth dessert.

TIPS

Prepare cakes ahead and freeze. Assemble when the need arises.

To separate an egg neatly, break it into a small funnel. The yolk stays in the funnel, and the white passes through.

- Preheat oven to 350°F (180°C)
- Two 8-inch (1.2 L) round cake pans, greased and floured

Cake

³⁄₄ cup	Robin Hood All-Purpose or Best For Cake & Pastry Flour	175 mL
2 tsp	baking powder	10 mL
½ tsp	salt	2 mL
1 cup	ground walnuts	250 mL
4	eggs, separated	4
2 tbsp	water	30 mL
1 tsp	vanilla	5 mL
1 cup	granulated sugar, divided	250 mL

Filling & Glaze

2 cups	whipping (35%) cream	500 mL
¼ cup	confectioner's (icing) sugar, sifted	50 mL
1	jar (7½ oz/213 mL) junior apricots (baby food)	1
½ cup	strained apricot jam	125 mL
2 tbsp	chopped walnuts, optional	30 mL

1. **Cake:** Combine flour, baking powder, salt and nuts in mixing bowl. Beat egg yolks, water and vanilla in small bowl on high speed of electric mixer until thick and light. Gradually add ³⁄₄ cup (175 mL) sugar, beating until thick and light, about 5 minutes. Beat egg whites and remaining ¼ cup (50 mL) sugar to stiff peaks. Fold dry ingredients into egg yolk mixture in four portions. Gently fold in meringue. Spread batter evenly in prepared pans. Bake for 25 to 30 minutes or until toothpick inserted in center comes out clean. Cool in pans for 5 minutes, then remove and cool completely on wire rack.

2. **Filling & Glaze:** Beat cream and confectioner's sugar to stiff peaks. Fold in apricots. Cut cake layers in half horizontally. Fill layers with apricot cream filling. Glaze top with apricot jam. Garnish with chopped walnuts, if desired. Refrigerate until serving.

Variation
Substitute pecans or hazelnuts for walnuts.

Divine Chocolate Raspberry Cake

Every bite of this luscious cake is like eating a chocolate raspberry truffle.

Makes about 10 servings

Preparation: 20 minutes
Baking: 28 minutes
Chilling: 30 minutes
Freezing: excellent

TIPS

Choose the finish to suit your taste. Use a chocolate glaze if you're appealing to chocolate lovers or top with a dollop of plain or Chocolate Whipped Cream (page 218). Scatter some fresh raspberries around the plate.

Place a doily on top of an unglazed cake and sift confectioner's (icing) sugar over top. Remove doily for an attractive sugar design. Or decorate with chocolate cutouts: Melt together 1 cup (250 mL) each semi-sweet and white chocolate chips and 1 tbsp (15 mL) vegetable oil. Cool slightly. Pour onto a baking sheet lined with waxed paper; spread chocolate about ¼ inch (0.5 cm) thick. Chill until almost set. Press small cookie cutters into chocolate. Chill until firm, then lift cutouts off the paper and arrange them on the cake or on serving plates.

- Preheat oven to 350°F (180°C)
- 8-inch (1.2 L) or 9-inch (1.5 L) round cake pan, greased and lined with a circle of parchment paper

Cake

2	squares (each 1 oz/28 g) unsweetened chocolate, chopped	2
½ cup	butter	125 mL
2	eggs	2
½ cup	granulated sugar	125 mL
½ cup	seedless raspberry jam	125 mL
2 tsp	vanilla extract	10 mL
1	square (1 oz/28 g) semi-sweet chocolate, finely chopped	1
⅔ cup	Robin Hood All-Purpose Flour	150 mL
½ tsp	baking powder	2 mL
¼ tsp	salt	1 mL

Chocolate Glaze, optional

¼ cup	butter	50 mL
4	squares (each 1 oz/28 g) semi-sweet chocolate, chopped	4

1. **Cake:** Melt unsweetened chocolate and butter in top of double boiler or small saucepan over low heat, stirring constantly, until smooth. Remove from heat.

2. Whisk together eggs, sugar, jam, vanilla, chopped semi-sweet chocolate and melted chocolate in a large bowl until blended.

3. Combine flour, baking powder and salt. Add to egg mixture, whisking until smooth. Spread batter evenly in prepared pan.

4. Bake for 23 to 28 minutes or until toothpick inserted in center comes out clean. Cool for 10 minutes in pan on rack, then remove cake from pan and transfer to rack to cool completely. When cool, remove paper from bottom of cake.

5. **Glaze (optional):** Melt butter and chocolate in a small saucepan over low heat, stirring until smooth. Cool slightly until mixture starts to thicken and is a soft, spreadable consistency. Leave cake on rack but place a sheet of waxed paper underneath. Pour glaze over top of cake, letting it drip down, covering the sides. Chill to set glaze, about 30 minutes.

Chocolate Toffee Candy Bar Cheesecake

This creamy cheesecake with chopped chocolate-covered toffee bars scattered throughout is rich and decadent.

Makes about 16 servings

Preparation: 30 minutes

Baking: 85 minutes

Chilling: 3 hours or overnight

Freezing: excellent

TIPS

If preparing the crust in a food processor, use cold butter cut into pieces.

Place the pan on a piece of aluminum foil in the oven to catch any drips, as the seal on springform pans is often less than perfect.

Run a knife around the edge of the pan to release the cake as soon as it comes out of the oven.

For the best texture, cool cheesecake completely, then chill in the refrigerator for at least 3 hours or overnight.

Cut cheesecakes with a warm wet knife.

Crush chocolate bars in their packages or in a plastic bag using a mallet or a rolling pin.

- Preheat oven to 350°F (180°C)
- 10-inch (25 cm) springform pan, greased

Crust

1 cup	Robin Hood All-Purpose Flour	250 mL
½ cup	cold butter	125 mL
⅓ cup	packed brown sugar	75 mL
⅓ cup	finely chopped almonds	75 mL

Filling

3	packages (each 8 oz/250 g) cream cheese, softened	3
¾ cup	granulated sugar	175 mL
1 tbsp	Robin Hood All-Purpose Flour	15 mL
1 tsp	vanilla	5 mL
3	eggs	3
⅓ cup	sour cream	75 mL
¾ cup	chopped crunchy toffee chocolate bars (3 bars, each 1.4 oz/39 g)	175 mL

1. **Crust:** Combine flour, butter, sugar and almonds in a food processor fitted with a metal blade and process until crumbly. (You can also do this in a mixing bowl, cutting the butter in.) Press firmly over bottom of prepared pan. Bake for 15 to 20 minutes or until light golden.

2. **Filling:** Beat cream cheese, sugar, flour and vanilla in a large bowl on medium speed of electric mixer until smooth. Add eggs, one at a time, beating lightly after each addition. Add sour cream and chocolate toffee pieces. Mix well. Spread mixture evenly over warm crust.

3. Bake for 15 minutes, then reduce temperature to 300°F (150°C) and bake for 45 to 50 minutes longer or until softly set. Remove from oven. Run knife around edge of pan. Cool completely in pan on rack. Chill for 3 hours or overnight before serving.

Variation

For an even more decadent dessert, serve with a drizzle of caramel or chocolate sauce.

Company Cheesecake

La crème de la crème of indulgence to serve with your favorite berry sauce.

Makes about 16 servings

Preparation: 40 minutes

Baking:
1 hour 22 minutes

Refrigeration:
3 hours or overnight

Freezing: excellent

TIPS

Run knife around pan rim to loosen edge of cheesecake from pan as soon as it comes out of the oven.

Serve cake at room temperature for optimum texture and flavor.

- Preheat oven to 400°F (200°C)
- 10-inch (25 cm) springform pan

Crust

1 cup	butter or margarine	250 mL
2 cups	Robin Hood All-Purpose Flour	500 mL
½ cup	granulated sugar	125 mL
2 tsp	grated lemon zest	10 mL
1	egg, beaten	1

Filling

5	packages (each 8 oz/250 g) cream cheese, softened	5
1¾ cups	granulated sugar	425 mL
3 tbsp	Robin Hood All-Purpose Flour	45 mL
2 tsp	grated lemon zest	10 mL
½ tsp	vanilla	2 mL
5	eggs	5
¼ cup	whipping (35%) cream	50 mL
	Fruit pie filling or fruit sauce	

1. **Crust:** Combine butter, flour, sugar and lemon zest in food processor or mixing bowl until crumbly. Add egg, mixing until dough forms. Remove ring from springform pan. With floured fingers, press one-third of the dough on pan bottom. Bake at 400°F (200°C) for 8 to 10 minutes or until golden. Cool. Return ring to pan. Pat remaining dough onto sides, at least 2 inches (5 cm) high.

2. **Filling:** Beat cream cheese in large bowl with electric mixer until smooth. Beat in sugar, flour, lemon zest and vanilla on high speed. Add eggs, one at a time, then cream, beating until smooth and light. Pour into prepared crust.

3. Place pan on baking sheet or piece of foil (grease will leak out slightly from crust). Bake at 425°F (220°C) for 12 minutes, then reduce heat to 300°F (150°C) and bake for 1 hour longer or until softly set. Cool completely. Refrigerate for 3 hours or overnight. Serve with fruit filling or sauce.

Chocolate Cream Hazelnut Meringue Torte

Serve this beautiful multilayered dessert in thin slices as it is so rich.

Makes about 12 servings
Preparation: 35 minutes
Baking: 35 minutes
Chilling: 1 to 6 hours
Freezing: not recommended

TIPS

Tortes differ from layer cakes in that they usually have more layers and are quite rich. They are spectacular to look at and can be served in thin slices. This cake definitely meets all those criteria.

Cream of tartar helps keep the beaten egg whites stiff.

Use a food processor or nut grinder to finely chop the nuts.

The Chocolate Cream is delightful. Try using it on other cakes, such as the Chocolate Raspberry Torte (see recipe, page 174) or Best-Ever Banana Cake (see recipe, page 192).

- Preheat oven to 350°F (180°C)
- Two 8-inch (1.2 L) or 9-inch (1.5 L) round cake pans, greased and floured

Cake

½ cup	butter, softened	125 mL
1½ cups	granulated sugar, divided	375 mL
4	eggs, separated	4
1 tsp	vanilla	5 mL
1 cup	Robin Hood All-Purpose Flour	250 mL
1 tsp	baking powder	5 mL
¼ tsp	salt	1 mL
⅓ cup	milk	75 mL
¼ tsp	cream of tartar	1 mL
¾ cup	finely chopped hazelnuts	175 mL

Chocolate Cream

¾ cup	granulated sugar	175 mL
⅓ cup	unsweetened cocoa powder, sifted	75 mL
1½ cups	whipping (35%) cream	375 mL

1. **Cake:** Cream butter and ½ cup (125 mL) sugar in a large bowl on medium speed of electric mixer until light. Add egg yolks, one at a time, beating for 1 minute after each addition. Stir in vanilla.

2. Combine flour, baking powder and salt. Add to creamed mixture alternately with milk, making three dry and two liquid additions, beating lightly on low speed after each. Spread in pans. Set aside.

3. Beat egg whites and cream of tartar in a small bowl until soft peaks form. Gradually add remaining 1 cup (250 mL) sugar, beating until stiff peaks form. Fold in hazelnuts. Spread over batter.

4. Bake for 30 to 35 minutes or until toothpick inserted in center comes out clean. Cool for 10 minutes in pans on rack, then transfer to rack, meringue-side up. Cool completely.

5. **Chocolate Cream:** Combine sugar and cocoa in a medium bowl. Gradually add whipping cream, stirring until blended, then beat on medium speed of electric mixer until soft peaks form.

6. **Assembly:** Place one cake layer, meringue-side up, on serving plate. Spread half of the Chocolate Cream on top (not on the sides). Repeat layers. Chill for at least 1 hour or for up to 6 hours.

Variation

Replace hazelnuts with almonds or pecans.

Orange Chiffon Cake

Light as a feather, chiffon cakes are especially nice to serve after a hearty meal.

Makes about 12 servings

Preparation: 20 minutes

Baking: 60 minutes

Freezing: excellent

TIPS

Chiffon cakes are quite versatile in their presentations. You can cut them in three layers and fill with whipped cream or a butter frosting. Or leave them whole and cover with a simple glaze.

When serving, cut the cake into wedges, and top with fresh fruit and a dollop of whipped cream or yogurt sauce.

For a quick vanilla sauce, defrost a premium-quality French vanilla ice cream, stirring to obtain a smooth saucelike consistency. Chill until ready to serve.

Don't grease the pan. The batter rises up by sticking to the pan, which it won't do if the sides are greased.

- Preheat oven to 350°F (180°C)
- 10-inch (4 L) tube pan, ungreased

1¾ cups	Robin Hood All-Purpose Flour	425 mL
1½ cups	granulated sugar, divided	375 mL
1 tbsp	baking powder	15 mL
1 tsp	salt	5 mL
6	eggs, separated	6
1 tbsp	grated orange zest	15 mL
¾ cup	orange juice	175 mL
½ cup	vegetable oil	125 mL
½ tsp	cream of tartar	2 mL

1. Combine flour, ¾ cup (175 mL) sugar, baking powder and salt in a large mixer bowl. Stir well. Add egg yolks, orange zest and juice, and oil. Beat on medium speed of electric mixer until smooth, about 30 seconds.

2. Beat egg whites and cream of tartar in a small bowl until soft peaks form. Gradually add remaining ¾ cup (175 mL) sugar, beating until stiff, shiny peaks form. Fold one-quarter of the egg whites into egg yolk mixture until thoroughly blended. Gently fold in remainder. Pour batter into pan.

3. Bake for 55 to 60 minutes or until toothpick inserted in center comes out clean. Invert pan and cool completely in pan on rack. Run a knife around the edge to loosen, then shake pan to remove cake.

Variation

Lemon Chiffon Cake: Replace orange zest with lemon zest and orange juice with 2 tsp (10 mL) lemon juice plus enough water to make ¾ cup (175 mL) liquid.

Raspberry Almond Cake with Cream Cheese Frosting

A very attractive presentation turns a simple white layer cake into a special treat.

Makes about 12 servings

Preparation: 40 minutes

Baking: 40 minutes

Freezing: excellent (without garnish)

TIPS

The cake mellows as it stands, so it improves if it is prepared a day ahead, then garnished when ready to serve.

Separate eggs when they are cold, but let the whites come to room temperature before beating to get the maximum volume.

For a smaller cake, freeze one layer for use at a later date and prepare only half of the frosting.

It is easier to cut cake layers if they are very cold. Chill thoroughly or freeze and partially thaw before slicing. Because chilling makes cakes less fragile, they are less likely to break as you cut them.

- Preheat oven to 350°F (180°C)
- Two 8-inch (1.2 L) round cake pans, greased and floured

Cake

¾ cup	butter, softened	175 mL
1½ cups	granulated sugar	375 mL
1 tsp	each vanilla and almond extract	5 mL
2 cups	Robin Hood All-Purpose Flour	500 mL
1 tbsp	baking powder	15 mL
½ tsp	salt	2 mL
1 cup	milk	250 mL
5	egg whites	5

Frosting

2	packages (each 8 oz/250 g) cream cheese, softened	2
6 tbsp	butter, softened	90 mL
1 tsp	vanilla	5 mL
1½ cups	confectioner's (icing) sugar, sifted	375 mL

Filling

¾ cup	seedless raspberry jam	175 mL

Garnish

	Fresh raspberries, optional	
1⅓ cups	sliced almonds, toasted	325 mL

1. **Cake:** Beat butter, sugar, vanilla and almond extract in a large bowl on medium speed of electric mixer until light and creamy.

2. Combine flour, baking powder and salt. Add to butter mixture alternately with milk, making three dry and two liquid additions, mixing on low speed lightly after each. Beat egg whites until stiff peaks form. Fold into batter gently until combined. Spread evenly in pans. Bake for 35 to 40 minutes or until toothpick inserted in center comes out clean. Cool for 10 minutes in pans on rack, then remove from pans and transfer to a rack to cool completely. Cut each layer in half horizontally to make four layers total.

3. **Frosting:** Beat cream cheese, butter and vanilla in a large bowl on high speed of electric mixer until blended. Reduce speed to low and gradually add icing sugar, beating until smooth.

4. **Assembly:** Place one halved cake layer, cut-side up, on plate. Spread about ½ cup (125 mL) frosting over top. Drizzle ¼ cup (50 mL) jam over top. Repeat layering, ending with top cake layer, cut-side down. Spread remaining frosting on top and sides of cake. Garnish top with fresh raspberries, if using, and press almonds onto the side of cake. Chill until ready to serve.

Old-Fashioned Raisin Spice Cake

A moist, spicy everyday cake that freezes well.

TIP

Do not use a plastic bowl when beating egg whites since oils retained in the plastic prevent the egg whites from forming stiff peaks. Be sure the beaters are clean and dry.

- Preheat oven to 375°F (190°C)
- 9-inch (2.5 L) square cake pan, greased

Cake

2	egg whites	2
1⅓ cups	Robin Hood All-Purpose Flour or 1½ cups (375 mL) Robin Hood Best For Cake & Pastry Flour	325 mL
1½ tsp	baking powder	7 mL
½ tsp	salt	2 mL
2 tsp	ground cinnamon	10 mL
1 tsp	ground allspice	5 mL
½ tsp	ground cloves	2 mL
½ cup	butter or margarine, softened	125 mL
1 cup	granulated sugar	250 mL
2	egg yolks	2
⅔ cup	milk	150 mL
1 tsp	vanilla	5 mL
¾ cup	raisins	175 mL

Frosting

¼ cup	butter or margarine, softened	50 mL
2 cups	confectioner's (icing) sugar, sifted	500 mL
1 tbsp	lemon juice	15 mL
1 to 2 tbsp	cream or milk	15 to 30 mL
	Chopped walnuts, optional	

1. **Cake:** Beat egg whites to stiff but moist peaks. Combine flour, baking powder, salt, cinnamon, allspice and cloves in large bowl. Stir well to blend. Add butter, sugar, egg yolks, milk and vanilla. Beat on low speed of electric mixer for 30 seconds to blend, then on medium speed until smooth, about 1½ minutes. Stir in raisins. Fold in stiff egg whites. Spread batter evenly in prepared pan. Bake for 30 to 35 minutes. Cool completely.

2. **Frosting:** Cream together butter, half of the confectioner's sugar and lemon juice until light. Gradually add remaining confectioner's sugar and enough cream to make a smooth, spreadable consistency. Spread over cooled cake. Sprinkle with walnuts, if desired.

Variation
Adjust spices to suit your own personal taste.

Frostings

This versatile frosting lends itself to a variety of flavours.

Makes about 2¾ cups (675 mL) frosting

Enough to fill and frost an 8-inch (20 cm) 2-layer cake

TIP

Prepare an extra batch of frosting. Store it in the refrigerator for up to a month and let come to room temperature before using.

This frosting has a light, creamy chocolate color that looks and tastes terrific on dark chocolate cake.

Makes about 2½ cups (625 mL) frosting

Enough to frost a 9-inch (23 cm) square cake

Basic Butter Frosting

½ cup	butter, softened	125 mL
4 cups	confectioner's (icing) sugar, sifted	1 L
⅓ cup	half-and-half (10%) cream or evaporated milk	75 mL
1 tsp	vanilla	5 mL

1. Beat butter and half of the sugar in a large mixer bowl on medium speed of electric mixer until light. Add cream and vanilla. Gradually add remaining sugar, beating until smooth.

Lemon or Orange Butter Frosting: Omit vanilla; add 1 tbsp (15 mL) grated lemon or orange zest and 1 tbsp (15 mL) lemon or orange juice.

Coffee Butter Frosting: Omit vanilla; add 1 tbsp (15 mL) instant coffee granules dissolved in 1 tsp (5 mL) warm water.

Chocolate Butter Frosting: Melt 2 squares (each 1 oz/ 28 g) unsweetened chocolate; cool completely. Add to mixture before adding the cream and vanilla. Beat until smooth.

Cocoa Butter Frosting: Replace ½ cup (125 mL) of the icing sugar with ½ cup (125 mL) unsweetened cocoa powder. Sift together cocoa and icing sugar before beating in.

Chocolate Sour Cream Frosting

¼ cup	butter	50 mL
3	squares (each 1 oz/28 g) semi-sweet chocolate	3
½ cup	sour cream	125 mL
3 cups	confectioner's (icing) sugar, sifted	750 mL
2 tbsp	warm water	30 mL
1 tsp	vanilla	5 mL

1. In a small saucepan over low heat, combine butter and chocolate. Heat, stirring constantly, until smooth and melted. Cool slightly, then transfer to a large mixer bowl. Stir in sour cream. Gradually add sugar alternately with warm water, beating on low speed of electric mixer until smooth and creamy. Beat in vanilla. Chill slightly, if necessary, to reach a spreadable consistency.

Whipped Creams

This is a basic, slightly sweetened whipped cream from which you can make many different flavors.

Makes about 2 cups (500 mL) whipped cream

Enough to fill and frost a 9-inch (23 cm) 2-layer cake

TIP

Chill the bowl, beaters and cream well before beating.

Makes about 4 cups (1 L)

Enough to fill and frost a 9-inch (23 cm) 4-layer cake

Basic Whipped Cream

1 cup	whipping (35%) cream	250 mL
2 tbsp	confectioner's (icing) sugar, sifted	30 mL

Flavor Variations

1 tsp	vanilla	5 mL
$\frac{1}{2}$ tsp	almond extract	2 mL
$\frac{1}{2}$ tsp	rum or brandy extract	2 mL
$\frac{1}{2}$ tsp	maple extract	2 mL
$\frac{1}{2}$ tsp	ground cinnamon	2 mL
$1\frac{1}{2}$ tsp	grated lemon or orange zest	7 mL
$1\frac{1}{2}$ tsp	instant coffee granules	7 mL

1. In a small mixer bowl, beat cream, icing sugar and one of the flavorings on high speed of electic mixer until stiff peaks form.

Variation

Fold $\frac{1}{4}$ cup (50 mL) crushed nut brittle, grated chocolate, chopped nuts, fruit or toasted coconut into whipped cream.

Chocolate Whipped Cream

2 cups	whipping (35%) cream	500 mL
$\frac{1}{2}$ cup	granulated sugar	125 mL
$\frac{1}{3}$ cup	unsweetened cocoa powder, sifted	75 mL

1. In a small mixer bowl, combine cream, sugar and cocoa. Chill for 15 minutes. Beat mixture until stiff peaks form.

Variation

Fold 1 cup (250 mL) crushed crunchy toffee chocolate bars into the whipped cream.

Glazes

Glazes are a nice alternative to frostings. They give a simple finishing touch in taste and appearance. They are quick and easy to prepare, too. They are usually drizzled over Bundt and tube cakes and will harden as they cool.

Vanilla or Almond Glaze

2 cups	confectioner's (icing) sugar, sifted	500 mL
1 tbsp	butter, softened	15 mL
1 tsp	vanilla or almond extract	5 mL
2 to 3 tbsp	hot water	30 to 45 mL

1. In a small bowl, combine icing sugar and butter. Add vanilla and enough of the hot water to make a smooth, pourable consistency.

Orange, Lemon or Lime Glaze: Omit vanilla and water. Add 2 tsp (10 mL) grated orange, lemon or lime zest and 2 to 4 tbsp (30 to 60 mL) orange, lemon or lime juice.

Pineapple-Orange Glaze: Omit vanilla and water. Add 1 tsp (5 mL) grated orange zest and 2 to 4 tbsp (30 to 60 mL) pineapple juice.

Coffee Glaze: Replace vanilla with 2 tsp (10 mL) instant coffee granules dissolved in 3 tbsp (45 mL) of the hot water.

There are many recipes for chocolate glaze, each a little different but all quite simple to make. They are warm when you spread or drizzle them and firm up as they cool. Here are two favorites.

Basic Chocolate Glaze

1	square (1 oz/28 g) unsweetened chocolate, chopped	1
¼ cup	water	50 mL
1 tbsp	butter	15 mL
2 cups	confectioner's (icing) sugar, sifted	500 mL

1. In a small saucepan over low heat, heat chocolate, water and butter, stirring constantly until chocolate is melted and smooth. Remove from heat. Gradually add icing sugar, stirring until smooth. Add a little more water, if necessary, to reach a pourable consistency.

Basic Chocolate Chip Glaze

1 cup	granulated sugar	250 mL
⅓ cup	butter	75 mL
⅓ cup	half-and-half (10%) cream	75 mL
1 cup	semi-sweet chocolate chips	250 mL
½ tsp	vanilla	2 mL

1. In a small saucepan, combine sugar, butter and cream. Cook over medium heat, stirring constantly, until mixture comes to a boil. Boil for 1 minute. Remove from heat. Add chocolate chips and vanilla, stirring until smooth and melted. Pour warm glaze over top of cake, letting it drizzle down sides.

*Prize-Winning Pecan Pie
and The Ultimate Butter Tart*

Pies & Pastry

Prize-Winning Pecan Pie

Top with a dollop of whipped cream or a scoop of vanilla ice cream.

Makes about 8 servings

Preparation: 20 minutes

Baking: 40 minutes

Freezing: excellent

TIP

Keep nuts right side up for the nicest appearance.

- Preheat oven to 425°F (220°C)
- 9-inch (23 cm) pie plate

Crust

Pastry for 9-inch (23 cm) single-crust pie (see recipes pages 247 to 249)

Filling

1 cup	pecan halves	250 mL
3	eggs	3
$\frac{2}{3}$ cup	granulated sugar	150 mL
1 cup	corn syrup	250 mL
$\frac{1}{3}$ cup	butter, melted	75 mL
Pinch	salt	Pinch

1. **Crust:** Prepare pastry for unbaked pie shell according to recipe instructions.
2. **Filling:** Spread pecans over pastry. Combine eggs, sugar, corn syrup, melted butter and salt. Beat well. Pour over pecans. Bake on lower oven rack at 425°F (220°C) for 10 minutes, then reduce temperature to 350°F (180°C) and bake for 25 to 30 minutes longer or just until set. Cool.

The Ultimate Butter Tart

If you like runny, gooey tarts, you'll love these. Try them warm with ice cream.

Makes 12 tarts

Preparation: 25 minutes

Baking: 15 minutes

Freezing: excellent

TIP

If you don't have a cookie cutter, use the lid from a large jar.

- *Preheat oven to 425°F (220°C)*
- *12-cup muffin pan*
- *4-inch (10 cm) cutter*

Crust

	Pastry for 9-inch (23 cm) single-crust pie (see recipes pages 247 to 249)	

Filling

½ cup	packed brown sugar	125 mL
½ cup	corn syrup	125 mL
¼ cup	butter, softened	50 mL
1	egg, lightly beaten	1
1 tsp	vanilla	5 mL
¼ tsp	salt	1 mL
¾ cup	raisins	175 mL

1. **Crust:** Prepare pastry according to recipe directions. Roll out thinly on lightly floured surface. Cut into rounds with 4-inch (10 cm) cutter. Fit into muffin cups.

2. **Filling:** Combine brown sugar, corn syrup, butter, egg, vanilla and salt. Mix well. Divide raisins evenly among pastry shells. Fill two-thirds full with syrup mixture. Bake on lower oven rack for 12 to 15 minutes or just until set. Don't overbake. Underbaking makes them runnier. Cool on wire rack, then remove from pans.

Variation
Replace raisins with chopped pecans for nut lovers.

Chilly Orange Cream Pie

Don't save this cool, refreshingly light pie for summer. Enjoy its delicious flavor year-round.

Makes about 8 servings

Preparation: 35 minutes

Baking: 15 minutes

Chilling: 6 hours

Freezing: not recommended

TIPS

Bake pie shells one or two days ahead for convenience.

Gelatin pies need at least four hours to set in order to slice properly. That makes them good choices for entertaining, as you can prepare dessert the day before you intend to serve it.

Canned mandarin oranges are a convenient choice for this pie. If desired, add slices of fresh orange for an attractive garnish.

If you love lemon, increase the lemon juice to ½ cup (125 mL).

Add 1 tbsp (15 mL) sesame seeds to the pie crust for a nice nutty flavor.

- Preheat oven to 425°F (220°C)
- 9-inch (23 cm) pie plate

Crust

	Pastry for 9-inch (23 cm) single-crust pie (see recipes, pages 247 to 249)	

Filling

1	envelope (1 tbsp/15 mL) unflavored gelatin	1
2 tbsp	cold water	30 mL
1	can (10 oz/284 mL) mandarin oranges, drained and coarsely chopped, juice reserved	1
¾ cup	granulated sugar	175 mL
⅓ cup	lemon juice	75 mL
1 cup	whipping (35%) cream	250 mL
	Whipped cream and orange slices, optional	

1. **Crust:** Prepare and bake pie shell according to recipe instructions. Cool completely.

2. **Filling:** Mix gelatin and cold water. Let stand for 10 minutes to soften.

3. Pour mandarin juice into a measuring cup and add enough water to make 1 cup (250 mL). In a saucepan, bring mixture to a boil. Add gelatin mixture, stirring until dissolved. Stir in sugar and lemon juice. Mix well. Refrigerate for 2 hours or until mixture just starts to thicken but does not set.

4. Beat cream until soft peaks form. Fold into gelatin mixture gently but thoroughly. Fold in mandarins. Spread evenly in pie shell. Chill for 4 hours or overnight or until set. Garnish with whipped cream and orange slices, if using.

Variations

Melt 2 squares (each 1 oz/28 g) semi-sweet chocolate and spread over pastry shell. Let set before filling.

Substitute clementines for the mandarins.

Raspberry Lattice Pie

There are few sights prettier than fresh red raspberries peeking through glistening golden pastry strips in this favorite pie.

Makes about 8 servings

Preparation: 20 minutes

Baking: 50 minutes

Freezing: excellent

TIPS

For a rich golden crust, brush lattice with the glaze. A sprinkle of sugar will add sparkle to the pastry.

Start pies in a hot oven (425°F/220°C) and place them on the bottom rack. This quickly creates steam in the pastry, which makes air pockets, creating a flaky crust.

Cool pies before cutting to allow time for the filling to set.

When fluting the edge, keep it high. This helps keep the juices in the pie.

Watch the pie carefully. If the pastry seems to be browning too quickly around the edges, cut the inside from a foil pie plate and place the rim over the pie to prevent over-browning. It stays in place and is reusable.

- Preheat oven to 425°F (220°C)
- 9-inch (23 cm) pie plate

Crust

	Pastry for 9-inch (23 cm) double-crust pie (see recipes, pages 247 to 249)	

Filling

4 cups	fresh raspberries	1 L
²⁄₃ to 1 cup	granulated sugar, depending on sweetness of fruit	150 to 250 mL
3 tbsp	quick-cooking tapioca or cornstarch	45 mL
1 tbsp	lemon juice	15 mL
2 tbsp	butter	30 mL

Glaze, optional

1	egg yolk	1
2 tsp	water	10 mL
	Granulated sugar	

1. **Crust:** Prepare pastry for double-crust pie. Roll out bottom crust and fit into pie plate.

2. **Filling:** Combine raspberries, sugar, tapioca and lemon juice in a large bowl. Toss gently until fruit is thoroughly coated. Turn into the pastry-lined pie plate and dot with butter.

3. Roll out pastry for top crust. Cut into strips about ½ inch (1 cm) wide. Arrange strips about 1 inch (2.5 cm) apart on top of the filling, weaving lengthwise and crosswise strips to form a lattice. Press strips against the edge of the bottom pastry and seal. Flute edge.

4. **Glaze (optional):** Beat egg yolk and water in a small bowl. Brush lightly over lattice strips. Sprinkle with sugar.

5. Bake on bottom rack of oven for 15 minutes, then reduce temperature to 350°F (180°C) and bake for 25 to 35 minutes longer or until crust is golden and fruit is tender and bubbly.

Walnut Raspberry Tart

This tart is a real dazzler. The tender, buttery crust and cinnamon-sugared walnut filling combined with a raspberry-and-cream topping has great taste, texture and eye appeal.

Makes about 12 servings

Preparation: 30 minutes

Baking: 45 minutes

Freezing: excellent (without topping)

TIPS

Prepare the tart a day ahead, then add the topping when you are ready to serve.

A shortbread crust usually needs to be kneaded with your hands. Work the dough to make it come together smoothly rather than adding more butter, which will cause it to shrink down the sides of the pan and become too crisp when baked.

Chop the walnuts in fairly chunky pieces, not finely.

- *Preheat oven to 400°F (200°C)*
- *10-inch (25 cm) fluted flan pan with removable bottom*

Crust

½ cup	butter, softened	125 mL
¼ cup	granulated sugar	50 mL
1½ cups	Robin Hood All-Purpose Flour	375 mL
¼ tsp	salt	1 mL
1	egg, beaten	1

Filling

2	eggs	2
1	egg yolk	1
1 cup	packed brown sugar	250 mL
½ cup	Robin Hood All-Purpose Flour	125 mL
¾ tsp	ground cinnamon	3 mL
½ tsp	baking powder	2 mL
2 cups	walnut pieces, coarsely chopped	500 mL

Topping

¾ cup	red currant jelly	175 mL
4 cups	fresh raspberries	1 L
1 cup	whipped cream, optional	250 mL

1. **Crust:** Cream butter and sugar in a large bowl until light and creamy. Add flour, salt and egg. Mix well then knead lightly to form a smooth dough. Press into bottom and 1 inch (2.5 cm) up side of pan.

2. Bake on bottom rack of oven for 8 to 10 minutes or until very light golden. Reduce heat to 350°F (180°C).

3. **Filling:** Beat eggs, egg yolk and brown sugar in a small bowl on medium speed of electric mixer until light and fluffy. Add flour, cinnamon and baking powder and mix until blended. Stir in walnuts. Pour into crust.

4. Bake at 350°F (180°C) for 30 to 35 minutes longer or until filling is set. Cool completely in pan on rack.

5. **Topping:** Melt jelly in a small saucepan over low heat. Add berries, stirring to coat. Spread evenly over top of cooled tart filling. Serve with dollops of whipped cream, if using.

Variations

Use a combination of raspberries and blackberries in the topping.

Replace the red currant jelly with raspberry or strawberry jelly. Red apple jelly is fine, too.

Chocolate Peanut Butter Cream Pie

This luscious dessert is like a chocolate peanut butter cup dressed up as a pie.

Makes about 8 servings

Preparation: 35 minutes

Baking: 15 minutes

Chilling: 2 hours or overnight

Freezing: excellent

TIPS

Use smooth peanut butter in the filling to maintain a creamy texture.

Sift the confectioner's (icing) sugar after measuring and add it gradually to the cheese mixture. Adding it all at once makes it more difficult to blend smoothly.

When adding melted butter to recipes, unless otherwise specified, the butter should be cooled but still liquid.

To get the maximum volume when whipping cream, chill the bowl and beaters.

Decorate the top of this pie with quartered chocolate peanut butter cups.

- Preheat oven to 425°F (220°C)
- 9-inch (23 cm) pie plate

Crust

	Pastry for 9-inch (23 cm) single-crust pie (see recipes, pages 247 to 249)	

Filling

1¼ cups	smooth peanut butter	300 mL
1	package (8 oz/250 g) cream cheese, softened	1
1 cup	confectioner's (icing) sugar, sifted, divided	250 mL
2 tbsp	butter, melted	30 mL
2 tsp	vanilla	10 mL
1¼ cups	whipping (35%) cream	300 mL

Glaze

⅓ cup	whipping (35%) cream	75 mL
3	squares (each 1 oz/28 g) semi-sweet chocolate, chopped	3

1. **Crust:** Prepare and bake pie shell according to recipe instructions. Cool completely.
2. **Filling:** Beat peanut butter and cream cheese in a large bowl on medium speed of electric mixer until smooth. Gradually add ¾ cup (175 mL) icing sugar, melted butter and vanilla; mix well.
3. Beat whipping cream and remaining ¼ cup (50 mL) icing sugar until stiff peaks form. Stir one-quarter of the whipped cream into peanut butter mixture and mix thoroughly. Fold in remaining cream gently but thoroughly. Spoon into prepared crust. Chill for 1 hour or until firm.
4. **Glaze:** Bring cream to a boil in a small saucepan over low heat. Remove from heat. Add chocolate, stirring until melted and smooth. Cool slightly. Pour over filling, tilting pie to cover top completely. Chill for at least 1 hour or overnight to set glaze.

Variation

For an even more decadent treat, chop two chocolate bars with peanut butter filling and spread them evenly over the baked pie shell before adding the filling.

Upside-Down Apple Pecan Pie

A novel twist on an old-fashioned favorite.

Makes about 8 servings

Preparation: 30 minutes

Baking: 45 minutes

Freezing: not recommended

TIPS

Place pie on foil or baking sheet to catch any juice that may run over.

Serve warm with ice cream or whipped cream.

- Preheat oven to 425°F (220°C)
- 9-inch (23 cm) pie plate

Glaze

¼ cup	packed brown sugar	50 mL
1 tbsp	butter, melted	15 mL
1 tbsp	corn syrup	15 mL
½ cup	pecan halves	125 mL

Crust

Pastry for 9-inch (23 cm) double-crust pie (see recipes, pages 247 to 249)

Filling

⅔ cup	granulated sugar	150 mL
3 tbsp	Robin Hood All-Purpose Flour	45 mL
1 tsp	ground cinnamon	5 mL
5 cups	sliced peeled apples	1.25 L

1. **Glaze:** Combine brown sugar, melted butter and corn syrup in pie plate. Spread evenly to coat bottom of pan. Arrange pecans over top.

2. **Crust:** Prepare pastry according to recipe directions for two-crust pie. Place bottom pastry over mixture in pan, gently pressing onto nuts.

3. **Filling:** Combine sugar, flour, cinnamon and spices. Turn into pastry-lined pan. Cover with top pastry. Fold edge under bottom crust. Press together to seal. Flute edges. Cut slits to allow steam to escape. Bake on lower oven rack at 425°F (220°C) for 10 minutes, then reduce temperature to 325°F (160°C) and bake for 25 to 35 minutes longer or until apples are tender. Let set for 5 minutes, then loosen edge of pie and carefully invert onto serving plate.

Peach 'n' Cranberry Apple Pie

A flavorful twist on an all-time favorite.

TIP

Brush top pastry with milk and sprinkle with sugar before baking.

- *Preheat oven to 450°F (230°C)*
- *9-inch (23 cm) pie plate*

Crust

Pastry for 9-inch (23 cm) double-crust pie (see recipes, pages 247 to 249)

Filling

¾ cup	granulated sugar	175 mL
¼ cup	Robin Hood All-Purpose Flour	50 mL
1 tsp	ground cinnamon	5 mL
¼ tsp	nutmeg	1 mL
4 cups	sliced peeled apples	1 L
2 cups	fresh or canned sliced peaches, drained	500 mL
1 cup	cranberries, fresh or frozen	250 mL
1 tbsp	lemon juice	15 mL
2 tbsp	butter	30 mL

1. **Crust:** Prepare pastry according to recipe directions for two-crust pie. Roll out bottom crust and fit into pie plate.
2. **Filling:** Mix together sugar, flour, cinnamon and nutmeg. Combine sugar mixture with apples, peaches, cranberries and lemon juice. Mix well. Fill bottom crust with fruit mixture. Dot with butter. Place top pastry crust over filling. Seal and flute edge. Slash top crust for steam to escape. Place pie on piece of foil to catch any drips. Bake on lower oven rack at 450°F (230°C) for 15 minutes, then reduce temperature to 350°F (180°C) and bake for 35 to 40 minutes longer or until fruit is tender and crust is golden.

Variation

Replace cranberries with blueberries.

Open Apple Plum Pie

A *year-round favorite —
especially warm with a
scoop of ice cream.*

TIP

The lemon juice will prevent apples from turning brown.

- Preheat oven to 450°F (230°C)
- 9-inch (23 cm) pie plate

Crust

Pastry for 9-inch (23 cm) single-crust pie
(see recipes, pages 247 to 249)

Filling

¾ cup	granulated sugar	175 mL
⅓ cup	Robin Hood All-Purpose Flour	75 mL
1 tsp	ground cinnamon	5 mL
¼ tsp	nutmeg	1 mL
5 cups	sliced peeled apples	1.25 L
2½ cups	sliced plums	625 mL
1 tbsp	lemon juice	15 mL
2 tbsp	butter	30 mL
	Milk and sugar to glaze, optional	

1. **Crust:** Prepare pastry according to recipe directions for one-crust pie. Wrap and set aside.

2. **Filling:** Combine sugar, flour, cinnamon and nutmeg. Stir in apples, plums and lemon juice. Mix well.

3. Roll out pastry on floured surface into 15-inch (38 cm) circle. Fit into pie plate, allowing pastry to overhang. Fill with fruit mixture. Dot with butter. Fold pastry over fruit, pleating into rough circle. If desired, brush pastry with milk and sprinkle with sugar. Bake on lower oven rack at 450°F (230°C) for 10 minutes, then reduce temperature to 350°F (180°C) and bake for 35 to 45 minutes longer or until crust is golden and fruit is tender.

Variation

Replace plums with peaches or apples for another great taste.

Lemon Meringue Pie

This is the ultimate pie, a favorite with lemon lovers everywhere.

TIPS

Serve pie the same day you make it for the best taste and appearance.

You can control the tartness. If you like a tart taste, increase the lemon juice to ¾ cup (175 mL) and decrease the water to 1¼ cups (300 mL).

One lemon will give you about ¼ cup (50 mL) juice and 2 tsp (10 mL) grated zest.

This meringue takes a little more time to prepare, but the results are worth it. The cornstarch stabilizes the meringue so it won't weep. The lower baking temperature produces a evenly browned crust.

The filling should be hot when you add it to the shell and cover it with meringue. If meringue is placed on a cool filling, it can cause condensation or weeping under the meringue.

- Preheat oven to 425°F (220°C)
- 9-inch (23 cm) pie plate

Crust

Pastry for 9-inch (23 cm) single-crust pie (see recipes, pages 247 to 249)

Filling

1½ cups	cold water	375 mL
1 cup	granulated sugar	250 mL
¼ cup	cornstarch	50 mL
Pinch	salt	Pinch
6	egg yolks	6
1 tbsp	grated lemon zest	15 mL
½ cup	lemon juice	125 mL
2 tbsp	butter	30 mL

Meringue

1 tbsp	cornstarch	15 mL
½ cup	granulated sugar	125 mL
¼ tsp	cream of tartar	1 mL
4	egg whites	4

1. **Crust:** Prepare and bake pie shell according to recipe instructions. Cool completely.

2. **Filling:** Combine water, sugar, cornstarch and salt in a large saucepan. Bring to a simmer over medium heat, whisking constantly. When mixture starts to simmer and turn translucent, add egg yolks, two at a time, whisking after each addition until thoroughly blended. Whisk in lemon zest and juice and butter. Bring mixture to a boil, whisking constantly. Remove from heat. Cover surface with plastic wrap to keep warm and prevent a skin from forming. Set aside.

3. **Meringue:** Mix ⅓ cup (75 mL) water and cornstarch in a small saucepan. Bring to a simmer, whisking constantly. When mixture starts to simmer and turn translucent, remove from heat. Cool while going on to next step.

4. Preheat oven to 325°F (160°C). Mix sugar and cream of tartar. Beat egg whites in a medium bowl until frothy. Add sugar mixture, 1 tbsp (15 mL) at a time, beating until soft peaks form. Add cornstarch mixture, 1 tbsp (15 mL) at a time, beating until stiff peaks form.

5. If necessary, return lemon filling to low heat for 1 minute or until hot. Pour hot filling into baked pie shell. Immediately spread meringue over the filling, sealing it to the crust. Make peaks using the back of a spoon. Bake for 15 to 20 minutes or until golden. Cool completely in plate on rack. Serve the same day.

Light and Lemony Cream Pie

Smooth, light and refreshing.

Preparation: 30 minutes

Baking: 15 minutes

Cooking: 6 minutes

Refrigeration time: 1 hour (crust) plus 3 hours (filling)

Freezing: not recommended

TIP

A thin layer of melted chocolate on a baked pie shell will keep the crust from getting soggy. It also adds a nice flavor but isn't a necessity.

- *Preheat oven to 450°F (230°C)*
- *9-inch (23 cm) pie plate*

Crust

	Pastry for 9-inch (23 cm) single-crust pie (see recipes, pages 247 to 249)	
2	squares (each 1 oz/28 g) bittersweet chocolate, melted	2

Filling

1	envelope (1 tbsp/15 mL) unflavored gelatin	1
1 cup	granulated sugar, divided	250 mL
Pinch	salt	Pinch
4	egg yolks	4
1/2 cup	lemon juice	125 mL
1 tbsp	grated lemon zest	15 mL
4	egg whites	4
1/2 cup	whipping (35%) cream, beaten stiff	125 mL
	Lemon slices to garnish, optional	

1. **Crust:** Prepare pastry according to recipe directions for one-crust pie. Crimp edges. Prick well. Refrigerate for 1 hour. Bake for 12 to 15 minutes or until golden. Cool completely. (Wrap and refrigerate remaining pastry for later use.) Spread melted chocolate evenly over pastry shell. Cool.

2. **Filling:** Combine gelatin, 1/2 cup (125 mL) sugar, salt, egg yolks and lemon juice in small saucepan. Cook, stirring constantly, over medium heat for about 6 minutes or until slightly thickened. (It thickens more on cooling.) Stir in zest. Refrigerate just until mixture starts to set, about 30 minutes. Beat egg whites and remaining 1/2 cup (125 mL) sugar to stiff peaks. Fold egg whites and whipped cream into lemon mixture gently but thoroughly. Pile into baked pie shell. Refrigerate for about 2 1/2 hours or until set, or overnight. Decorate with lemon slices, if desired.

Variation

Use white or semi-sweet chocolate to spread on the crust.

Fabulous Fruit Flan

This all-year-round dessert changes its look constantly, depending on what fruits are in season. Enjoy fresh berries in the summer and canned fruit in the winter.

Preparation: 35 minutes

Baking: 10 minutes

Freezing: not recommended

TIPS

When using canned fruits, such as mandarin oranges and peach slices, set them on a paper towel to drain well before arranging them over the filling.

Make this flan as simple (all one fruit) or as colorful and elaborate (several kinds of fruit) as you like.

Prepare the crust a few days ahead for easy entertaining.

Because this crust is like shortbread, only butter will do. Work the dough with your hands until it melds into a smooth ball.

If using red fruit, such as berries, use red currant jelly for the glaze.

- Preheat oven to 425°F (220°C)
- 9-inch (23 cm) fluted flan pan with removable bottom

Crust

1¼ cups	Robin Hood All-Purpose Flour	300 mL
2 tbsp	icing sugar, sifted	30 mL
½ cup	butter, softened	125 mL

Filling

1	package (8 oz/250 g) cream cheese, softened	1
½ cup	confectioner's (icing) sugar, sifted	125 mL
1 tsp	vanilla	5 mL
½ cup	whipping (35%) cream	125 mL
3 cups	fruit	750 mL

Glaze, optional

½ cup	apricot jam, put through a sieve	125 mL
1 tbsp	lemon juice	15 mL

1. **Crust:** Combine flour and icing sugar. Cream butter in a bowl and gradually blend in flour mixture. Use your hands to form a smooth dough. Press evenly onto bottom and up side of pan; prick well with fork and chill for 15 minutes.

2. Bake on bottom rack of oven for 7 to 10 minutes or until light golden. Cool completely in pan on rack.

3. **Filling:** Beat cream cheese, icing sugar and vanilla until smooth. Whip cream until stiff peaks form and fold into cheese mixture. Spread evenly in baked crust.

4. Arrange fruit attractively over filling.

5. **Glaze (optional):** If desired, melt jam and lemon juice together until smooth and brush over fruit. Serve at room temperature.

Variation

Use your favorite fresh or canned fruit: strawberries, raspberries, blueberries, blackberries, kiwifruit, grapes, apricots, mandarins, pineapple, peaches and so on; they're all scrumptious.

Lemon Tart

If you like lemon, you'll love this.

Makes about 12 servings

Preparation: 20 minutes

Refrigeration: 30 minutes

Baking: 42 minutes

Freezing: not recommended

TIPS

Garnish with fresh berries, if desired.

If you prefer a not-so-tart tart, reduce lemon juice to ¾ cup (175 mL).

- Preheat oven to 375°F (190°C)
- 9-inch (23 cm) flan pan with removable sides

Crust

1 cup	Robin Hood All-Purpose Flour	250 mL
¼ cup	granulated sugar	50 mL
¼ cup	butter	50 mL
1	egg, beaten	1

Filling

3	eggs	3
½ cup	granulated sugar	125 mL
1 tbsp	grated lemon zest (1 to 2 lemons)	15 mL
1 cup	lemon juice (3 to 4 lemons)	250 mL
¾ cup	ground almonds	175 mL
⅓ cup	melted butter, cooled	75 mL
	Fresh berries, optional	

1. **Crust:** Combine flour and sugar. Cut in butter until mixture resembles coarse crumbs. Stir in egg. Working with hands, mix well to form smooth dough. Press into sides and bottom of pan. Prick pastry well with fork. Refrigerate for 30 minutes. Bake on lower oven rack for 10 to 12 minutes. Cool.

2. **Filling:** Whisk together eggs, sugar, lemon zest and juice. Stir in almonds and cooled melted butter. Pour carefully into pastry shell. Bake for 25 to 30 minutes or until filling is set and pastry is light golden. Cool completely. Serve with fresh berries, if desired.

Chewy Cherry Coconut Tarts

The name says it all.

Makes 12 tarts

Preparation: 20 minutes
Baking: 23 minutes
Freezing: excellent

TIPS

Work dough with hands to make smooth.

Use floured fingers to press dough into pan.

Use your favorite kind of nut.

- *Preheat oven to 325°F (160°C)*
- *12-cup muffin pan*

Crust

½ cup	butter, softened	125 mL
½ cup	packed brown sugar	125 mL
1	egg yolk	1
1 cup	Robin Hood All-Purpose Flour	250 mL

Filling

2	egg whites	2
½ cup	packed brown sugar	125 mL
½ cup	flaked coconut	125 mL
⅓ cup	chopped maraschino cherries, drained	75 mL
¼ cup	finely chopped nuts	50 mL
1 tsp	vanilla	5 mL

1. **Crust:** Combine butter, brown sugar, egg yolk and flour, mixing to form smooth dough. Press into muffin cups to form tart shells.

2. **Filling:** Beat egg whites to stiff peaks. Fold in brown sugar, coconut, cherries, nuts and vanilla until blended. Mix well. Spoon into prepared shells. Bake on lower oven rack for 18 to 23 minutes or until golden. Cool.

Creamy Peach Crumble Pie

The crumbly oat topping and creamy filling bring out the best in fresh peaches.

Makes about 8 servings

Preparation: 20 minutes

Baking: 60 minutes

Freezing: not recommended

TIPS

Large-flake oats look great in toppings and have a nice oat flavor that is enhanced by butter and brown sugar. If you don't have any, use regular or quick oats.

If you have leftover peaches, sauté the peeled slices in a little butter and brown sugar until tender.

When filling an unbaked pie shell with fruit, sprinkle it lightly with fine dry bread crumbs before filling to prevent a soggy crust.

- Preheat oven to 350°F (180°C)
- 9-inch (23 cm) pie plate

Crust

	Pastry for 9-inch (23 cm) single-crust pie (see recipes, pages 247 to 249)	

Topping

¾ cup	Robin Hood All-Purpose Flour	175 mL
½ cup	packed brown sugar	125 mL
⅓ cup	Robin Hood Large-Flake Oats	75 mL
1 tsp	ground cinnamon	5 mL
⅓ cup	butter	75 mL

Filling

¾ cup	sour cream	175 mL
½ cup	granulated sugar	125 mL
¼ cup	Robin Hood All-Purpose Flour	50 mL
6	medium peaches, peeled, pitted and sliced	6

1. **Crust:** Prepare pastry for unbaked pie shell. Roll out and fit into pie plate.
2. **Topping:** Combine flour, brown sugar, oats and cinnamon in a bowl. Using two knives, a pastry blender or your fingers, cut in butter until mixture resembles coarse crumbs. Set aside.
3. **Filling:** Mix sour cream, sugar and flour in a bowl until smooth. Stir in peaches. Spread in bottom of pie shell. Sprinkle topping evenly over filling. Place pie on a piece of aluminum foil to catch any drips.
4. Bake on bottom rack for 50 to 60 minutes or until peaches are tender. Cool completely on rack.

Variation
Replace half or all of the peaches with apples.

Easy Bumbleberry Pie

This mixture of apples and berries brings out the best in all the fruits. The pie looks fabulous as well.

Makes about 8 servings

Preparation: 30 minutes

Baking: 65 minutes

Freezing: excellent

TIPS

Toss apples with the lemon juice as soon as you slice them to prevent browning.

After the filling is mixed, let it stand for 5 minutes, then mix it again before adding it to the pastry. This gives the flour and sugar a better chance to become thoroughly blended with the fruit, which helps the filling thicken during baking.

- *Preheat oven to 425°F (220°C)*
- *9-inch (23 cm) pie plate*

Crust

Pastry for 9-inch (23 cm) double-crust pie (see recipes, pages 247 to 249)

Filling

¾ cup	granulated sugar	175 mL
6 tbsp	Robin Hood All-Purpose Flour	90 mL
4 cups	sliced peeled cored apples	1 L
1 cup	raspberries	250 mL
1 cup	blueberries	250 mL
1 tbsp	lemon juice	15 mL
2 tbsp	butter	30 mL

1. **Crust:** Prepare pastry for double-crust pie. Roll out bottom crust and fit into pie plate.
2. **Filling:** Mix sugar and flour in a large bowl. Add apples, raspberries, blueberries and lemon juice. Toss gently until fruit is thoroughly coated. Turn into the pastry-lined pie plate and dot with butter.
3. Roll out pastry for top crust. Arrange over filling. Seal and flute the edge. Slash the top to allow steam to escape. Place pie on a piece of aluminum foil to catch drips.
4. Bake on bottom rack of oven for 15 minutes, then reduce temperature to 350°F (180°C) and bake for 40 to 50 minutes longer or until crust is golden and apples are tender and bubbly.

Variation
Replace apples with peaches.

Best Blueberry Pie

Blueberries are a plentiful treat during Canadian summers. Enjoy the bounty in this simple double-crust pie.

Makes about 8 servings

Preparation: 25 minutes

Baking: 1 hour

Freezing: excellent

TIPS

If using frozen fruit, thaw just enough to separate the berries. Replace the flour with cornstarch, which has twice as much thickening power — it's necessary to accommodate the additional juice in the frozen fruit. Also, increase the baking time by about 20 minutes. Watch carefully and cover the top with aluminum foil during baking if it's browning too quickly.

For a nicely browned top, brush the crust with an egg glaze (see page 23).

If you have trouble rolling and placing the top crust on a pie (or you just want a fun alternative to a plain top), cut the pastry into attractive shapes with a cookie cutter and arrange the pieces, slightly overlapping, over the filling.

- *Preheat oven to 425°F (220°C)*
- *9-inch (23 cm) pie plate*

Crust

	Pastry for 9-inch (23 cm) double-crust pie (see recipes, pages 247 to 249)	

Filling

5 cups	fresh or frozen blueberries (see Tips, left)	1.25 L
¾ cup	granulated sugar	175 mL
⅓ cup	Robin Hood All-Purpose Flour	75 mL
2 tsp	grated lemon zest	10 mL
1 tbsp	lemon juice	15 mL
2 tbsp	butter	30 mL

1. **Crust:** Prepare pastry for double-crust pie. Roll out bottom crust and fit into pie plate.
2. **Filling:** Combine blueberries, sugar, flour and lemon zest and juice. Toss gently until fruit is thoroughly coated. Turn into the pastry-lined pie plate and dot with butter.
3. Roll out pastry for top crust. Arrange over filling. Seal and flute edge. Slash top crust to allow steam to escape. Place pie on a piece of aluminum foil to catch drips. (As an added safeguard, press the floured tines of a fork into the fluted edge that rests on the plate rim. This keeps the fruit in place and helps seal in the juices.)
4. Bake on bottom rack of oven for 15 minutes, then reduce heat to 350°F (180°C) and bake for 35 to 45 minutes longer or until crust is golden and fruit is tender and bubbly.

Variations

Replace half of the blueberries with raspberries.

A pinch of ground nutmeg or ginger adds an intriguing hint of flavor to fruit pies.

Mixed Nut Tart

If you like nuts, you'll love this tart, which is loaded with them. It has a similar flavor to pecan pie.

Makes about 12 servings

Preparation: 25 minutes

Baking: 45 minutes

Freezing: excellent

TIPS

Buy deluxe mixed nuts with no peanuts or make your own blend using pecans, almonds, hazelnuts, cashews and Brazil nuts.

Use nuts that are similar in size. If using large Brazil nuts, cut them in half.

Use salted nuts. The combination of sweet and salty is particularly appealing.

Take the time to turn some of the nuts in the filling right side up for the most attractive presentation.

Pastry made with butter shrinks more and is not as flaky as that made with shortening.

To transfer dough to the pan, drape it over the rolling pin or fold it in half for easy moving.

- Preheat oven to 400°F (200°C)
- 11-inch (27 cm) fluted flan pan with removable bottom

Crust

1½ cups	Robin Hood All-Purpose Flour	375 mL
2 tbsp	granulated sugar	30 mL
¼ tsp	salt	1 mL
½ cup	cold shortening or butter	125 mL
4 to 5 tbsp	cold water	60 to 75 mL

Filling

2	eggs	2
½ cup	packed brown sugar	125 mL
½ cup	corn syrup	125 mL
3 tbsp	butter, melted	45 mL
2 tsp	vanilla	10 mL
2 cups	deluxe mixed nuts (11 oz/300 g)	500 mL
	Whipped cream, optional	

1. **Crust:** Combine flour, sugar and salt in a mixing bowl. Using a pastry blender, two knives or your fingers, cut in shortening until mixture resembles coarse crumbs. Add water, 1 tbsp (15 mL) at a time, mixing lightly with a fork until dough comes together. Add just enough water to hold dough together. Press into a ball.

2. Roll dough out on lightly floured surface to a 14-inch (35 cm) round. Transfer to pan. Press into bottom and up side of pan. Fold overhang in and press against side of pan to form a rim slightly taller than the edge of the pan. Prick bottom with a fork.

3. Bake for 15 minutes or until set but not golden. Reduce temperature to 375°F (190°C).

4. **Filling:** Whisk eggs, brown sugar, corn syrup, butter and vanilla in a medium bowl until smoothly blended. Stir in nuts. Pour mixture into tart shell.

5. Bake on bottom rack of oven for 25 to 30 minutes or until set and golden. Cool completely in pan on rack. Serve with whipped cream, if using.

Variation

If you prefer, use a mixture of nuts that contains peanuts, but keep the peanuts to a minimum for the best flavor and appearance.

Fresh Strawberry Pie

The fresh strawberries create an explosion of color and flavor in this dynamite pie.

Makes about 8 servings

Preparation: 30 minutes

Baking: 15 minutes

Chilling: 2 hours

Freezing: not recommended

TIPS

Drizzle melted chocolate over the filling for a special treat.

The berries can be soft for the cooked sauce but should be firmer for the uncooked portion.

If the berries seem very wet, add another teaspoon (5 mL) of cornstarch.

- Preheat oven to 400°F (200°C)
- 9-inch (23 cm) pie plate

Crust

1 cup	Robin Hood All-Purpose Flour	250 mL
½ cup	butter, softened	125 mL
¼ cup	confectioner's (icing) sugar, sifted	50 mL
¼ cup	ground pecans	50 mL

Filling

5½ cups	fresh strawberries	1.375 L
1 cup	granulated sugar	250 mL
3 tbsp	cornstarch	45 mL
1 tbsp	lemon juice	15 mL

1. **Crust:** Combine flour, butter, icing sugar and pecans, mixing until smooth. Turn out onto a floured board and knead lightly to form a smooth dough. Press firmly into bottom and up sides of pie plate. Prick well with a fork. Chill for 20 minutes.
2. Bake on bottom rack of oven for 12 to 15 minutes or until golden. Cool completely.
3. **Filling:** Cut 2 cups (500 mL) of the strawberries in half. Combine with sugar and cornstarch in a small saucepan. Cook over medium-high heat, stirring constantly, until mixture starts to bubble. Reduce heat to low and cook, stirring often, until berries soften and mixture thickens slightly. Chill to lukewarm.
4. Leave remaining berries whole if small or halve if large. Mix with thickened berry mixture. Cool completely. Pour mixture into baked pie shell. Chill for 1 hour before serving.

Variations

Replace pecans with hazelnuts or almonds.

Replace some of the fresh strawberries with blueberries, raspberries or a mixture of berries.

Basic Pastry

This-tried-and-true recipe makes tender, flaky pastry every time.

TIPS

Robin Hood Best for Cake & Pastry Flour helps take the worry out of making pastry, as it is more forgiving of little mistakes. If you are using all-purpose flour, handle the dough as little as possible, because too much handling will make it tough.

When assembling double-crust pies, you can flute the edges by pinching the evenly trimmed top and bottom crusts together in a crimped pattern, or simply seal them together using the tines of a fork.

Start pies in a hot oven (425°F/220°C) and place them on the bottom rack. This quickly creates steam in the pastry, which makes air pockets that push up the flakes of fat-coated starch, creating a flaky crust.

For convenience, make pastry dough ahead of time. Unrolled pastry dough can be stored in the refrigerator for up to 3 days or frozen for up to 6 months. Thaw frozen dough overnight in the refrigerator before rolling it out.

● *9-inch (23 cm) pie plate*

Single Crust

1 cup + 2 tbsp	Robin Hood Best for Cake & Pastry Flour	280 mL
$\frac{1}{2}$ tsp	salt	2 mL
$\frac{1}{2}$ cup	cold shortening	125 mL
2 to 3 tbsp	cold water	30 to 45 mL

Double Crust

$2\frac{1}{4}$ cups	Robin Hood Best for Cake & Pastry Flour	550 mL
$\frac{3}{4}$ tsp	salt	3 mL
$\frac{3}{4}$ cup	cold shortening	175 mL
4 to 6 tbsp	cold water	60 to 90 mL

1. Combine flour and salt in a mixing bowl. Using two knives, a pastry blender or your fingers, cut in shortening until mixture is uniform and resembles large peas. Don't overblend.

2. Sprinkle with water, 1 tbsp (15 mL) at a time, mixing lightly with a fork after each addition. Add just enough water to hold dough together. Press into a ball. Chill for 15 to 30 minutes for easy rolling.

3. Divide dough into 2 portions for double-crust pie. Flatten into round disc(s). Place 1 disc on a floured surface or pastry cloth.

4. Roll out dough to a uniform thickness (about $\frac{1}{8}$ inch/3 mm), starting in the center and rolling, spoke-fashion, toward the edge with light, even strokes. If dough sticks, dust the bottom of the pastry or the board lightly with flour. Roll pastry loosely around the rolling pin, then unroll over the pie plate; ease into the plate without stretching. Trim dough $\frac{1}{2}$ inch (1 cm) beyond the edge of the pie plate.

5. For a single crust, fold under the edge and flute.

6. For a double crust, fill bottom crust, then roll out remaining dough as for bottom crust and flip over filling. Fold edge of top crust under the overhang of bottom crust; seal and flute edge. Cut slits in the center of the top crust to allow steam to escape.

Variations

Replace $\frac{1}{4}$ cup (50 mL) shortening with cold butter. Shortening makes the pastry tender, flaky and easy to handle, while butter adds flavor and color.

All-Purpose Flour: Use 1 cup (250 mL) for a single crust and 2 cups (500 mL) for a double crust.

Oil Pastry

Here is an easy way to make pastry that is very tender and tasty.

TIPS

Pastry made with oil is not as flaky as that made with shortening or butter, but it is very tender and easy to mix.

Using liquid oils (such as safflower, sunflower, canola and olive) instead of solid fats (such as lard, shortening and solid margarine) will help you to reduce the saturated and trans fats in your diet.

When making savory recipes, add dried herbs to the pastry for enhanced flavor. Try basil, oregano, parsley and dill — whatever complements the filling. Grated or shredded cheese, such as Parmesan or Cheddar (about 1/2 cup/125 mL, added to the dry ingredients), also works.

For dessert pastries, try adding sesame seeds, cinnamon, nutmeg, ginger, grated chocolate, orange or lemon zest, or finely chopped nuts to the dry ingredients, to taste, when making this pastry.

- 9-inch (23 cm) pie plate

Single Crust

1 cup + 2 tbsp	Robin Hood All-Purpose Flour	280 mL
1/2 tsp	salt	2 mL
6 tbsp	vegetable oil	90 mL
2 tbsp	cold water	30 mL

Double Crust

2 1/4 cups	Robin Hood All-Purpose Flour	550 mL
1 tsp	salt	5 mL
3/4 cup	vegetable or canola oil	175 mL
1/4 cup	cold water	50 mL

1. Combine flour and salt in a mixing bowl.

2. Combine oil and water. Add to flour all at once. Stir lightly with a fork until the dough comes together, then shape into a ball. If making a double-crust pie, divide into two portions. Using your hand, flatten slightly into disc(s). Place one disc of dough between two large squares of waxed paper.

3. Place paper and dough on a moistened surface to prevent paper from moving. Roll out to a uniform thickness (about 1/8 inch/3 mm), starting in center and rolling, spoke-fashion, toward the edge with light, even strokes until dough reaches the desired size. Peel off top paper and flip dough over onto pie plate. Gently peel off the remaining paper. Ease dough into the plate without stretching. Trim dough 1/2 inch (1 cm) beyond the edge of the pie plate.

4. For a single crust, fold under the edge and flute.

5. For a double crust, fill bottom crust, then roll out remaining dough as for top crust and flip over filling. Fold edge of top crust under the edge of bottom crust; seal and flute. Cut slits in center of top crust to allow steam to escape. Bake as directed in recipe.

Easy-as-Pie Pastry

If you make a lot of pies, this larger-batch recipe makes life easy. It makes enough pastry for five 9-inch (23 cm) pie shells, or two double-crust pies and one single-crust pie.

TIPS

The egg and vinegar tenderize the pastry and make it very easy to work with.

Although shortening can be stored at room temperature, it works better in pastry if it is cold.

For convenience, prepare shells or pies ahead and refrigerate or freeze them. Rolled pastry dough can be kept in the fridge for up to 3 days or frozen for up to 6 months. Wrap tightly in plastic before freezing. It isn't necessary to thaw rolled dough before baking.

5 cups	Robin Hood All-Purpose Flour	1.25 L
1½ tsp	salt	7 mL
1	package (1 lb/454 g) shortening, chilled (2⅓ cups/575 mL)	1
1	egg	1
1 tbsp	vinegar	15 mL
½ cup	cold water	125 mL

1. Combine flour and salt in a large mixing bowl.
2. Using two knives, a pastry blender or your fingers, cut in shortening until mixture is uniform and resembles large peas. Don't overblend.
3. Beat egg and vinegar in a measuring cup. Add enough cold water to make ¾ cup (175 mL) liquid and add all at once to flour mixture. Stir with fork until dough holds together, then form into a ball using your hands.
4. Roll out for use in recipe.

Baking Pastry

The following general directions are for baking pastry. If there are specific directions in your recipe, follow those.

Double Crust: Cut slits in top crust or prick with a fork. Bake in a 425°F (220°C) oven for 40 to 50 minutes or until the top is golden.

Unbaked Shell (for fillings such as custard, pumpkin or quiche): Do not prick the dough. Fill and bake in a 450°F (230°C) oven for 10 minutes. Reduce heat to 350°F (180°C) and bake for 30 to 40 minutes longer.

Baked Shell (lemon or cream filling): Prick the dough all over with a fork. Bake in a 425°F (220°C) oven for 12 to 15 minutes. Cool then fill.

To Bake Blind: Pie crusts tend to shrink when they are baked because the strands of gluten, which have been stretched by rolling, retract when heated. Here's a foolproof way to bake a pastry shell without shrinkage. Cut a 12-inch (30 cm) circle of aluminum foil or parchment paper. Fit into pastry shell. Fill with pie weights or dried beans. Bake on bottom rack in 425°F (220°C) oven for 10 minutes. Cool for 5 minutes, then remove beans. Reduce heat to 350°F (180°C) and bake for 15 to 20 minutes longer or until golden.

Cream Puffs

Desserts

Cream Puffs

It's a challenge to purchase prepared cream puffs or chocolate éclairs filled with real whipped cream, because they need to be eaten soon after the puffs are filled. Serve these to your guests and you'll be a star.

Makes about 12 servings

Preparation: 20 minutes
Baking: 35 minutes
Freezing:
not recommended

Tips

Cream puffs and éclairs are made from the same choux pastry dough and are filled and topped in a similar way; they are just shaped differently. Cream puffs are round mounds, and éclairs are long tubes. For best results, use a pastry bag to make éclairs. When making cream puffs, just drop the dough onto the prepared baking sheet.

Prepare cream puffs ahead of time and assemble just before serving.

Serve these delectable morsels on a dessert plate, drizzled with chocolate sauce. For a change, fill puffs with ice cream.

- Preheat oven to 400°F (200°C)
- Baking sheet, greased

Puffs

1 cup	water	250 mL
1/2 cup	butter	125 mL
1 cup	Robin Hood All-Purpose Flour	250 mL
Pinch	salt	Pinch
4	eggs, at room temperature	4

Filling

4 cups	sweetened whipped cream	1 L

Topping

2 cups	chocolate, caramel or fruit sauce	500 mL

1. **Puffs:** Combine water and butter in a medium saucepan over medium heat; bring to a rolling boil. Add flour and salt all at once. Stir vigorously over low heat for 1 minute or until mixture pulls away from the side of the pan and forms a ball. Remove from heat and cool for 5 minutes.

2. Add eggs, one at a time, beating vigorously after each addition on high speed of an electric mixer or with a wooden spoon until smooth and glossy. Drop dough by scant 1/4 cupfuls (50 mL), 2 inches (5 cm) apart, onto prepared baking sheet.

3. Bake for 30 to 35 minutes or until puffed and golden. Cut a small slit in the side of each puff to allow steam to escape. Bake for 2 minutes longer. Transfer from pan to rack and cool completely.

4. **Filling:** To serve, cut puff in half horizontally. Fill with whipped cream.

5. **Topping:** Top with warm or cool sauce. Serve immediately.

Variations

Éclairs: Spoon cream puff dough into a pastry bag fitted with a 1/2-inch (1 cm) round tip. Pipe 2-inch (5 cm) strips, 2 inches (5 cm) apart, onto prepared baking sheet. Bake and assemble as for cream puffs.

For a party, try finishing the puffs with Basic Chocolate Glaze (see recipe, page 219) or a sprinkle of icing sugar, rather than with the sauce, to simplify serving.

If you're serving these as a plated dessert, fill them with ice cream for a change.

Make smaller puffs for bite-size treats.

Apple Peach Blueberry Crisp

This tasty dessert is easy to make. Change it to accommodate seasonal fruits and your family's tastes.

Makes about 6 servings

Preparation: 10 minutes

Baking: 40 minutes

Freezing: not recommended

TIPS

Vary the fruit but keep the total amount to 5 cups (1.25 L).

You may have to adjust the sugar and flour in the filling depending upon how sweet and juicy the fruit is. Use more sugar if the fruit is less sweet, more flour if it is juicy.

Serve this crisp warm with a big scoop of vanilla ice cream or a dollop of whipped cream. If you prefer a lighter version, top with vanilla yogurt.

You can use Robin Hood Whole Wheat Flour and large-flake oats in this recipe.

- Preheat oven to 375°F (190°C)
- 6-cup (1.5 L) baking dish, greased

Crisp Topping

¾ cup	Robin Hood Oats	175 mL
⅓ cup	Robin Hood All-Purpose Flour	75 mL
½ cup	packed brown sugar	125 mL
1 tsp	ground cinnamon	5 mL
¼ cup	butter	50 mL

Fruit

2 cups	sliced peeled cored apples	500 mL
2 cups	sliced peeled pitted peaches	500 mL
1 cup	blueberries	250 mL
½ cup	granulated sugar	125 mL
3 tbsp	Robin Hood All-Purpose Flour	45 mL
1 tbsp	lemon juice	15 mL

1. **Crisp Topping:** Combine oats, flour, brown sugar and cinnamon in a mixing bowl. Using two knives, a pastry blender or your fingers, cut in butter until mixture resembles coarse crumbs. Set aside.
2. **Fruit:** Combine apples, peaches, blueberries, sugar, flour and lemon juice in a bowl. Mix thoroughly. Let stand for 5 minutes then mix again. Turn into prepared baking dish. Sprinkle topping evenly over fruit.
3. Bake for 35 to 40 minutes or until fruit is tender.

Variation
Almost any fruit works well in this recipe. Leave softer fruits, such as berries, whole or in larger pieces and cut firmer fruits, such as apples, into thin slices so they will cook to tender in approximately the same time.

Bumbleberry Cobbler

Once a favorite, always a favorite.

TIP

Choose a tart crisp apple like Granny Smith. Decrease water if fruit is juicy.

- Preheat oven to 400°F (200°C)
- 9-inch (2.5 L) square cake pan or 2½-quart (2.5 L) baking dish, greased

Fruit

5 cups	thinly sliced peeled apples	1.25 L
1 cup	fresh or frozen cranberries	250 mL
1 cup	fresh or frozen raspberries	250 mL
¾ cup	granulated sugar	175 mL
¼ cup	Robin Hood All-Purpose Flour	50 mL
⅓ cup	water	75 mL

Topping

1¾ cups	Robin Hood All-Purpose Flour	425 mL
2 tbsp	granulated sugar	30 mL
4 tsp	baking powder	20 mL
½ tsp	salt	2 mL
½ cup	butter or margarine	125 mL
1 cup	milk	250 mL

1. **Fruit:** Combine apples, cranberries, raspberries, sugar, flour and water in a large bowl. Mix well. Spread in prepared pan.

2. **Topping:** Mix together flour, sugar, baking powder and salt. Cut in butter with pastry blender until mixture resembles coarse meal. Add milk all at once. Stir with fork until all ingredients are moistened. Drop spoonfuls of batter over fruit, covering surface. Place pan on piece of foil to catch any drips that boil over. Bake for 25 to 30 minutes or until top is golden. Serve warm.

Variation

Try other fruit mixtures, keeping total amount the same.

Lemon-Glazed Cheesecake Squares

A lemon lover's delight.

TIP

Prepare a day ahead for convenience and optimum texture and flavor.

- Preheat oven to 350°F (180°C)
- 13- by 9-inch (3.5 L) cake pan, greased

Crust

2 cups	Robin Hood All-Purpose Flour	500 mL
½ cup	confectioner's (icing) sugar, sifted	125 mL
1 cup	butter	250 mL

Filling

3	packages (each 8 oz/250 g) cream cheese, softened	3
¾ cup	granulated sugar	175 mL
3	eggs	3
⅓ cup	lemon juice	75 mL
2 tsp	vanilla	10 mL

Topping

2 cups	sour cream	500 mL
3 tbsp	granulated sugar	45 mL

Glaze

½ cup	granulated sugar	125 mL
2 tbsp	cornstarch	30 mL
¾ cup	water	175 mL
⅓ cup	lemon juice	75 mL
1	egg yolk, beaten	1
1 tbsp	butter	15 mL

1. **Crust:** Combine flour, sugar and butter in food processor or with pastry blender until crumbly. Press in prepared pan. Bake for 15 to 20 minutes or until light golden.

2. **Filling:** Beat cream cheese and sugar on high speed of electric mixer until smooth. Add eggs, lemon juice and vanilla, beating until smooth. Spread over crust. Bake for 35 minutes or until set.

3. **Topping:** Combine sour cream and sugar. Spread over cheesecake. Return to oven for 5 minutes. Cool for 1 hour.

4. **Glaze:** Combine sugar and cornstarch in saucepan. Stir in water, lemon juice and egg yolk. Cook on medium heat, stirring constantly, until mixture comes to a boil and thickens. Stir in butter. Cool slightly. Spread over cheesecake. Store in refrigerator. Cut into squares.

Variation

Top each square with a small piece of fruit.

Strawberry Cheesecake Squares

Nice on a cookie tray as well as for dessert.

Makes about 36 squares

Preparation: 30 minutes

Baking: 45 minutes

Refrigeration: 3 hours or overnight

Freezing: excellent

TIP

Line pan with foil for easy removal of cooled squares.

- Preheat oven to 350°F (180°C)
- 13- by 9-inch (3.5 L) cake pan, greased

Crust

2 cups	Robin Hood All-Purpose Flour	500 mL
¾ cup	packed brown sugar	175 mL
¾ cup	finely chopped almonds	175 mL
¾ cup	butter or margarine	175 mL

Filling

2	packages (each 8 oz/250 g) cream cheese, softened	2
⅔ cup	granulated sugar	150 mL
2	eggs	2
½ tsp	almond extract	2 mL
1 cup	strawberry jam	250 mL
¾ cup	sliced almonds	175 mL

1. **Crust:** Combine flour, sugar, almonds and butter until crumbly. Reserve ¾ cup (175 mL) for topping. Press remainder into prepared pan. Bake for 12 to 15 minutes or until edges are golden.

2. **Filling:** Beat cream cheese, sugar, eggs and almond extract on medium speed of electric mixture until smooth. Spread evenly over hot crust. Bake for 15 minutes. Stir jam until smooth. Spread over filling. Stir sliced almonds into reserved crumble mixture. Sprinkle over jam. Bake for 15 minutes longer. Cool completely on wire rack. Refrigerate for at least 3 hours or overnight before cutting into squares. Store in refrigerator.

Variation

Try raspberry or apricot jam in place of strawberry.

Buttery Apple Torte

A *year-round dessert that's easy to make for family and company, too.*

TIPS

Toast almonds and sprinkle on torte just before serving to keep them crunchy.

A sprinkling of confectioner's (icing) sugar before serving adds a nice finishing touch.

- Preheat oven to 450°F (230°C)
- 10-inch (25 cm) springform pan, greased

Crust

¾ cup	butter, softened	175 mL
½ cup	granulated sugar	125 mL
1⅔ cups	Robin Hood All-Purpose Flour	400 mL
½ cup	apricot or raspberry jam	125 mL

Filling

8 oz	spreadable cream cheese	250 g
¼ cup	granulated sugar	50 mL
1	egg	1
1 tsp	vanilla	5 mL

Topping

3 cups	thinly sliced peeled apples	750 mL
⅓ cup	granulated sugar	75 mL
1 tsp	cinnamon	5 mL
⅓ cup	sliced almonds	75 mL

1. **Crust:** Cream together butter and sugar. Blend in flour. Working with hands, mix well to form smooth dough. Press evenly onto bottom and 1½ inches (3.5 cm) up sides of prepared pan. Spread jam evenly over crust.

2. **Filling:** Beat together cream cheese, sugar, egg and vanilla with electric mixer until smooth. Spread carefully over jam.

3. **Topping:** Toss together apples, sugar and cinnamon to coat apples well. Spoon over filling. Sprinkle with almonds. Bake at 450°F (230°C) for 10 minutes, then reduce heat to 400°F (200°C) and bake for 25 to 30 minutes longer or until apples are tender-crisp. Serve warm or cool.

Variation
Any flavor of jam works well.

Mixed Berry Cheese Torte

A not-too-sweet dessert that tastes as great as it looks.

Makes about 12 servings

Preparation: 25 minutes
Baking: 55 minutes
Freezing: excellent

TIP

For an attractive presentation, sift confectioner's (icing) sugar on top just before serving.

● Preheat oven to 350°F (180°C)
● 10-inch (25 cm) springform pan, greased

Crust

1¾ cups	Robin Hood All-Purpose Flour	425 mL
½ cup	granulated sugar	125 mL
½ tsp	baking powder	2 mL
½ tsp	baking soda	2 mL
¼ tsp	salt	1 mL
¾ cup	butter, softened	175 mL
2	eggs	2
1 tsp	vanilla	5 mL

Filling

1	package (8 oz/250 g) cream cheese, softened	1
1	egg	1
¼ cup	granulated sugar	50 mL
1	can (19 oz/540 mL) mixed berry pie filling, divided	1

1. **Crust:** Combine flour, sugar, baking powder, baking soda, salt, butter, eggs and vanilla in large bowl of electric mixer. Beat at medium speed for about 2 minutes or until smooth. Spread over bottom and 2 inches (5 cm) up side of prepared pan.

2. **Filling:** Beat together cream cheese, egg and sugar in small bowl at medium speed until smooth and creamy. Reserve ¾ cup (175 mL) of the pie filling for top. Spread remainder over prepared crust. Pour cheese mixture evenly on top. Spoon reserved pie filling evenly over cheese mixture. Bake for 45 to 55 minutes or until set and light golden brown. Serve slightly warm or cool.

Raspberry Clafouti

Clafouti is usually made with tart cherries, but this raspberry version seems even more delicious than the traditional one. Clafouti is also one of the quickest desserts in this book, so if you're short on time, try this.

Makes about 8 servings

Preparation: 15 minutes
Baking: 35 minutes
Freezing:
not recommended

TIPS

Garnish with a dollop of whipped cream for a special treat and enjoy plain for a lighter, everyday dessert.

Use a glass or ceramic pie plate for the best appearance. They are also easy to clean.

Check your pan size. You need a regular 10-inch (25 cm) pie plate or a 9-inch (23 cm) deep-dish pie plate.

- Preheat oven to 375°F (190°C)
- 10-inch (25 cm) pie plate, greased

Fruit

3 cups	fresh raspberries	750 mL
2 tbsp	granulated sugar	30 mL

Batter

3	eggs	3
¾ cup	milk	175 mL
2 tbsp	butter, melted	30 mL
¾ cup	Robin Hood All-Purpose Flour	175 mL
¼ cup	granulated sugar	50 mL
½ tsp	baking powder	2 mL
¼ tsp	salt	1 mL

Topping

¼ cup	granulated sugar	50 mL

1. **Fruit:** Scatter raspberries over bottom of prepared pie plate. Sprinkle 2 tbsp (30 mL) sugar over top.
2. **Batter:** Whisk eggs, milk and melted butter in a medium bowl. Combine flour, sugar, baking powder and salt. Gradually add to egg mixture, whisking constantly until smooth. Pour evenly over berries.
3. Bake for 35 to 40 minutes or until set, puffed and golden. Let cool for 10 minutes in pan on rack.
4. **Topping:** Sprinkle with ¼ cup (50 mL) sugar. Cut into wedges and serve warm.

Variation
Replace raspberries with blackberries or pitted tart cherries.

Bumbleberry Cream-Filled Crêpes

Here's a smashing dessert crêpe that is delicious made with any seasonal berries.

**Makes about
8 servings**

Preparation: 20 minutes

Freezing: excellent
(crêpes only, not filled)

TIPS

Six-inch (15 cm) crêpes are a perfect size to handle and to serve. You can make larger 8-inch (20 cm) crêpes if you have the proper pan. Larger ones work well on a buffet table as a single serving, supplemented with other desserts. If you're serving smaller crêpes, two usually constitute a serving.

Reserve the most attractive fruit for garnish. A mint leaf adds a nice finishing touch.

If you use strawberries in the filling, garnish each serving with a whole berry dipped in chocolate and a drizzle of chocolate sauce.

For convenience, make a sugar shaker for dusting baked goods. Fill a large salt shaker with confectioner's (icing) sugar and a few grains of rice to keep the sugar dry.

Crêpes

1	batch Basic Crêpe Batter (see recipe, page 352)	1

Filling

²⁄₃ cup	raspberries	150 mL
²⁄₃ cup	blueberries	150 mL
²⁄₃ cup	sliced strawberries	150 mL
1 cup	whipping (35%) cream	250 mL
2 tbsp	confectioner's (icing) sugar, sifted	30 mL
1 tsp	vanilla	5 mL
½ cup	strawberry jam	125 mL
	Icing sugar	
	Fresh berries	

1. **Crêpes:** Prepare crêpes; set aside.
2. **Filling:** Combine raspberries, blueberries and strawberries. Whip cream, icing sugar and vanilla in a bowl until stiff peaks form. Fold in berry mixture. Spread each crêpe with a thin layer of jam. Spoon filling down the center of each; roll up. Place two crêpes, seam-side down, on a dessert plate. Sprinkle with icing sugar and garnish with fresh berries. Serve immediately.

Variation

Use whatever berries you prefer. You can't go wrong with this recipe.

Raspberry Almond Cream Crêpes

Having a stack of crêpes in your freezer makes entertaining easy.

Makes about 8 servings

Preparation: 40 minutes

Refrigeration: 1 hour

Cooking: 30 minutes

Sauce: 10 minutes

TIP

To store crêpes, cool completely and stack between waxed paper; enclose in an airtight plastic bag and freeze.

- 6-inch (15 cm) crêpe or frying pan

Crêpe Batter

1	batch Basic Crêpe Batter (see recipe, page 352)	1

Crêpe Filling

1	package (8 oz/250 g) cream cheese, softened	1
¼ cup	confectioner's (icing) sugar, sifted	50 mL
½ tsp	almond extract	2 mL
½ cup	ground almonds	125 mL
1 cup	whipping (35%) cream, whipped stiff	250 mL

Raspberry Sauce

1	package (15 oz/425 g) frozen whole raspberries in syrup, thawed	1
	Cranberry juice	
⅓ cup	granulated sugar	75 mL
3 tbsp	cornstarch	45 mL
1 tbsp	lemon juice	15 mL

1. **Crêpes:** Prepare crêpes; set aside.
2. Heat lightly greased 6-inch (15 cm) crêpe pan or frying pan. Remove from heat. Spoon in about 2 tbsp (30 mL) batter. Lift and tilt pan to cover bottom with batter. Return to heat. Brown lightly, then turn over and brown other side. Repeat with remaining batter. Cover cooked crêpes and keep warm if using immediately or cool completely, then stack between waxed paper and refrigerate or freeze in an airtight container.
3. **Filling:** Beat together cream cheese, confectioner's (icing) sugar and almond extract. Fold in almonds and whipped cream.
4. **Raspberry Sauce:** Drain raspberries, reserving juice. Add cranberry juice to raspberry juice to make 2 cups (500 mL). Combine sugar, cornstarch and juice in saucepan. Cook over medium heat, stirring constantly, until mixture comes to a boil. Stir in lemon juice and raspberries. Keep warm or cool to room temperature.
5. **Assembly:** Fill crêpes. Roll up. Top with warm or cooled sauce.

Variation

Try strawberries instead of raspberries.

Raspberry Hazelnut Cream Crêpes

With a stack of prepared crêpes in the freezer, this dessert is a snap.

Makes about 8 servings

Preparation: 15 minutes

Cooking: 10 minutes

Freezing: excellent (crêpes only, not filled)

TIPS

To store cooked crêpes, cool them completely, then stack each one between squares of waxed paper. Store in an airtight plastic bag and freeze for up to 3 months. Defrost overnight in the refrigerator or for 2 hours at room temperature.

Prepare filling and sauce the day before, then assemble the crêpes when you are ready to serve.

Light cream cheese works very well in this filling.

Freshly ground nuts have the best flavor. Use a food processor or a nut grinder to make the job easy. Toast nuts lightly to bring out their flavor.

Serve the sauce warm or cool.

Crêpes

1	batch Basic Crêpe Batter (see recipe, page 352)	1

Filling

1	package (8 oz/250 g) cream cheese, softened	1
1/4 cup	confectioner's (icing) sugar, sifted	50 mL
1 tsp	vanilla	5 mL
1 cup	whipping (35%) cream, whipped until stiff peaks form	250 mL
1/2 cup	ground hazelnuts	125 mL

Raspberry Sauce

1	package (15 oz/425 g) frozen whole raspberries in syrup, thawed Cranberry juice	1
1/3 cup	granulated sugar	75 mL
3 tbsp	cornstarch	45 mL
1 tbsp	lemon juice	15 mL

1. **Crêpes:** Prepare crêpes; set aside.
2. **Filling:** Beat together cream cheese, icing sugar and vanilla in a bowl until smooth. Fold in whipped cream and hazelnuts.
3. **Raspberry Sauce:** Drain raspberries, reserving juice. Add cranberry juice to raspberry juice to make 2 cups (500 mL). Combine sugar, cornstarch and juice mixture in saucepan. Cook over medium heat, stirring constantly, until mixture comes to a boil. Stir in lemon juice and raspberries. Keep warm or cool to room temperature.
4. **Assembly:** Fill crêpes with filling. Roll up. Top with warm or cool sauce.

Variations

Replace raspberries with sliced strawberries.

Replace ground hazelnuts with ground pecans or almonds.

Triple-Berry Shortcake

Quicker and easier to prepare than the biscuit-type cake, this version of the classic dessert is often preferred because it's light and tender.

Makes about 6 servings

Preparation: 20 minutes

Baking: 23 minutes

Freezing: excellent (cake only)

TIPS

Prepare the cake a day ahead or keep one on hand in the freezer. Thaw before assembling.

Fresh fruit in season is sensational, but frozen berries, including those packed in syrup, are also delicious in this cake.

Coarse granulated sugar, which is often available in bulk stores, adds a special touch to the top of shortcake.

- Preheat oven to 400°F (200°C)
- 8-inch (2 L) square cake pan, greased

Shortcake

2 cups	Robin Hood All-Purpose Flour	500 mL
1/2 cup	granulated sugar	125 mL
1 tbsp	baking powder	15 mL
1/2 tsp	baking soda	2 mL
1/2 tsp	salt	2 mL
1/2 cup	butter	125 mL
1 cup	buttermilk	250 mL

Filling

Triple-berry mixture (any combination of strawberries, raspberries, blackberries and/or blueberries)
Whipped cream

1. **Shortcake:** Combine flour, sugar, baking powder, baking soda and salt in a mixing bowl. Using a pastry blender, two knives or your fingers, cut in butter until mixture resembles coarse crumbs. Add buttermilk to flour mixture, stirring just until moistened. Spread dough in prepared pan.

2. Bake for 17 to 23 minutes or until light golden. Cool in pan on rack.

3. **Filling:** To serve, cut cake into 6 rectangles; cut each in half horizontally. Spoon berries over bottom half; add a spoonful of whipped cream. Repeat layering, ending with a generous dollop of whipped cream.

Variations

Although this cake is made with a mixture of berries, strawberries, raspberries, blueberries or blackberries on their own look and taste great. For a change, try using sliced peaches.

Replace whipped cream with slightly softened vanilla ice cream.

Cranberry Strawberry Rhubarb Dessert

Delicious warm with ice cream or whipped cream.

Makes about 12 servings

Preparation: 25 minutes

Baking: 1 hour

Freezing: not recommended

TIP

If fresh rhubarb is not available, use frozen. Thaw and pat dry first.

- Preheat oven to 350°F (180°C)
- 13- by 9-inch (3.5 L) cake pan, greased

Cake

1½ cups	Robin Hood All-Purpose Flour	375 mL
½ cup	Robin Hood Oats	125 mL
¼ cup	packed brown sugar	50 mL
2½ tsp	baking powder	12 mL
¼ tsp	salt	1 mL
¼ cup	butter or margarine	50 mL
1	egg, beaten	1
¾ cup	milk	175 mL
6 cups	thinly sliced rhubarb	1.5 L
6 oz	sweetened dried cranberries (1 cup/250 mL)	170 g
1	package (3 oz/85 g) strawberry-flavored gelatin dessert mix	1

Topping

6 tbsp	butter or margarine	90 mL
1½ cups	granulated sugar	375 mL
⅔ cup	Robin Hood Oats	150 mL
¼ cup	Robin Hood All-Purpose Flour	50 mL
1 tsp	cinnamon	5 mL

1. **Cake:** Combine flour, oats, brown sugar, baking powder and salt in mixing bowl. Cut in butter until crumbly. Add egg and milk, stirring until moistened. Spread evenly in prepared pan. Combine rhubarb and cranberries. Sprinkle evenly over cake. Sprinkle powdered gelatin over fruit.

2. **Topping:** Combine butter, sugar, oats, flour and cinnamon. Sprinkle over fruit. Bake for 60 minutes or until fruit is tender.

Chocolate Lime Mousse Dessert

A rich chocolate base offset with a light, tart lime mousse.

TIP

Warm limes slightly in microwave to get maximum amount of juice.

- Preheat oven to 350°F (180°C)
- 10-inch (25 cm) springform pan, greased

Chocolate Base

½ cup	butter or margarine	125 mL
3	squares (each 1 oz/28 g) unsweetened chocolate	3
1 ¼ cups	granulated sugar	300 mL
3	eggs	3
⅔ cup	Robin Hood All-Purpose Flour	150 mL
¼ tsp	baking powder	1 mL

Topping

1	envelope (1 tbsp/15 mL) unflavored gelatin	1
1 cup	granulated sugar, divided	250 mL
4	egg yolks	4
½ cup	lime juice	125 mL
2 tsp	grated lime zest	10 mL
4	egg whites	4
½ cup	whipping (35%) cream, whipped stiff	125 mL
	Lime slices	

1. **Chocolate Base:** Melt butter and chocolate in saucepan over low heat, stirring until smooth. Remove from heat. Add sugar, eggs, flour and baking powder, stirring until smooth. Spread in prepared pan. Bake for 20 to 25 minutes or just until set. Cool in pan.

2. **Topping:** Combine gelatin, ½ cup (125 mL) sugar, egg yolks and lime juice in small saucepan. Cook, stirring constantly, over medium heat for about 5 minutes or until slightly thickened (it thickens more on cooling). Stir in zest. Refrigerate until mixture starts to set. Beat egg whites and remaining ½ cup (125 mL) sugar to stiff peaks. Fold egg whites and whipped cream into lime mixture gently but thoroughly. Spread over chocolate base. Refrigerate for about 3 hours or until set, or overnight. Decorate with lime slices.

Variation

Replace lime juice and zest with lemon.

Chocolate Strawberry Mousse Delight

Prepare a day ahead for easy entertaining.

TIP

Desserts containing gelatin and whipped cream don't freeze well.

● *Preheat oven to 350°F (180°C)*
● *9-inch (23 cm) springform pan, greased*

Chocolate Base

½ cup	shortening	125 mL
3	squares (each 1 oz/28 g) unsweetened chocolate	3
1¼ cups	granulated sugar	300 mL
1 tsp	vanilla	5 mL
3	eggs	3
⅔ cup	Robin Hood All-Purpose Flour	150 mL
½ tsp	baking powder	2 mL

Topping

1	package (15 oz/425 g) frozen sliced strawberries in syrup, thawed	1
1	envelope (1 tbsp/15 mL) unflavored gelatin	1
½ cup	granulated sugar	125 mL
2 tbsp	lemon juice	30 mL
2 cups	whipping (35%) cream, divided	500 mL
	Fresh strawberries	

1. **Chocolate Base:** Melt shortening and chocolate in saucepan over low heat, stirring until smooth. Remove from heat. Add sugar, vanilla and eggs. Mix well. Combine flour and baking powder. Add to chocolate mixture, stirring until well blended. Spread in prepared pan. Bake for 22 to 27 minutes or just until set. Cool in pan.

2. **Topping:** Drain strawberries, reserving liquid. Add enough water to liquid to make 1¼ cups (300 mL). Combine gelatin and sugar in saucepan over medium heat. Stir in strawberry liquid and lemon juice. Bring mixture to a boil, stirring constantly to dissolve sugar and gelatin. Remove from heat. Chill until starting to set, about 1½ hours. Beat 1¼ cups (300 mL) of the whipping cream to stiff peaks. Beat gelatin mixture in small bowl on high speed of electric mixer until light. Fold in whipped cream. Fold in drained strawberries. Spread evenly over base in pan. Refrigerate for 3 hours or until set, or overnight. To serve, beat remaining whipping cream to stiff peaks. Decorate mousse attractively with whipped cream and fresh berries.

Variation

Replace strawberries with raspberries.

Peach Pastry Squares

These delicious squares taste like a fresh peach tart. They are very easy to make and ideal for feeding a crowd, making them a great potluck dessert.

Makes about 16 servings

Preparation: 20 minutes

Baking: 40 minutes

Freezing: not recommended

TIPS

To peel peaches, dip them in boiling water for 30 seconds. Immediately plunge into a bowl of ice water for a few seconds. The skin should peel off easily.

A jelly roll pan is like a cookie sheet with ½-inch (1 cm) sides. Be sure you have the right size; this is the smaller version.

Don't peel and slice the peaches until you are ready to bake. Exposure to air turns them brown. Toss with a little lemon juice to prevent browning.

You can use a food processor fitted with a metal blade to make the crust. Pulse the dry ingredients, then add cold butter and pulse until the mixture resembles coarse crumbs. Add the egg and pulse until blended.

- Preheat oven to 400°F (200°C)
- 15- by 10 (2 L) jelly roll pan, greased

Crust

2½ cups	Robin Hood All-Purpose Flour	625 mL
⅔ cup	granulated sugar	150 mL
½ tsp	salt	2 mL
1 cup	butter	250 mL
1	egg, beaten	1

Topping

⅓ cup	granulated sugar	75 mL
1 tsp	ground cinnamon	5 mL
6 cups	sliced peeled pitted peaches (about 8)	1.5 L
1	egg, beaten	1
1 cup	sour cream	250 mL
1 tbsp	granulated sugar	15 mL

1. **Crust:** Combine flour, sugar and salt in a large bowl. Using two knives, a pastry blender or your fingers, cut in butter until mixture resembles coarse crumbs. Add egg and mix lightly to blend. Press firmly into prepared pan to form a thin, even layer.
2. Bake on bottom oven rack for 10 to 15 minutes or until golden.
3. **Topping:** Combine sugar and cinnamon in a bowl. Add peaches and toss well. Arrange evenly over crust.
4. Bake for 15 minutes longer. Reduce temperature to 350°F (180°C).
5. Combine egg, sour cream and sugar. Drizzle over peaches. Bake for 10 minutes longer or just until fruit is tender and topping is set. Serve warm or cool.

Variation
Replace peach slices with sliced nectarines, plums or apples. A mixture of any two of these fruits is also tasty.

Lemon Sponge Pudding

With a soufflé-like crust resting on a creamy yet tangy lemon sauce, this delicious dessert is the ultimate comfort food.

Makes about 6 servings

Preparation: 20 minutes

Baking: 45 minutes

Freezing: not recommended

TIPS

When serving, be sure to dip the spoon all the way down to the bottom of the dish so that each helping is a blend of the crusty top and saucy bottom.

Garnish each plate with fresh berries for an attractive finish.

This very light dessert is a great choice when you want a little something to end a hearty meal.

Plan to serve this the same day it is prepared. In fact, for optimum taste and texture, it is best served warm from the oven.

- *Preheat oven to 350°F (180°C)*
- *8-cup (2 L) baking dish, greased*
- *Larger pan to hold baking dish*

1 cup	granulated sugar	250 mL
1/3 cup	Robin Hood All-Purpose Flour	75 mL
1 1/2 tbsp	grated lemon zest	22 mL
1/4 tsp	salt	1 mL
1 1/2 cups	half-and-half (10%) cream	375 mL
1/3 cup	lemon juice	75 mL
3	egg yolks, beaten	3
3	egg whites	3

1. Combine sugar, flour, lemon zest and salt in a large bowl. Add cream, lemon juice and egg yolks, whisking until smooth.

2. Beat egg whites in a bowl until stiff peaks form. Gently fold into batter. Carefully pour into prepared baking dish. Set dish in a large pan filled with hot water to 1-inch (2.5 cm) depth.

3. Bake for 40 to 45 minutes or until top is set and golden. Serve warm.

Variation

Replace lemon juice and zest with orange or lime. A combination of lemon and lime is also good.

Mix 'n' Match Ice Cream Dessert

The variety is endless. Use your favorite ice cream and sundae sauce for an effortless dessert.

Makes about 15 servings

Preparation: 15 minutes

Baking time: 25 minutes

Freezing: necessary

TIP

Thaw 10 minutes before serving to soften slightly for easy cutting.

- Preheat oven to 400°F (200°C)
- 13- by 9-inch (3.5 L) cake pan, greased

1 1/2 cups	Robin Hood All-Purpose Flour	375 mL
1 cup	Robin Hood Oats	250 mL
1 cup	chopped pecans	250 mL
1/2 cup	packed brown sugar	125 mL
1 cup	butter or margarine, melted	250 mL
1 cup	butterscotch or chocolate chips	250 mL
1 1/2 cups	butterscotch or chocolate sundae sauce	375 mL
8 cups	ice cream, softened	2 L

1. Combine flour, oats, pecans and brown sugar in large bowl. Stir in melted butter. Mix well. Spread evenly on large baking sheet with sides. Bake, stirring occasionally, for 20 to 25 minutes or until golden. Crumble while warm; cool completely.

2. Press half of the oat mixture into prepared pan. Stir chips into remaining oat mixture. Drizzle half of the sauce over crumbs in pan. Spread with softened ice cream. Drizzle remaining sauce over ice cream. Cover with butterscotch chip crumb mixture. Cover and freeze. Cut into pieces as needed.

Variation
Try vanilla, butterscotch ripple, cherry, strawberry or chocolate ice cream. Almost any flavor is great.

Deep-Fried Apple Rings

Serve warm with ice cream and maple syrup for a yummy dessert.

Makes about 3 dozen rings

Preparation: 20 minutes

Refrigeration: 1 hour

Frying: 4 minutes per batch

TIP

Brush peeled apples with lemon juice to prevent browning.

- Preheat oil to 375°F (190°C)
- Deep-fryer

1 cup	Robin Hood All-Purpose Flour	250 mL
2 tbsp	cornstarch	30 mL
1 tbsp	granulated sugar	15 mL
½ tsp	baking powder	2 mL
½ tsp	salt	2 mL
1	egg	1
1 cup	milk	250 mL
½ cup	granulated sugar	125 mL
½ tsp	cinnamon	2 mL
5	medium apples	5
	Oil or shortening for deep-frying	

1. Combine flour, cornstarch, 1 tbsp (15 mL) sugar, baking powder and salt in mixing bowl. Set aside.

2. Beat together egg and milk. Add to dry ingredients and whisk until well blended. Refrigerate for 1 hour.

3. Mix together ½ cup (125 mL) sugar and cinnamon. Set aside. Peel and core apples. Cut crosswise into ¼-inch (0.5 cm) thick rings.

4. Heat 2 to 3 inches (5 to 7.5 cm) oil in deep-fryer. Dip apple slices in batter, allowing excess to drip back into bowl. Fry two to three at a time in hot oil, turning frequently, for 3 to 4 minutes or until golden brown. Drain on paper towels. Roll in cinnamon-sugar mixture. Serve warm.

Orange Cranberry Spiral

Breads

Orange Cranberry Spiral

This loaf looks amazingly complicated but is actually very easy and fun to shape. Quick-rise yeast makes it faster to prepare than traditional breads.

Makes 2 loaves (about 12 slices per loaf)

Preparation: 65 minutes

Rising: 65 minutes

Baking: 35 minutes

Freezing: excellent

TIPS

A glaze of egg and milk before baking gives this loaf a beautiful, shiny golden surface.

Quick-rise yeast is finely granulated yeast that is mixed directly with the other dry ingredients. It produces a quick first rise.

As a twist, add a drizzle of orange icing on top.

After brushing the strips with butter, sprinkle lightly with cinnamon-sugar. It looks and tastes great!

Replace dried cranberries with raisins.

- *Preheat oven to 350°F (180°C) during second rising*
- *Two 9-inch (23 cm) springform pans, greased*

Dough

5 to 6 cups	Robin Hood Best for Bread Homestyle White or All-Purpose Flour	1.25 to 1.5 L
⅓ cup	granulated sugar	75 mL
4½ tsp	quick-rise instant yeast (2 envelopes, each ¼ oz/8 g)	22 mL
1 tsp	salt	5 mL
¾ tsp	ground nutmeg	3 mL
1¾ cups	milk	425 mL
1½ cups	dried cranberries	375 mL
¾ cup	butter	175 mL
1 tbsp	grated orange zest	15 mL
1	egg, beaten	1

Filling and Glaze

2 tbsp	butter, melted	30 mL
1	egg	1
1 tbsp	milk	15 mL

1. **Dough:** Combine 2 cups (500 mL) of the flour, sugar, yeast, salt and nutmeg in a large mixer bowl.

2. Heat milk, cranberries, butter and orange zest in a saucepan over medium heat until hot (125°F/50°C) and butter is melted. Add to flour mixture along with egg. Beat on low speed of electric mixer for 1 minute, then on high speed for 3 minutes. Stir in enough of the remaining flour to make a soft dough. Turn out onto a floured surface. Knead for about 10 minutes, adding enough flour to make dough smooth and elastic. Divide dough in half. Shape each into a ball. Cover and let rest for 20 minutes.

3. **Filling and Glaze:** To shape bread, roll one ball of dough into a 16- by 12-inch (40 x 30 cm) rectangle. Cut lengthwise into six 2-inch (5 cm) wide strips. Brush with 1 tbsp (15 mL) of the melted butter. Roll up one strip loosely and place, cut side up in center of prepared pan. Coil remaining strips loosely around the center roll, covering the bottom of pan. Repeat with remaining dough and melted butter to make a second loaf.

4. Cover with a tea towel and let rise in a warm place (75 to 85°F/ 24 to 29°C) until doubled in bulk, about 45 minutes. Beat egg and milk together in a small bowl. Brush over loaves.

5. Bake on center rack of oven for 30 to 35 minutes or until golden. Cover with foil for last 10 minutes if the top is becoming too brown. Cool in pans for 20 minutes, then turn out onto rack and cool completely.

Cheery Cherry Bread

This ruby-studded loaf is festive enough for the holiday season but delicious all year round. You have to try this to believe how great it is.

Makes 1 loaf (about 12 slices)

Preparation: 30 minutes

Rising: 4 hours

Baking: 55 minutes

Freezing: excellent

TIPS

Use candied cherries, not maraschino, which are quite different in flavor.

The cherries will leak moisture when you're kneading the dough, so don't be alarmed if you need to add more flour during this step.

For a browner crust, brush the top with melted butter just before baking.

For a soft crust, brush the top of the loaf with melted butter as soon as it comes out of the oven.

- Preheat oven to 350°F (180°C) during second rising
- 9- by 5-inch (2 L) loaf pan, greased

1 tsp	granulated sugar	5 mL
1 cup	warm water (105°F to 115°F/40°C to 46°C)	250 mL
2¼ tsp	active dry yeast (1 envelope, ¼ oz/8 g)	11 mL
3 to 3½ cups	Robin Hood Best for Bread Homestyle White or All-Purpose Flour	750 to 875 mL
1 tbsp	butter, softened	15 mL
⅓ cup	granulated sugar	75 mL
1 tsp	salt	5 mL
½ tsp	ground cinnamon	2 mL
¼ tsp	ground nutmeg	1 mL
1 cup	whole candied cherries	250 mL

1. Dissolve 1 tsp (5 mL) sugar in warm water in a large bowl. Sprinkle with yeast; let stand for 10 minutes. Stir well. Add 1 cup (250 mL) of the flour, ⅓ cup (75 mL) sugar, butter, salt, cinnamon and nutmeg to dissolved yeast mixture. Beat with a wooden spoon or on medium speed of an electric mixer until smooth and elastic. Stir in cherries.

2. Gradually stir in 2 cups (500 mL) of the remaining flour. If necessary, add more flour to make a soft dough that leaves sides of the bowl and forms a ball. Turn out onto a lightly floured surface. Form into a ball. Knead, adding enough of the remaining flour to make the dough smooth, elastic and no longer sticky, about 10 minutes. Place in a lightly greased bowl and turn to grease top. Cover with plastic wrap. Let rise in a warm place (75 to 85°F/24 to 29°C) until doubled, 1½ to 2 hours.

3. Punch down dough. Turn out onto a lightly floured surface. Cover and let rest for 10 minutes.

4. **Shaping:** Shape dough into a loaf. Place in prepared loaf pan. Cover with a tea towel and let rise in a warm place until dough doubles in bulk, 1½ to 2 hours.

5. Bake on bottom rack of oven for 45 to 55 minutes or until top is golden and loaf sounds hollow when tapped on the bottom. Remove from pan immediately and cool on rack.

Variation
Use red or green cherries or a combination of both.

Double Cheese Bread

Double the cheese means double the flavor.

TIPS

Use freshly grated Parmesan cheese for the best flavor.

When you add cubes of cheese to a yeast dough, the bread will have holes where the cheese melts. If you use shredded cheese, you won't have this effect. The choice is yours.

Make individual mini loaves by dividing dough into six portions and place in six 5³/₄- by 3¹/₄-inch (500 mL) pans. Reduce rising and baking times by 10 minutes each.

Recipes for breads usually give a range for the amount of flour. Start with the least and add only as much as is necessary to make a smooth dough.

On hot, humid days bread dough will take more flour than on cool, dry days.

- *Preheat oven to 375°F (190°C) during second rising*
- *Two 8¹/₂- by 4¹/₂-inch (1.5 L) loaf pans, greased*

1 tsp	granulated sugar	5 mL
1¹/₂ cups	warm water (105°F to 115°F/40°C to 46°C)	375 mL
2¹/₄ tsp	active dry yeast(1 envelope, ¹/₄ oz/8 g)	11 mL
¹/₃ cup	vegetable oil	75 mL
1 tsp	salt	5 mL
1 tsp	hot sauce, or to taste	5 mL
1	egg, beaten	1
2¹/₂ cups	shredded old Cheddar cheese	625 mL
¹/₂ cup	grated Parmesan cheese	125 mL
4¹/₄ to 4³/₄ cups	Robin Hood Best for Bread Homestyle White or All-Purpose Flour	1.05 to 1.175 L

1. Dissolve sugar in warm water in a large bowl. Sprinkle with yeast; let stand for 10 minutes. Stir well. Beat in oil, salt, hot sauce and egg. Stir in 1 cup (250 mL) of the Cheddar cheese and Parmesan cheese. Beat well.

2. Stir in 2 cups (500 mL) of the flour. Add more flour until mixture becomes too stiff to stir. Turn out onto a lightly floured surface. Knead for 8 to 10 minutes, adding enough of the remaining flour to make the dough smooth and elastic. Place in greased bowl and turn to grease top. Cover with plastic wrap. Let rise in warm place (75 to 85°F/24 to 29°C) until doubled in bulk, about 1 hour.

3. Punch down dough. Turn out onto a lightly floured surface. Knead in remaining Cheddar cheese until well distributed. Divide into six equal portions. Shape each portion into a ball. Place three balls side by side in the bottom of each greased pan. Cover with a tea towel. Let rise in a warm place until doubled in bulk, 50 to 60 minutes.

4. Bake on bottom rack of oven for 30 to 35 minutes or until golden and loaves sound hollow when tapped on the bottom. Remove from pans immediately and cool on rack.

Variations

For a "chunky cheese" look, shred 1¹/₂ cups (375 mL) of the Cheddar cheese and cut the rest into cubes to make 1 cup (250 mL). Add the cubed cheese and the remaining ¹/₂ cup (125 mL) of the shredded cheese to the dough in Step 3.

Add diced cooked bacon and/or chives to the dough along with the second portion of cheese.

Cheese 'n' Tomato Grain-Filled Bread

A versatile dough that's delicious any way you shape it.

Makes 1 loaf or 16 rolls

Preparation: 20 minutes

Rising: 1 hour for loaf, 40 minutes for rolls

Baking: 25 minutes for loaf, 23 minutes for rolls

Freezing: excellent

TIP

Sun-dried tomatoes are available packed in oil at deli counters or in bottles.

- *Preheat oven to 375°F (190°C)*
- *8¹/₂- by 4¹/₂-inch (1.5 L) loaf pan or 9-inch (2.5 L) square cake pan, greased*
- *Bread machine*

1	egg, beaten	1
1 cup	water	250 mL
2 tbsp	butter or margarine	30 mL
2 tbsp	liquid honey	30 mL
1¹/₂ cups	Robin Hood Best For Bread Homestyle White Flour	375 mL
1 cup	Robin Hood Best For Bread Whole Wheat Flour	250 mL
¹/₂ cup	Robin Hood Oats	125 mL
¹/₂ cup	Red River Cereal	125 mL
1 tsp	salt	5 mL
1¹/₄ tsp	bread machine yeast	6 mL
²/₃ cup	chopped sun-dried tomatoes	150 mL
¹/₄ cup	grated Parmesan cheese	50 mL

1. Add ingredients to bread machine according to manufacturer's directions. Add tomatoes and cheese at "add ingredients" signal or with other dry ingredients. Select Whole Wheat cycle for bread machine loaf; or select Dough cycle to shape and bake in conventional oven.

2. **Loaf:** Shape dough into three or four balls. Place in prepared loaf pan and cover with tea towel. Let rise in warm place (75° to 85°F/24° to 29°C) for about 1 hour. Bake for 25 minutes. Cover with foil if becoming too brown.

3. **Rolls:** Shape dough into 16 balls. Place in prepared square pan. Cover with tea towel and let rise for 30 to 40 minutes. Bake for 18 to 23 minutes.

Multigrain Seed Bread

Moist, dense and hearty, this loaf is a healthy choice for sandwiches and toast.

Makes 2 loaves (about 12 slices per loaf)

Preparation: 30 minutes
Rising: 2¹⁄₂ hours
Baking: 30 minutes
Freezing: excellent

TIPS

If you like the top crusty, spritz it lightly with water three times during baking.

Enhance the appearance of any grainy loaf by brushing the top with milk and sprinkling with oats just before baking.

- Preheat oven to 375°F (190°C) during second rising
- Two 8¹⁄₂- by 4¹⁄₂-inch (1.5 L) or 9- by 5-inch (2 L) loaf pans, greased

1 tsp	granulated sugar	5 mL
2 cups	warm water (105°F to 115°F/40°C to 46°C)	500 mL
2¹⁄₄ tsp	active dry yeast (1 envelope, ¹⁄₄ oz/8 g)	11 mL
¹⁄₄ cup	fancy molasses	50 mL
2 tbsp	vegetable oil	30 mL
1 cup	Robin Hood Best for Bread or regular Whole Wheat Flour	250 mL
²⁄₃ cup	Robin Hood Oats	150 mL
²⁄₃ cup	sunflower seeds, toasted	150 mL
¹⁄₃ cup	flaxseeds	75 mL
¹⁄₃ cup	Red River Cereal	75 mL
1¹⁄₂ tsp	salt	7 mL
3 to 3¹⁄₂ cups	Robin Hood Best for Bread Homestyle White or All-Purpose Flour	750 to 875 mL

1. Dissolve sugar in warm water in a large bowl. Sprinkle with yeast; let stand for 10 minutes. Stir in molasses and oil.

2. Combine 1 cup (250 mL) flour, oats, sunflower seeds, flaxseeds, cereal and salt. Stir into yeast mixture. Stir in enough of the 3 to 3¹⁄₂ cups (750 mL to 875 mL) white flour to form a slightly sticky dough. Turn out onto a lightly floured surface. Knead for 8 to 10 minutes, adding enough of the remaining flour to make dough smooth and elastic. Place in a greased bowl and turn to grease the top. Cover with plastic wrap. Let rise in a warm place (75 to 85°F/24 to 29°C) until doubled in bulk, 1 to 1¹⁄₂ hours.

3. Punch down dough. Divide in half. Shape each half into a loaf. Place in prepared pans. Cover with a tea towel and let rise in a warm place until doubled in bulk, about 1 hour.

4. Bake on bottom rack of oven for 25 to 30 minutes or until top is golden and loaf sounds hollow when tapped on the bottom. Remove from pans and cool on rack.

Variation

Dinner rolls: After the first rising, shape dough into 15 balls and place on a greased baking sheet, about 2 inches (5 cm) apart. Cover and let rise until doubled in size, about 1 hour. Bake in 375°F (190°C) oven until golden, about 20 minutes.

Batter Rolls

Not only tender, light and delicious but easy to make, too!

TIP

Dough is very elastic and sticky. Use floured fingers to shape dough.

- *Preheat oven to 375°F (190°C)*
- *Two 12-cup muffin pans, greased*

1 tsp	granulated sugar	5 mL
½ cup	warm water (105° to 115°F/40° to 46°C)	125 mL
2¼ tsp	active dry yeast (1 envelope ¼ oz/8 g)	11 mL
1½ cups	milk	375 mL
¼ cup	granulated sugar	50 mL
¼ cup	shortening	50 mL
2 tsp	salt	10 mL
2	eggs	2
4 cups	Robin Hood All-Purpose or Best For Bread Homestyle White Flour	1 L

1. Dissolve 1 tsp (5 mL) sugar in warm water in large bowl. Sprinkle in yeast. Let stand for 10 minutes, then stir well.

2. Combine milk, ¼ cup (50 mL) sugar, shortening and salt in saucepan. Heat until lukewarm and shortening is melted. Stir well. Add to yeast mixture along with eggs. Add 2¾ cups (675 mL) of the flour and beat vigorously with wooden spoon or electric mixer until smooth, about 3 minutes. Gradually stir in remaining 1½ cups (375 mL) flour. (Batter will be soft.) Cover with greased waxed paper and tea towel. Let rise in warm place (75° to 85°F/24° to 29°C) until doubled, about 1 hour.

3. Stir down dough and let stand for 10 minutes. Fill prepared muffin cups three-quarters full. Let rise until doubled, 25 to 40 minutes. Bake for 15 to 20 minutes or until golden. Turn out of pans immediately. Serve warm or cool.

Old-Fashioned Cloverleaf Potato Rolls

Moist and flavourful, this traditional favorite will never go out of style.

Makes 2 dozen rolls

Preparation: 30 minutes
Rising: 80 minutes
Baking: 12 minutes
Freezing: excellent

TIPS

In addition to a tender texture, mashed potatoes give yeast bread extra moistness and a subtle, rich, creamy flavor.

Grandmothers made extra mashed potatoes so they would have them on hand to make these rolls. If you prefer, you can make them using instant mashed potatoes for convenience.

Use a thermometer to check the temperature of the liquid. If it's too hot, the yeast will be killed. If it's too cool, the action of the yeast will slow down.

If you prefer a shiny top, brush the rolls lightly with butter or an egg wash just before baking.

Sprinkle sesame or poppy seeds over top, if desired.

- *Preheat oven to 400°F (200°C) during second rising*
- *Two 12-cup muffin pans, greased*

1¼ cups	milk	300 mL
½ cup	butter	125 mL
½ cup	mashed potatoes	125 mL
4¾ to 5 cups	Robin Hood Best for Bread Homestyle White or All-Purpose Flour	1.175 to 1.25 L
¼ cup	granulated sugar	50 mL
2¼ tsp	quick-rise instant yeast (1 envelope, ¼ oz/8 g)	11 mL
1½ tsp	salt	7 mL
1	egg, beaten	1
	Melted butter, optional	

1. Heat milk, butter and mashed potatoes in a saucepan over medium heat until mixture is hot (125°F/50°C) and butter is melted.

2. Combine 3 cups (750 mL) of the flour, sugar, yeast and salt in a large bowl. Stir in milk mixture and egg. Stir vigorously with a wooden spoon until blended. Gradually add enough of the remaining flour to make a soft dough. Turn out onto a floured surface and knead dough for about 10 minutes, adding enough flour to make the dough smooth and elastic. Cover and let rest for 20 minutes.

3. **Shaping:** Divide dough into eight portions. Cut each portion into nine pieces to make 72 pieces total. Shape each piece into a ball. Place 3 balls in the bottom of each prepared muffin cup. Repeat, using all the balls to fill the 24 cups. Cover with a tea towel and let stand in a warm place (75 to 85°F/24 to 29°C) until doubled in size, about 1 hour. Brush with melted butter, if using.

4. Bake on center rack of oven for 10 to 12 minutes or until golden. Remove from pans immediately. Cool for 10 minutes on rack.

Variation

Try other shapes, such as snails, spirals, crescents and small balls but remember to keep them all about the same size to ensure that the dough rises and bakes uniformly.

Hearty Oatmeal Raisin Bread

Wonderful fresh from the oven, but delicious toasted, too.

Makes 2 loaves

Preparation: 30 minutes
Rising: 2½ hours
Baking: 1 hour
Freezing: excellent

TIP

Plump raisins in boiling water if very hard. Pat dry before using.

- *Preheat oven to 375°F (190°C)*
- *Two 9- by 5-inch (2 L) loaf pans, greased*

2 cups	milk	500 mL
2 cups	Robin Hood Oats	500 mL
⅓ cup	molasses	75 mL
¼ cup	packed brown sugar	50 mL
¼ cup	shortening	50 mL
4 tsp	salt	20 mL
1 tsp	cinnamon	5 mL
¼ tsp	ground nutmeg	1 mL
2 tsp	granulated sugar	10 mL
1 cup	warm water (105° to 115°F/40° to 46°C)	250 mL
4½ tsp	active dry yeast (2 envelopes ¼ oz/8 g each)	22 mL
3 cups	Robin Hood Whole Wheat or Best For Bread Whole Wheat Flour	750 mL
3 to 3½ cups	Robin Hood All-Purpose or Best For Bread Homestyle White Flour	750 to 875 mL
1½ cups	raisins	375 mL

1. Heat milk to very hot but not boiling.
2. Combine oats, molasses, brown sugar, shortening, salt, cinnamon and nutmeg in large bowl. Pour hot milk over oat mixture. Cool to lukewarm.
3. Dissolve granulated sugar in warm water. Sprinkle in yeast. Let stand for 10 minutes, then stir well. Add yeast mixture to oats mixture. Add 2 cups (500 mL) of the whole wheat flour, beating vigorously until well mixed. Stir in remaining 1 cup (250 mL) whole wheat flour and enough of the white flour to form dough that comes away from sides of bowl.
4. Turn out dough onto lightly floured surface. Knead for 10 to 12 minutes, adding enough flour to make dough smooth and elastic. Flatten on floured board to height of about 1 inch (2.5 cm). Sprinkle raisins on top and knead into dough. Place in greased bowl. Cover with greased waxed paper and tea towel. Let rise in warm place (75° to 85°F/24° to 29°C) until doubled, 1 to 1½ hours.
5. Punch down dough. Turn out onto lightly floured board and cut into two equal portions. Shape each into loaf. Place in prepared loaf pans. Cover with tea towel and let rise until doubled, about 1 hour. Bake for 15 minutes, then reduce oven temperature to 350°F (180°C) and bake for 35 to 45 minutes. Cover tops of bread with foil during last 15 minutes if becoming too brown. Remove from pan and cool on rack.

Cheese Puffs

A fun-to-eat treat, these puffs are delicious served warm.

Makes about 40 rolls

Preparation: 25 minutes

Rising: 1 hour 10 minutes

Baking: 50 minutes

Freezing: excellent

TIP

Bread machine yeast works well, too.

- *Preheat oven to 375°F (190°C)*
- *10-inch (4 L) tube pan, greased*

6½ cups	Robin Hood All-Purpose or Best For Bread Homestyle White Flour	1.625 L
1½ cups	shredded sharp Cheddar cheese	375 mL
2½ tsp	salt	12 mL
2¼ tsp	quick-rise instant yeast (1 envelope ¼ oz/8 g)	11 mL
1 tsp	granulated sugar	5 mL
1½ cups	milk	375 mL
½ cup	water	125 mL
3 tbsp	butter or margarine	45 mL
	Melted butter	
1½ cups	grated Parmesan cheese	375 mL

1. Set aside 1 cup (250 mL) of the flour. Combine remaining flour, Cheddar cheese, salt, yeast and sugar in large mixing bowl.

2. Heat milk, water and 3 tbsp (50 mL) butter until hot to touch (125° to 130°F/50° to 55°C). Stir hot liquid into yeast mixture. Knead dough for about 10 minutes, adding reserved flour as necessary to make smooth, elastic and no longer sticky. Cover and let rest for 10 minutes.

3. Cut dough into 40 pieces. Shape into balls. Dip in melted butter, then roll in Parmesan cheese. Arrange in two layers in prepared pan. Cover with tea towel. Let rise in warm place (75° to 85°F/24° to 29°C) until balls come almost to top of pan, about 1 hour.

4. Bake for 40 to 50 minutes or until crisp. Cover with foil for last 10 minutes, if necessary, to prevent overbrowning of crust. Cool for 5 minutes, then remove from pan. Pull apart individual balls or slice.

Make-Ahead Sticky Buns

Prepare the day before and enjoy fresh from the oven the next morning.

Makes 15 buns

Preparation: 25 minutes

Rising: first 1¼ hours, second 1½ hours, or 12 to 48 hours

Baking time: 30 minutes

Freezing: excellent

TIP

Use dark brown sugar for a more caramel taste.

- Preheat oven to 350°F (180°C)
- 13- by 9-inch (3.5 L) cake pan, greased

Dough

3½ to 4 cups	Robin Hood Best For Bread Homestyle White Flour	875 mL to 1 L
⅓ cup	granulated sugar	75 mL
1 tsp	salt	5 mL
4½ tsp	quick-rise instant yeast (2 envelopes ¼ oz/8 g each)	22 mL
1 cup	warm milk (100° to 110°F/38° to 45°C)	250 mL
⅓ cup	butter or margarine	75 mL
1	egg	1

Topping

1 cup	packed brown sugar	250 mL
½ cup	butter or margarine	125 mL
¼ cup	corn syrup	50 mL
1 cup	pecan halves	250 mL

Filling

2 tbsp	butter or margarine, softened	30 mL
¾ cup	chopped pecans	175 mL
¼ cup	packed brown sugar	50 mL
1½ tsp	cinnamon	7 mL

1. **Dough:** Combine 2 cups (500 mL) of the flour, sugar, salt and yeast in large bowl. Add milk, butter and egg. Beat for 1 minute. Stir in enough of the remaining flour to make soft dough. Knead dough on floured board for 5 minutes. Place in greased bowl. Cover with plastic wrap. Let rise in warm place (75° to 85°F/24° to 29°C) until doubled, about 1¼ hours.

2. **Topping:** Bring brown sugar and butter to a boil. Stir in corn syrup. Pour into prepared pan. Sprinkle pecan halves on top.

3. **Filling:** Punch down dough. Roll out into 15- by 10-inch (37 x 25 cm) rectangle. Spread with butter. Combine pecans, brown sugar and cinnamon. Sprinkle over dough. Starting at long side, roll up tightly, pinching seam to seal. Cut into 15 pieces. Place in pan. Cover tightly with plastic wrap. Let rise in warm place for 1½ hours or in refrigerator for 12 to 48 hours or until doubled. Bake, uncovered, for 25 to 30 minutes or until golden. Let stand for 3 minutes in pan, then invert onto serving platter.

Apricot Cheese Coffee Cake

An easy twisted dough top rises and puffs during baking to a very attractive finish.

Makes about 10 servings

Preparation: 25 minutes

Rising: approximately 3 hours

Baking: 35 minutes

Freezing: excellent

TIP

Cool bread for about 30 minutes to let filling set before slicing.

- Preheat oven to 375°F (190°C)
- 9½-inch (24 cm) springform pan, side ring removed
- Bread machine

Sweet Dough

¾ cup	warm milk	175 mL
1	egg, beaten	1
2 tbsp	butter	30 mL
2 cups	Robin Hood Best For Bread Homestyle White Flour	500 mL
¼ cup	granulated sugar	50 mL
¾ tsp	salt	3 mL
2 tsp	grated orange zest	10 mL
1½ tsp	bread machine yeast	7 mL

Filling

4 oz	spreadable cream cheese	125 g
1½ tbsp	Robin Hood Best For Bread Homestyle White Flour	22 mL
⅓ cup	apricot jam	75 mL
1	egg, beaten	1
2 tbsp	sliced almonds	30 mL

1. **Sweet Dough:** Add all ingredients to bread machine according to manufacturer's directions. Select Dough cycle. Remove dough from pan. Cover and let rest for 10 minutes.

2. **Filling:** Roll out dough on lightly floured surface into 15-inch (37 cm) circle. Place dough on pan bottom. Combine cream cheese and flour. Spread cheese mixture in center of dough, covering area over top of pan. Spread jam over cheese. Make cuts about 1 inch (2.5 cm) apart around dough to about 1 inch (2.5 cm) away from filling. Twist pairs of dough strips together. Bring up to center covering filling. Place greased ring on pan bottom. Cover with tea towel. Let rise in warm place for 50 to 60 minutes or until almost doubled. Brush lightly with beaten egg. Sprinkle almonds on top. Bake for 30 to 35 minutes or until golden. Cover with foil after 20 minutes if becoming too brown.

Date and Nut Loaf

This loaf, which was a favorite in the 1920s, remains popular and has stood the test of time.

TIPS

Because it is so moist, this loaf is easy to slice very thinly. Enjoy it lightly buttered or spread with cream cheese. It is also good toasted.

Buy pitted dates that are fairly soft for easy cutting.

Spray knife with cooking spray or lightly oil to prevent dates from sticking.

- Preheat oven to 325°F (160°C)
- 9- by 5-inch (2 L) loaf pan, greased

1 cup	chopped pitted dates	250 mL
1 cup	boiling water	250 mL
1 tsp	baking soda	5 mL
1 cup	packed brown sugar	250 mL
1/4 cup	butter, melted	50 mL
1	egg, beaten	1
1 3/4 cups	Robin Hood All-Purpose Flour	425 mL
1 tsp	baking powder	5 mL
1/2 tsp	salt	2 mL
3/4 cup	chopped walnuts	175 mL

1. Combine dates, boiling water and baking soda in a large bowl. Stir well; let cool. Stir in brown sugar, butter and egg, mixing until blended.

2. Combine flour, baking powder and salt. Stir into date mixture along with walnuts. Mix well. Spread in prepared pan.

3. Bake for 65 to 75 minutes or until toothpick inserted in center comes out clean. Cool for 15 minutes in pan, then turn out onto rack and cool completely.

Variation
Add 1 tbsp (15 mL) grated orange or lemon zest to the batter.

Glazed Lemon Nut Bread

Passed down from generation to generation, this wonderful loaf has passed the test of time.

Makes 1 loaf

Preparation: 15 minutes

**Baking time:
1 hour 5 minutes**

Freezing: excellent

TIP

Try it toasted!

- *Preheat oven to 350°F (180°C)*
- *9- by 5-inch (2 L) loaf pan, greased*

2 cups	Robin Hood All-Purpose Flour	500 mL
1 tsp	baking powder	5 mL
1/2 tsp	baking soda	2 mL
1/4 tsp	salt	1 mL
1 1/4 cups	granulated sugar	300 mL
1/2 cup	shortening	125 mL
3	eggs	3
1/2 cup	lemon juice	125 mL
1/2 cup	milk	125 mL
3/4 cup	chopped pecans	175 mL

Lemon Glaze

1/3 cup	confectioner's (icing) sugar, sifted	75 mL
1/4 cup	lemon juice	50 mL

1. Stir together flour, baking powder, baking soda and salt. Set aside.

2. Beat sugar and shortening in large bowl on medium speed of electric mixer until fluffy. Add eggs, one at a time, beating well after each addition. Gradually beat in lemon juice. Add milk alternately with dry ingredients. Stir in nuts. Pour into prepared pan. Bake for 60 to 65 minutes or until toothpick inserted in center comes out clean. Remove from oven. While still in pan, poke holes with toothpick or fork in bread 1 inch (2.5 cm) apart.

3. **Lemon Glaze:** Stir together sugar and juice. Slowly pour half of the glaze over warm bread. Cool for 10 minutes. Remove from pan. Place on rack over piece of waxed paper. Pour remaining glaze over bread. Cool completely.

Lemon Poppy Seed Loaf

The tart taste of lemon together with the crunch of poppy seeds makes this delicious loaf a real winner.

Makes 1 loaf

Preparation: 15 minutes

Baking: 65 minutes

Freezing: excellent

TIPS

Be sure to remove the zest first, then cut the lemon in half to juice.

Remove only the yellow part of the zest. The white pith will be bitter.

To extract the maximum amount of juice, warm lemons slightly before juicing by immersing them in hot water for 30 seconds. One lemon will yield at least 2 tbsp (30 mL) juice.

- Preheat oven to 350°F (180°C)
- 8¹/₂- by 4¹/₂-inch (1.5 L) loaf pan, greased

Loaf

¹/₃ cup	butter, softened	75 mL
1 cup	granulated sugar	250 mL
2	eggs	2
1¹/₂ cups	Robin Hood All-Purpose Flour	375 mL
1¹/₂ tsp	baking powder	7 mL
1 tsp	grated lemon zest	5 mL
¹/₂ tsp	salt	2 mL
¹/₂ cup	milk	125 mL
2 tbsp	poppy seeds	30 mL

Lemon Glaze

¹/₄ cup	granulated sugar	50 mL
2 tbsp	lemon juice	30 mL

1. **Loaf:** Cream butter and sugar in a large mixer bowl on medium speed of electric mixer until fluffy. Add eggs, one at a time, beating well after each addition.
2. Combine flour, baking powder, lemon zest and salt. Add to creamed mixture alternately with milk, beating lightly after each addition. Stir in poppy seeds. Spread in prepared pan.
3. Bake for 55 to 65 minutes or until toothpick inserted in center comes out clean. Remove from oven. While still warm in pan, poke holes with toothpick or fork in top of loaf, 1 inch (2.5 cm) apart.
4. **Lemon Glaze:** Heat sugar and lemon juice in a small saucepan or microwave until sugar is dissolved. Brush glaze over loaf. Cool for 15 minutes in pan, then turn out onto rack and cool completely.

Variations

Omit poppy seeds, if desired.

Substitute ¹/₂ cup (125 mL) chopped pecans, walnuts or hazelnuts for the poppy seeds.

Pineapple Banana Loaf

A moist, tender banana loaf with bits of crushed pineapple throughout. Enjoy one now and freeze one loaf for unexpected company.

Makes 2 loaves

Preparation: 15 minutes

Baking: 1 hour 10 minutes

Freezing: excellent

TIP

Brands of pineapple vary. Choose coarsely chopped fruit with a high proportion of fruit to juice.

- Preheat oven to 350°F (180°C)
- Two 8½- by 4½-inch (1.5 L) or 9- by 5-inch (2 L) loaf pans, greased

3 cups	Robin Hood All-Purpose Flour	750 mL
2 cups	granulated sugar	500 mL
1 tsp	baking powder	5 mL
1 tsp	baking soda	5 mL
1 tsp	salt	5 mL
2 cups	mashed ripe banana (about 5 bananas)	500 mL
1¼ cups	vegetable oil	300 mL
1 cup	crushed pineapple, undrained	250 mL
3	eggs	3
2 tsp	vanilla	10 mL

1. Combine flour, sugar, baking powder, baking soda and salt.
2. Beat together banana, oil, pineapple, eggs and vanilla in large bowl until blended. Add dry ingredients, stirring until thoroughly combined. Divide evenly between prepared pans. Bake for 60 to 70 minutes or until toothpick inserted in center comes out clean. Cool for 15 minutes in pan, then transfer to rack and cool completely.

Variation

Stir 1 cup (250 mL) chopped nuts into batter, if desired. Macadamia or Brazil nuts are nice.

Rhubarb Bread

If you don't know what to do with all that fresh rhubarb in the garden, here's an ideal way to use it up. If you're not a gardener, it's worth purchasing rhubarb for this mouthwatering recipe.

Makes 2 loaves

Preparation: 10 minutes

Baking: 60 minutes

Freezing: excellent

TIPS

If you use frozen rhubarb, thaw and pat dry with paper towels to remove excess moisture before using in baking.

For foolproof removal of loaves, line the pan bottom and sides with greased aluminum foil or parchment paper. To remove, simply lift the loaves out of the pan — they won't stick. Remove paper and let cool.

If you are making a gift of this or any other bread, leave it in the pan. Cool completely, then wrap pan and loaf in colorful plastic wrap or an airtight bag. Attach a recipe card with the recipe written on it.

- *Preheat oven to 350°F (180°C)*
- *Two 9- by 5-inch (2 L) loaf pans, greased*

Loaf

1½ cups	packed brown sugar	375 mL
1 cup	buttermilk	250 mL
⅔ cup	vegetable oil	150 mL
1	egg	1
2 tsp	grated orange zest	10 mL
2½ cups	Robin Hood All-Purpose Flour	625 mL
1 tsp	baking soda	5 mL
1 tsp	salt	5 mL
1¾ cups	chopped rhubarb	425 mL
½ cup	chopped pecans	125 mL

Topping

½ cup	granulated sugar	125 mL
1 tbsp	butter, softened	15 mL
2 tsp	grated orange zest	10 mL

1. **Loaf:** Combine brown sugar, buttermilk, oil, egg and orange zest in a large bowl. Mix well.
2. Combine flour, baking soda and salt. Add to sugar mixture, mixing until smooth. Fold in rhubarb and pecans. Spread batter in prepared pans, dividing evenly.
3. **Topping:** Mix sugar, butter and orange zest together with a fork until blended. Sprinkle over batter.
4. Bake for 55 to 60 minutes or until toothpick inserted in center comes out clean. Cool for 15 minutes in pan, then turn out onto rack and cool completely.

Variations

Replace half of the rhubarb with sliced strawberries.

Adding 1 tsp (5 mL) ground cinnamon to the batter along with the salt adds terrific flavor.

Mini Banana Loaves

These mini-loaves are a nice size to give as gifts. They also make a great item for bake sales.

Makes 6 mini-loaves

Preparation: 20 minutes

Baking: 45 minutes

Freezing: excellent

TIPS

Use ripe bananas for the best flavor in loaves and muffins. Plan ahead by purchasing bananas in advance of baking and allowing them to ripen.

You can freeze mashed bananas, but keep in mind that they are much wetter than freshly mashed. The extra moisture will affect the recipe by producing a soggy loaf that is sunken in the center. To avoid this problem, bake banana loaves with fresh bananas and freeze them. Reserve frozen mashed bananas for smoothies and shakes.

- Preheat oven to 350°F (180°C)
- Six 5¾- by 3¼-inch (500 mL) mini-loaf pans, greased

3 cups	mashed ripe banana (about 7 large)	750 mL
½ cup	lemon juice	125 mL
⅔ cup	butter, softened	150 mL
1 cup	granulated sugar	250 mL
4	eggs	4
1 tsp	vanilla	5 mL
3¾ cups	Robin Hood All-Purpose Flour	925 mL
2 tsp	baking soda	10 mL
1½ tsp	baking powder	7 mL
1 tsp	salt	5 mL
¾ tsp	ground nutmeg	3 mL

1. Combine mashed banana and lemon juice in a bowl; set aside.
2. Cream butter and sugar in a large bowl until light and creamy. Add eggs, one at a time, beating lightly after each addition. Add banana mixture and vanilla. Stir well.
3. Combine flour, baking soda, baking powder, salt and nutmeg. Stir into banana mixture gradually, mixing until smooth. Spread in prepared pans, dividing evenly.
4. Bake for 40 to 45 minutes or until toothpick inserted in center comes out clean. Cool for 15 minutes in pans, then turn out onto rack and cool completely.

Variations

Add 1 cup (250 mL) dried cranberries to the batter.

Add 1 cup (250 mL) chopped nuts to the batter.

Add ⅔ cup (150 mL) flaked coconut to the batter.

Zucchini Bread

A tasty recipe that's always popular. Moist and delicious, this loaf tastes great thinly sliced and buttered or spread with cream cheese.

Makes 2 loaves

Preparation: 15 minutes

Baking: 1 hour

Freezing: excellent

TIP

Use small zucchini. Large ones have tougher skins and a lot of seeds.

- *Preheat oven to 350°F (180°C)*
- *Two 8¹⁄₂- by 4¹⁄₂-inch (1.5 L) loaf pans, greased*

1¹⁄₂ cups	Robin Hood All-Purpose Flour	375 mL
1¹⁄₂ cups	Robin Hood Whole Wheat Flour	375 mL
1¹⁄₂ tsp	ground cinnamon	7 mL
1 tsp	baking powder	5 mL
1 tsp	baking soda	5 mL
1 tsp	salt	5 mL
¹⁄₂ tsp	ground nutmeg	2 mL
3	eggs	3
1¹⁄₂ cups	granulated sugar	375 mL
1 cup	vegetable oil	250 mL
2 tsp	vanilla	10 mL
2 cups	shredded unpeeled zucchini	500 mL
¹⁄₂ cup	chopped walnuts	125 mL
¹⁄₂ cup	raisins	125 mL

1. Combine all-purpose and whole wheat flours, cinnamon, baking powder, baking soda, salt and nutmeg. Stir well to blend.

2. Beat eggs in large mixing bowl. Gradually beat in sugar, then oil and vanilla. Add dry ingredients gradually, mixing well. Stir in zucchini, walnuts and raisins. Pour batter into prepared pans. Bake for 55 to 60 minutes or until toothpick inserted in center comes out clean. Cool in pans for 10 minutes, then turn out onto rack to cool completely.

Variation
Replace zucchini with grated carrot.

Wheaten Bread

This healthy bread stays moist for days. It has lots of flavor on its own but makes great sandwiches, too.

Makes 1 loaf

Preparation: 10 minutes

Baking: 55 minutes

Freezing: excellent

TIPS

The batter will be very stiff.

If you don't have buttermilk, here is a substitute. To make 1 cup (250 mL) buttermilk, mix 1 tbsp (15 mL) vinegar or lemon juice with enough milk to make 1 cup (250 mL). Let stand for 5 minutes, then stir.

Sprinkle a little (1 tbsp/ 15 mL) whole wheat flour on top of the batter before baking to give the loaf a homemade look.

● *Preheat oven to 350°F (180°C)*
● *$8^{1}/_{2}$- by $4^{1}/_{2}$-inch (1.5 L) loaf pan, greased*

$1^{1}/_{2}$ cups	Robin Hood All-Purpose Flour	375 mL
$1^{1}/_{2}$ cups	Robin Hood Whole Wheat Flour	375 mL
$^{1}/_{2}$ cup	granulated sugar	125 mL
2 tsp	baking powder	10 mL
1 tsp	baking soda	5 mL
1 tsp	salt	5 mL
1 cup	buttermilk	250 mL
$^{3}/_{4}$ cup	milk	175 mL

1. Combine white and whole wheat flours, sugar, baking powder, baking soda and salt in a mixing bowl. Add buttermilk and milk. Mix well.
2. Spread batter in prepared pan.
3. Bake for 30 minutes, then lower oven temperature to 325°F (160°C) and bake for 20 to 25 minutes longer or until toothpick inserted in center comes out clean. Cool for 10 minutes in pan, then turn out onto rack and cool completely.

Variation
Add 2 tbsp (30 mL) each flaxseeds and sesame seeds.

Buttermilk Biscuits

Enjoy these homey biscuits warm with butter, jam or preserves. In season, sweeten them up and use as a base for individual shortcakes, topped with fresh berries and whipped cream. Or serve them with dinner for a down-home treat.

Makes about 12 biscuits

Preparation: 15 minutes

Baking: 15 minutes

Freezing: excellent

TIPS

To simplify last-minute preparation, prepare the dry mixture, cut in the shortening and chill until needed. When ready to serve, preheat the oven while you are mixing and shaping the biscuits. Then pop them in the oven to bake.

A sour milk product, such as buttermilk, yogurt or sour cream, is used in doughs that contain baking soda. Plain milk is usually used when baking powder is the only leavening.

Biscuits made with shortening have a light, tender texture.

- Preheat oven to 425°F (220°C)
- Baking sheet, ungreased

2 cups	Robin Hood All-Purpose Flour	500 mL
2½ tsp	baking powder	12 mL
1 tsp	salt	5 mL
½ tsp	baking soda	2 mL
½ cup	shortening	125 mL
1 cup	buttermilk	250 mL

1. Combine flour, baking powder, salt and baking soda in a mixing bowl. Using two knives, a pastry blender or your fingers, cut in shortening until mixture resembles coarse crumbs.

2. Add buttermilk all at once to dry ingredients and stir with a fork until a soft dough forms. Turn dough out onto a lightly floured surface and knead gently eight to 10 times. Roll or pat to ¾-inch (2 cm) thickness. Cut with a 1¾-inch (4.5 cm) round cutter dipped in flour. Place on baking sheet. (Place biscuits close together for soft-sided biscuits or about 1 inch/2.5 cm apart for crusty-sided biscuits.)

3. Bake for 12 to 15 minutes or until light golden. Serve warm.

Variations

Brush tops with melted butter and sprinkle with sugar for a finishing touch.

Stir in about 1 cup (250 mL) shredded Cheddar cheese for a savory biscuit.

Add 2 tbsp (30 mL) sugar to the dough for a sweet biscuit that you can use as a base for shortcake.

Nutty Seed Bread

A wonderful flavored loaf with lots of crunchy seeds. Try it toasted with honey.

Makes 1 loaf

Preparation: 15 minutes

Baking: 1 hour

Freezing: excellent

TIP

Store whole wheat flour well wrapped in the freezer to retain its freshness.

- *Preheat oven to 350°F (180°C)*
- *9- by 5-inch (2 L) loaf pan, greased*

1	egg	1
1 cup	buttermilk or soured milk	250 mL
1/3 cup	vegetable oil	75 mL
1 cup	Robin Hood All-Purpose Flour	250 mL
1 cup	Robin Hood Whole Wheat Flour	250 mL
1 cup	packed brown sugar	250 mL
1/3 cup	finely chopped nuts	75 mL
2 tbsp	wheat germ	30 mL
2 tbsp	flaxseeds	30 mL
2 tbsp	sesame seeds	30 mL
2 tbsp	sunflower seeds	30 mL
2 tbsp	poppy seeds	30 mL
1 tsp	baking powder	5 mL
1 tsp	baking soda	5 mL
1/2 tsp	salt	2 mL

1. Combine egg, buttermilk and oil in large mixing bowl.

2. Mix together all-purpose and whole wheat flours, brown sugar, nuts, wheat germ, flaxseeds, sesame seeds, sunflower seeds, poppy seeds, baking powder, baking soda and salt. Add to liquid ingredients, mixing to moisten all ingredients. Spread in prepared pan. Bake for 50 to 60 minutes or until toothpick inserted in center comes out clean. Cool for 10 minutes in pan, then remove and cool completely on rack.

Variation
Vary the type of nuts and seeds to suit your personal taste.

Cornbread

Warm cornbread is a quite a delicacy in the American South. This tasty version has extra corn and peppers to make it particularly appetizing.

Makes about 12 servings

Preparation: 15 minutes
Baking: 25 minutes
Freezing: excellent

TIPS

Peaches-and-cream corn has a pleasant mild flavor and tender texture. Yellow corn is a bit firmer and slightly stronger in taste. Use whatever variety you prefer.

Fresh, canned or thawed frozen corn kernels work well in this recipe.

Use old Cheddar cheese for a strong cheese flavor or medium for a more mellow taste.

For individual servings, spoon batter into 12 greased muffin cups and bake for about 18 minutes.

- Preheat oven to 400°F (200°C)
- 8-inch (2 L) square cake pan, greased

2	eggs	2
1 cup	buttermilk	250 mL
1/4 cup	butter, melted	50 mL
1 cup	fresh, canned or thawed frozen corn kernels	250 mL
1 cup	shredded Cheddar cheese	250 mL
1/4 cup	finely chopped sweet red pepper	50 mL
1 cup	Robin Hood All-Purpose Flour	250 mL
1 cup	cornmeal	250 mL
1 tbsp	granulated sugar	15 mL
1 tbsp	baking powder	15 mL
1 tsp	salt	5 mL
1/2 tsp	baking soda	2 mL

1. Whisk eggs, buttermilk and melted butter in a large bowl. Stir in corn, cheese and pepper.
2. Combine flour, cornmeal, sugar, baking powder, salt and baking soda. Add to liquid ingredients all at once, stirring just until moistened. Spread batter in prepared pan.
3. Bake for 20 to 25 minutes or until toothpick inserted in center comes out clean. Cut into squares and serve warm or cool.

Variations

Replace peppers with green or black olives.
Add minced jalapeño pepper to taste for added zip.

Butterscotch Pecan Rolls

Warm from the oven, these sticky buns made with tender biscuit dough and covered in crunchy, sugary nuts are impossible to resist.

Makes 12 rolls

Preparation: 25 minutes
Baking: 23 minutes
Freezing: excellent

TIPS

Biscuit dough should be soft. You can always add a little more flour if it's too sticky, but a soft dough is much more tender than one that is too stiff.

Store nuts in the freezer to keep them fresh.

- Preheat oven to 425°F (220°C)
- 9-inch (2.5 L) square cake pan, greased

Topping
½ cup	corn syrup	125 mL
⅓ cup	packed brown sugar	75 mL
3 tbsp	butter	45 mL
1 tbsp	water	15 mL
½ cup	chopped pecans	125 mL

Dough
2 cups	Robin Hood All-Purpose Flour	500 mL
4 tsp	baking powder	20 mL
1 tsp	salt	5 mL
½ cup	shortening	125 mL
1 cup	milk	250 mL

Filling
2 tbsp	packed brown sugar	30 mL
1 tbsp	butter, softened	15 mL
1 tsp	ground cinnamon	5 mL

1. **Topping:** Mix syrup, brown sugar, butter and water in cake pan. Cook on top of stove over medium heat until sugar is dissolved. Sprinkle with pecans. Set aside.

2. **Dough:** Combine flour, baking powder and salt in a mixing bowl. Using two forks, a pastry blender or your fingers, cut in shortening until mixture resembles coarse crumbs. Add milk all at once and stir with a fork until ingredients are moistened and a soft dough forms. Turn out onto a floured surface. Form into a ball and knead gently about 10 times. Roll out or pat dough to a 9-inch (23 cm) square.

3. **Filling:** Mix brown sugar, softened butter and cinnamon until well combined. Spread evenly over dough. Roll up jelly-roll fashion. Cut into nine 1-inch (2.5 cm) slices with a sharp knife. Place over topping in prepared pan.

4. Bake for 18 to 23 minutes or until golden brown and the center of each biscuit is firm. Invert pan onto serving plate immediately. Let stand for 5 minutes, then remove pan. Serve warm.

Variation

Use your favorite nut. Walnuts and hazelnuts also work well in this recipe.

Sesame Crisp Bread

A unique homemade cracker to serve with a dill dip or pâté at your next party.

Makes four 12-inch (30 cm) round flat breads

Preparation: 15 minutes

Resting: 2 hours

Baking: 15 minutes

Freezing: excellent

TIP

Black sesame seeds add interest.

- *Preheat oven to 425°F (220°C)*
- *Baking sheet, ungreased*

1½ cups	Robin Hood All-Purpose Flour	375 mL
1 cup	Robin Hood Whole Wheat Flour	250 mL
½ tsp	salt	2 mL
1 cup	warm water	250 mL
1	egg, beaten	1
	Sesame seeds	
	Garlic powder	
	Finely chopped fresh dill or dried dillweed	

1. Combine all-purpose and whole wheat flours and salt in mixing bowl. Stir well to blend.
2. Add water to flour mixture. Stir with wooden spoon until mixture forms soft dough. Turn out dough onto floured surface and knead well for about 10 minutes or until smooth. Place in greased bowl; cover with damp cloth and allow to rest at room temperature for 2 hours.
3. Divide dough into four equal portions. Roll each piece into very thin round, approximately 12 inches (30 cm) in diameter. (Don't worry about an uneven shape. It's more interesting if circle isn't perfectly round.)
4. Transfer to baking sheet and brush lightly with beaten egg. Sprinkle lightly with sesame seeds, garlic powder and dill or other desired seasonings. Prick dough well with fork. Bake for 10 to 15 minutes or until crisp and lightly browned. Serve whole and break off pieces for eating.

Variation
Try different seasoning variations such as dried pepper flakes, sautéed onion and bacon, poppy seeds, finely chopped onion, grated Parmesan cheese and seasoning salt.

Popovers That Pop

These popovers, which make a great substitute for Yorkshire pudding, stay puffed, unlike Yorkshire pudding, which starts to deflate as soon as it comes out of the oven. They also have a delicious butter-and-egg flavor. Serve these tasty treats with roast beef and gravy or enjoy them with soup or salad in place of rolls.

Makes 12 popovers

Preparation: 10 minutes

Baking: 40 minutes

Freezing: not recommended

TIPS

The key to making popovers puff is to start them in a hot oven and reduce the heat after they have cooked for a while. If the initial heat is too low, they will never puff.

Heated butter in each cup aids the puffing and adds flavor.

Use a wire whisk to get the batter smooth.

Don't peek. If you open the door during baking, the popovers will collapse.

- *Preheat oven to 400°F (200°C)*
- *12-cup muffin pan, ungreased*

¼ cup	butter, melted	50 mL
1 cup + 2 tbsp	Robin Hood All-Purpose Flour	280 mL
4	eggs	4
1 cup	milk	250 mL
1 tsp	salt	5 mL

1. Put 1 tsp (5 mL) melted butter in each muffin cup. Place in oven for 5 minutes to heat.
2. Combine flour, eggs, milk and salt in a small bowl, beating until thick and smooth. Pour batter into heated pan, filling cups about half full.
3. Bake for 20 minutes, then reduce heat to 375°F (190°C) and bake for 10 to 15 minutes longer or until puffed. Remove from pan immediately.

Variation
Replace butter with oil.

Raisin Scones

Two different textures can be obtained in a matter of minutes!

TIP

Brush top with beaten egg and sprinkle with sugar for an appealing golden color.

- Preheat oven to 425°F (220°C)
- Baking sheet, ungreased

2 cups	Robin Hood All-Purpose Flour or 2¼ cups (550 mL) Robin Hood Best For Cake & Pastry Flour	500 mL
¼ cup	granulated sugar	50 mL
2½ tsp	baking powder	12 mL
½ tsp	baking soda	2 mL
½ tsp	salt	2 mL
¼ cup	shortening	50 mL
¾ cup	raisins	175 mL
1 cup	buttermilk or soured milk	250 mL

1. Combine flour, sugar, baking powder, baking soda and salt in mixing bowl. Cut in shortening with pastry blender until mixture resembles coarse crumbs. Add raisins and buttermilk, stirring with fork until all ingredients are moistened. (Dough should be sticky.)

2. Turn out dough onto well-floured surface and knead for 1 minute. Shape dough into ball. Pat down onto baking sheet to form circle ¾ inch (2 cm) thick and about 8 inches (20 cm) in diameter. Gently mark round into eight wedges with knife. Let rest for 10 minutes for scone-like texture or bake immediately for more cake-like texture. Bake for 20 to 25 minutes or until golden and set in center. Cover with foil if becoming too brown during baking. Serve warm.

Variation

Replace raisins with dried cranberries and add 1 tbsp (15 mL) grated orange zest to dry ingredients.

Cheesy Drop Biscuits

These easy-to-make biscuits are like tea biscuits that don't require kneading, rolling and cutting.

Makes 12 biscuits

Preparation: 15 minutes
Baking: 20 minutes
Freezing: excellent

TIPS

Prepare more of these biscuits than you think you'll need. They will vanish quickly.

Be sure your baking powder is fresh. As it ages, it loses its leavening power. If you don't bake often, purchase it in small amounts.

Bake the biscuits as soon as they are mixed. Once the liquid combines with the baking powder, the leavening starts to work.

Use old Cheddar cheese. A five- or six-year-old Cheddar has a flavorful nip that works well in these biscuits.

Expect the dough to be slightly sticky — that's what makes the biscuits moist and tender.

The shape will vary with each biscuit. Their unique appearance gives the biscuits homemade appeal.

- *Preheat oven to 400°F (200°C)*
- *Baking sheet, greased*

2 cups	Robin Hood All-Purpose Flour	500 mL
1 tbsp	baking powder	15 mL
³⁄₄ tsp	salt	3 mL
¹⁄₃ cup	butter	75 mL
1¹⁄₂ cups	shredded old Cheddar cheese	375 mL
1	green onion, chopped	1
1¹⁄₄ cups	milk	300 mL

1. Combine flour, baking powder and salt in a large bowl. Using two knives, a pastry blender or your fingers, cut in butter until mixture resembles coarse crumbs. Stir in cheese and green onion.

2. Add milk all at once, stirring to make a soft, sticky dough. Divide dough into 12 portions, about ¹⁄₃ cup (75 mL) each. Drop onto prepared baking sheet.

3. Bake for 18 to 20 minutes or until edges are golden. Serve warm or cool.

Variations

Replace Cheddar with Swiss cheese.

Add some diced cooked bacon or ham (about ¹⁄₂ cup/125 mL) to the dough, along with the cheese.

Use chives in place of the green onion.

Cranberry Apricot Granola

Family Favorites

Cranberry Apricot Granola

It's always a treat to find a wholesome snack and/or breakfast that tastes so good.

Makes about 5 cups (1.25 L)

Preparation: 10 minutes

Baking: 35 minutes

Freezing: not necessary (store at room temperature)

TIPS

Try this granola as a dessert. Top it with ice cream or frozen yogurt and finish with a drizzle of maple syrup or honey.

Use any dried fruit you like in this recipe. You can add other ingredients, such as fresh berries, to granola just before serving and enjoy a different breakfast every morning.

Be sure your pan has sides that are about 1 1/2 inches (4 cm) high so the ingredients won't spill over while you are stirring.

- Preheat oven to 300°F (150°C)
- 13- by 9-inch (3.5 L) baking pan, ungreased

2 cups	Robin Hood Large-Flake Oats	500 mL
1 1/2 cups	bran flake cereal, slightly crushed	375 mL
1/2 cup	flaked coconut	125 mL
1/2 cup	chopped dried apricots	125 mL
1/2 cup	dried cranberries	125 mL
1/3 cup	sunflower seeds	75 mL
1/3 cup	packed brown sugar	75 mL
1/4 cup	vegetable oil	50 mL
3 tbsp	apple or orange juice	45 mL
1 tsp	vanilla	5 mL

1. Combine oats, bran flakes, coconut, apricots, cranberries, sunflower seeds and brown sugar in a large bowl. Mix well.
2. Combine oil, juice and vanilla. Add to cereal mixture. Toss until thoroughly mixed. Spread out in pan.
3. Bake for 30 to 35 minutes, stirring frequently until light golden. Cool completely in pan on rack. Store in airtight containers or plastic bags in a cool place for up to 1 month.

Variations

Add fruit and nuts to suit your taste, such as raisins, dates, dried apples or cherries.

Use water in place of juice.

Double-Decker Granola Bars

Two granola-like mixtures make up the crust and topping of this delightful bar.

Makes about 16 bars

Preparation: 20 minutes

Baking: 30 minutes

Freezing: excellent

TIPS

Use regular clover honey for making cookies and bars. Some varieties, such as buckwheat, have a strong flavor that can be overpowering.

If your honey has crystallized, heat it gently in a pan of hot water until the crystals dissolve.

For added fiber, use whole wheat flour instead of all-purpose.

- Preheat oven to 325°F (160°C)
- 8-inch (2 L) square cake pan, greased

Crust

1/2 cup	Robin Hood All-Purpose or Whole Wheat Flour	125 mL
1/2 cup	Robin Hood Oats	125 mL
3 tbsp	packed brown sugar	45 mL
1/4 tsp	baking powder	1 mL
3 tbsp	butter, melted	45 mL

Topping

1/4 cup	butter, melted	50 mL
2 tbsp	packed brown sugar	30 mL
2 tbsp	honey	30 mL
1/2 cup	Robin Hood Oats	125 mL
1/2 cup	finely chopped nuts	125 mL
1/3 cup	flaked coconut	75 mL
1/4 cup	sunflower seeds	50 mL
1/4 cup	raisins	50 mL

1. **Crust:** Combine flour, oats, brown sugar and baking powder in a medium bowl. Add melted butter. Mix well. Press firmly into prepared pan. Bake for 10 minutes or until light golden at edges and set.
2. **Topping:** Combine melted butter, brown sugar and honey in a medium bowl. Stir until well blended. Add oats, nuts, coconut, sunflower seeds and raisins. Mix well. Spread mixture over crust. Press down gently.
3. Bake for 15 to 20 minutes longer or until golden and set. Cool completely in pan on rack, then cut into bars.

Variations

Use any nuts you have on hand or a combination of them. Just be sure they are finely chopped to make cutting the bars easy.

Replace the raisins with dried cranberries, chopped pitted dates or chopped dried apricots.

Soft 'n' Chewy Chocolate Oat Squares

These chewy bars combine two perennial favorites, chocolate and peanut butter, with an abundance of oats to make a treat that everyone will enjoy.

Makes about 4 dozen squares

Preparation: 15 minutes

Baking: 18 minutes

Freezing: excellent

TIPS

Quick-cooking oats work well in these squares, but you can use whatever variety you have on hand.

To remove bars easily from the pan, line the pan completely with greased aluminum foil or parchment paper. Once the bars have cooled completely, lift them out of the pan and place on a cutting board. Remove the paper and cut into bars. Bars and squares are much easier to cut after they have been removed from the pan.

If you plan to pack these bars in lunches, omit the topping.

- Preheat oven to 350°F (180°C)
- 13- by 9-inch (3.5 L) cake pan, greased

Squares

½ cup	butter, softened	125 mL
1 cup	packed brown sugar	250 mL
½ cup	corn syrup	125 mL
½ tsp	salt	2 mL
1 tsp	vanilla	5 mL
4 cups	Robin Hood Oats	1 L
½ cup	creamy peanut butter	125 mL

Topping

8	squares (each 1 oz/28 g) semi-sweet chocolate	8
¼ cup	butter	50 mL

1. **Squares:** Cream butter and brown sugar in a large bowl until light and creamy. Add corn syrup, salt, vanilla and oats. Mix well. Spread mixture evenly in prepared pan.

2. Bake for 13 to 18 minutes or until set and golden. Cool slightly on rack. Spread peanut butter evenly over top.

3. **Topping:** Heat chocolate and butter in a saucepan over low heat, stirring until smooth. Spread over peanut butter. Cool until chocolate is set, then cut into squares.

Variation

For a lighter treat, prepare only half of the chocolate topping and drizzle it over the peanut butter.

No-Bake Marshmallow Oat Balls

Fun to shape and great to simply pop in your mouth!

TIPS

Choose marshmallows carefully. The fresher and softer they are, the easier it is to melt them.

Cook butter and marshmallows over low heat. Be patient — if you try to hurry, they'll burn on the bottom.

Use wet hands to shape the mixture into balls. This will help keep it from sticking to every finger.

- *Baking sheet or tray, lined with waxed paper*

Oat Balls

6 cups	miniature marshmallows	1.5 L
¼ cup	butter	50 mL
2½ cups	Robin Hood Oats	625 mL
1½ cups	chopped walnuts	375 mL
1 cup	flaked coconut	250 mL

Garnish, optional

2	squares (each 1 oz/28 g) semi-sweet chocolate optional	2

1. **Oat Balls:** Heat marshmallows and butter together in a large saucepan over low heat, stirring, until melted. Remove from heat. Stir in oats, nuts and coconut. Mix well.
2. With wet hands, shape mixture into small balls. Place on prepared baking sheet.
3. **Garnish (optional):** Melt chocolate and drizzle over balls. Let set. Store uncovered at room temperature for up to 1 week.

Variations

Add finely chopped dried apricots, dates or dried cranberries to taste.

For a special treat, press a chocolate kiss candy on top in place of the chocolate drizzle.

Oats and Seeds Bars

These delicious bars make a great treat to pack in knapsacks for a school snack, a hike or a bicycle ride.

Makes about 3 dozen bars

Preparation: 10 minutes

Baking: 12 minutes

Freezing: excellent

TIPS

Melted chocolate on top tastes great, but leave the bars plain if you intend to pack or store them.

Dark brown sugar has a mild molasses flavor; golden brown sugar tastes more like butterscotch. Both work well in this recipe.

If you don't feel like cutting these bars, try breaking them into irregular shapes. It's easier than cutting them.

- *Preheat oven to 375°F (190°C)*
- *15- by 10-inch (2 L) jelly roll pan, greased*

¾ cup	butter	175 mL
1¼ cups	packed brown sugar	300 mL
1½ tsp	vanilla	7 mL
2¼ cups	Robin Hood Oats	550 mL
½ cup	sesame seeds	125 mL
¼ cup	flaxseeds	50 mL
¾ tsp	baking powder	3 mL

1. Melt butter in a large saucepan. Stir in brown sugar and vanilla. Cook over medium heat, stirring often, for 2 minutes or until mixture is bubbly. Remove from heat and stir in oats, sesame seeds, flaxseeds and baking powder; mix well. Press firmly with the back of a spoon into prepared pan.

2. Bake for 7 to 12 minutes or until golden. Cool completely in pan on rack. Cut into bars or break into pieces.

Variations

Replace flaxseeds with sunflower seeds.

Add ¼ cup (50 mL) sunflower seeds.

Apple Crumble Muffin Bites

Snacks in small sizes, like these tasty muffin bites, are a perfect solution for school lunch boxes.

Makes
30 mini-muffins

Preparation: 20 minutes

Baking: 15 minutes

Freezing: excellent

TIPS

You can make a dozen regular-size muffins with the same recipe. Bake for approximately 20 minutes.

Either sweetened or unsweetened applesauce will work in this recipe.

Use quick-cooking, not large-flake, oats in this recipe.

Increase the fiber by using all or half Robin Hood Whole Wheat Flour in place of the all-purpose.

Shred apples on the coarse side of a grater. Using one that is too fine will make the job much more difficult.

- Preheat oven to 400°F (200°C)
- Three 12-cup mini-muffin pans, greased or lined with paper liners

Topping

$^1/_2$ cup	Robin Hood Quick-Cooking Oats	125 mL
$^1/_4$ cup	packed brown sugar	50 mL
2 tbsp	butter, melted	30 mL
$^1/_4$ tsp	ground cinnamon	1 mL

Batter

1 $^1/_4$ cups	Robin Hood All-Purpose Flour	300 mL
1 cup	Robin Hood Quick-Cooking Oats	250 mL
$^1/_3$ cup	packed brown sugar	75 mL
1 tbsp	baking powder	15 mL
$^1/_2$ tsp	salt	2 mL
$^1/_2$ tsp	ground cinnamon	2 mL
1	egg	1
1 cup	shredded peeled apple (about 2)	250 mL
$^2/_3$ cup	applesauce	150 mL
$^1/_3$ cup	milk	75 mL
$^1/_4$ cup	vegetable oil	50 mL

1. **Topping:** Combine oats, brown sugar, melted butter and cinnamon in a small bowl. Mix well; set aside.

2. **Batter:** Combine flour, oats, brown sugar, baking powder, salt and cinnamon. In a large bowl, beat egg, apple, applesauce, milk and oil. Add dry ingredients and stir just until moistened. Spoon into prepared pans. Sprinkle with topping.

3. Bake for 12 to 15 minutes or until tops spring back when lightly touched. Cool for 5 minutes in pan, then transfer to rack and cool completely.

Variation

Add raisins or dried cranberries (about 1 cup/250 mL) to the batter.

Toonie Pancakes

These mini-pancakes don't take long to cook, and kids can have fun trying them with different syrups and toppings.

Makes about forty 2-inch (5 cm) or ten 6-inch (15 cm) pancakes

Preparation: 15 minutes

Cooking: 4 minutes per batch

Freezing: excellent

TIPS

To test pan for the correct temperature (375°F/190°C), heat over medium-high heat. Sprinkle a few drops of cold water on the surface. When the drops bounce and evaporate, it's ready to use.

To keep cooked pancakes warm, place them in a single layer on a baking sheet. Cover loosely with foil and keep in a warm oven (200°F/100°C).

If the batter thickens as it stands, thin with a little milk to the proper consistency.

You can also make regular-size pancakes using $\frac{1}{4}$ cup (50 mL) batter for each. They will take a bit longer to cook.

- *Preheat griddle to 375°F (190°C)*
- *Griddle or skillet, lightly greased*

1$\frac{1}{3}$ cups	Robin Hood All-Purpose Flour	325 mL
2 tbsp	granulated sugar	30 mL
1 tbsp	baking powder	15 mL
$\frac{1}{2}$ tsp	salt	2 mL
1	egg	1
1$\frac{1}{4}$ cups	milk	300 mL
3 tbsp	melted butter or vegetable oil	45 mL
	Butter	
	Maple syrup	

1. Combine flour, sugar, baking powder and salt. Set aside
2. Beat egg, milk and melted butter in a medium bowl. Add dry ingredients. Whisk until smooth.
3. Pour batter by tablespoonfuls (15 mL) onto prepared griddle. Cook for 2 minutes or until bubbles break on the tops and bottoms are golden; turn and cook for 1 to 2 minutes or until bottoms are golden. Serve warm with butter and syrup.

Variations

As soon as you put the batter on the griddle, sprinkle the pancakes with mini chocolate chips.

Try serving plain pancakes with butter and cinnamon-sugar.

Oat Pancakes with Cinnamon Honey Butter

A wonderful weekend treat the whole family can enjoy making and eating. Keep a supply of the Cinnamon Honey Butter on hand. It's great on toast and waffles, too.

Makes about eighteen 6-inch (15 cm) pancakes

Preparation: 10 minutes

Cooking: 5 minutes per batch

Freezing: excellent

TIPS

Prepare honey butter ahead. Refrigerate, then bring to room temperature to use.

These pancakes are light but hearty. With bacon or sausage, they are a meal in themselves.

To test pan for the correct temperature (375°F/190°C), heat over medium-high heat. Sprinkle a few drops of cold water on the surface. When drops bounce and evaporate, it's ready to use.

Save any leftover pancakes. Cool completely, wrap well and store in freezer. Pop into toaster for a quick breakfast.

Try these pancakes with chunky applesauce on the side.

- *Preheat griddle to 375°F (190°C)*
- *Griddle or skillet, lightly greased*

Cinnamon Honey Butter
1 cup	butter, softened	250 mL
1 cup	honey	250 mL
2 tsp	ground cinnamon	10 mL

Pancakes
2 cups	milk	500 mL
1 ½ cups	Robin Hood Oats	375 mL
1 cup	Robin Hood All-Purpose Flour	250 mL
2 tbsp	brown or granulated sugar	30 mL
2 tbsp	baking powder	30 mL
¾ tsp	salt	3 mL
3	eggs	3
¼ cup	vegetable oil	50 mL

1. **Cinnamon Honey Butter:** Beat butter, honey and cinnamon until smooth and blended. Set aside.
2. **Pancakes:** Mix milk and oats in a small bowl. Set aside until milk is absorbed.
3. Combine flour, sugar, baking powder and salt in a mixing bowl. Stir well.
4. Add eggs and oil to oat mixture. Beat well. Add oat mixture to flour mixture all at once, mixing until smooth.
5. Spoon batter by ¼ cupfuls (50 mL) onto griddle. Cook for 2 to 3 minutes or until bubbles break on the surface and bottoms are golden; turn and cook for 1 to 2 minutes or until bottoms are lightly browned. Serve hot with Cinnamon Honey Butter.

Variations
If you're a big fan of cinnamon, add ½ tsp (2 mL) to the batter.

Serve with maple syrup instead of the Cinnamon Honey Butter.

Banana Softies

These cake-like squares are particularly appealing to young children, who enjoy their soft texture and mellow flavor.

Makes about 16 squares

Preparation: 15 minutes

Baking: 20 minutes

Freezing: excellent

TIPS

To make measuring easier, measure any oil that is required first. Then measure honey in the same cup. It will slip out cleanly and easily.

Kids love to mash bananas. It's especially easy to do when the bananas are very ripe. Just squish them on a plate with the tines of a fork.

Add some nuts or mini chocolate chips (about 1/2 cup/125 mL) to the batter.

- *Preheat oven to 350°F (180°C)*
- *8-inch (2 L) square cake pan, greased*

1	ripe banana, mashed	1
2 tbsp	packed brown sugar	30 mL
2 tbsp	vegetable oil	30 mL
2 tbsp	liquid honey	30 mL
1	egg white	1
1 tsp	vanilla	5 mL
1/3 cup	Robin Hood All-Purpose Flour	75 mL
1/2 tsp	baking soda	2 mL
1/2 tsp	ground cinnamon	2 mL
1 1/4 cups	Cranberry Apricot Granola (see recipe, page 314)	300 mL

1. Combine banana, brown sugar, oil, honey, egg white and vanilla in a large bowl. Beat with a wooden spoon until smooth. Combine flour, baking soda and cinnamon. Add to banana mixture along with granola. Mix well. Spread mixture evenly in prepared pan.

2. Bake for 15 to 20 minutes or until set and golden. Cool completely in pan on rack, then cut into squares.

Oatmeal Sesame Sticks

Great for lunch boxes, your knapsack or a treat during a fall bicycle ride.

Makes about 60 bars

Preparation: 10 minutes

Baking: 10 minutes

Freezing: excellent

TIP

One pan goes a long way.

- *Preheat oven to 375°F (190°C)*
- *15- by 10-inch (2 L) jelly roll pan, greased*

¾ cup	butter	175 mL
1½ cups	packed brown sugar	375 mL
1½ tsp	vanilla	7 mL
2¼ cups	Robin Hood Oats	550 mL
¾ cup	sesame seeds	175 mL
¾ tsp	baking powder	3 mL

1. Melt butter in large saucepan. Stir in brown sugar and vanilla. Cook for 2 minutes or until mixture is bubbly. Remove from heat and stir in oats, sesame seeds and baking powder. Mix well. Press firmly with back of spoon into prepared pan. Bake for 7 to 10 minutes or until golden. Cool completely, then cut into bars.

Variation
Add a layer of melted chocolate on top for a more decadent taste.

Fruit Puff

Serve this unique dish for breakfast, brunch or dessert. Fill with any fresh or canned fruit to fit the season or the ingredients you have on hand.

Makes about 6 servings

Preparation: 25 minutes

Baking: 25 minutes

Freezing: not recommended

TIPS

Let children watch this dessert while it bakes. It puffs up and then collapses when it comes out of the oven.

Have confectioner's (icing) sugar in a small sieve ready to sprinkle on top just before serving.

Children love to drizzle maple syrup over top of this puff, which is like a pancake.

You can halve the recipe to make one puff, if desired.

Plan to serve your puff as soon as it comes out of the oven.

- *Preheat oven to 425°F (220°C)*
- *Two 9-inch (23 cm) pie plates*

3 tbsp	butter	45 mL
4	eggs	4
1 cup	milk	250 mL
1 tsp	grated lemon zest	5 mL
1 cup	Robin Hood All-Purpose Flour	250 mL
2 tbsp	granulated sugar	30 mL
½ tsp	salt	2 mL
	Fresh berries (such as strawberries, raspberries and/or blueberries)	
	Confectioner's (icing) sugar	

1. Divide butter evenly between two pie plates. Place plates in oven while preparing the batter.
2. Place eggs, milk and lemon zest in a blender and process until blended. Add flour, sugar and salt and blend until smooth. Pour batter into hot butter in pie plates, dividing evenly.
3. Bake for 18 to 25 minutes or until puffed and golden. Remove from oven. Fill with fruit. Dust with icing sugar. Cut puff into wedges and serve immediately.

Variation

Enjoy this dessert year-round using frozen fruit, such as sliced peaches.

Apple Pecan Cake

Let kids do the mixing themselves. This cake doesn't require a mixer — all you need is a wooden spoon and a little effort.

Makes about 8 servings

Preparation: 20 minutes

Baking: 45 minutes

Freezing: excellent

TIPS

This is a good cake for snacks and lunch boxes.

The raw cake mixture will be thick and pasty — not your normal cake batter.

Serve this cake warm with ice cream and caramel sauce for a delicious dessert.

Use Golden Delicious or Granny Smith apples, which hold their shape, for the best result.

- *Preheat oven to 350°F (180°C)*
- *8-inch (2 L) square cake pan, greased*

2 cups	diced peeled apple (about 2 or 3)	500 mL
1	egg, beaten	1
⅔ cup	granulated sugar	150 mL
½ cup	coarsely chopped pecans	125 mL
¼ cup	vegetable oil	50 mL
1 cup	Robin Hood Whole Wheat Flour	250 mL
1 tsp	baking soda	5 mL
1 tsp	ground cinnamon	5 mL
½ tsp	salt	2 mL
¼ tsp	ground nutmeg	1 mL

1. Beat apple, egg, sugar, pecans and oil thoroughly in a large bowl.
2. Combine flour, baking soda, cinnamon, salt and nutmeg. Add to apple mixture. Stir well to blend. Spread evenly in prepared pan.
3. Bake for 40 to 45 minutes or until toothpick inserted in center comes out clean. Let cool for 10 minutes in pan on rack, then serve warm, or transfer cake to rack to cool completely.

Variations

Replace pecans with walnuts.

Replace whole wheat flour with Robin Hood All-Purpose Flour.

Mix-in-the-Pan Chocolate Cake

This cake is especially suited to kids. They love the easy cleanup as much as the cake.

Makes about 12 servings

Preparation: 15 minutes
Baking: 40 minutes
Freezing: excellent

TIPS

Don't be surprised — there is no egg in this cake. Keep it in mind if you bake for people with egg allergies.

You can mix the cake with a fork right in the pan or in a bowl with a whisk. Either way, no mixer is required.

To pour melted butter easily, put the measured amount in a glass measure and melt it in the microwave. The measure has a spout for easy pouring.

If your frosting recipe makes more than you need, store any extra in the refrigerator for up to 2 weeks. Bring to room temperature before using.

- Preheat oven to 350°F (180°C)
- 8-inch (2 L) square cake pan, ungreased

1½ cups	Robin Hood All-Purpose Flour	375 mL
1 cup	granulated sugar	250 mL
¼ cup	unsweetened cocoa powder, sifted	50 mL
1 tsp	baking powder	5 mL
1 tsp	baking soda	5 mL
½ tsp	salt	2 mL
⅓ cup	butter, melted	75 mL
1 tbsp	vinegar	15 mL
1 cup	warm water	250 mL

1. Combine flour, sugar, cocoa, baking powder, baking soda and salt in pan. Stir well to blend. Make two holes in flour mixture. Pour melted butter into one hole, vinegar into the other. Pour water over top. Mix well with a fork until smooth.

2. Bake for 35 to 40 minutes or until toothpick inserted in center comes out clean. Cool completely in pan on rack.

Variations

Replace warm water with brewed coffee.

Leave cake plain or frost with Cocoa Buttercream Frosting (see recipe, below) or Basic, Coffee or Chocolate Butter Frosting (see recipes, page 216).

Cocoa Buttercream Frosting

- Makes about 3 cups (750 mL) frosting
- Enough to fill and frost a 9-inch (23 cm) 2-layer cake

3 cups	confectioner's (icing) sugar	750 mL
¾ cup	unsweetened cocoa powder	175 mL
⅔ cup	butter, softened	150 mL
5 to 6 tbsp	half-and-half (10%) cream or milk	75 to 90 mL
1½ tsp	vanilla	7 mL

1. Sift icing sugar and cocoa together; set aside. In a large mixer bowl, beat butter on medium speed until smooth. Gradually add cocoa mixture alternately with cream, beating until smooth and creamy. (Add only enough of the cream to make a soft, spreadable consistency.) Beat in vanilla. Gradually add a little more cream if frosting is too stiff or a little more icing sugar if frosting is too soft.

Kaleidoscope Cookies

These colorful cookies are fun to make and attractive to look at — and they taste great, too!

Makes about 2½ dozen cookies

Preparation: 25 minutes
Chilling: 1 hour
Baking: 12 minutes
Freezing: excellent

TIPS

Use bright primary colors for the most impact. For some occasions, pastels may be more appropriate. Let children decide what to use.

This is a good cookie to involve younger children in making, because there is no wrong way to blend the balls of dough. Every cookie will have a different look.

Paste cake-decorating colors are quite strong compared to regular liquid colorings. If using, add 1 drop at a time and work into the dough — a very small amount will give you a vibrant color.

You can prepare a few rolls of dough ahead and refrigerate them to bake at another time.

● *Preheat oven to 350°F (180°C)*
● *Cookie sheet, ungreased*

½ cup	butter, softened	125 mL
½ cup	confectioner's (icing) sugar, sifted	125 mL
1 cup	Robin Hood All-Purpose Flour	250 mL
4	food coloring bottles or tubes — red, blue, green and yellow	4

1. Cream butter and icing sugar in a medium bowl until smooth and creamy. Gradually add flour, mixing until a smooth dough forms.

2. Divide dough into four equal portions. Using a different color for each portion, work in enough food coloring to make a deep color. Work dough with hands to incorporate color thoroughly. Divide each piece of colored dough in half. Shape each into a ball. You'll have eight balls, two of each color.

3. Place two different colored balls side by side on a board, then arrange the remaining balls on top of them, alternating colors and pressing them together. Roll into a 8-inch (20 cm) long log. Chill for 1 hour or until dough is firm enough to slice.

4. Cut log into thin slices, about ¼ inch (0.5 cm) thick, and place slices on cookie sheet, about 1 inch (2.5 cm) apart.

5. Bake for 10 to 12 minutes or until cookies are set and just starting to brown around edges. Cool for 5 minutes on sheet, then transfer to rack and cool completely.

Chocolate Oatmeal Funny Face Cookies

Be sure to have this recipe on hand for rainy days. It will entertain children for hours, and moms and dads will be impressed with the creative results.

<table>
<tr><td colspan="2">Makes about 2 dozen cookies</td></tr>
</table>

Preparation: 20 minutes

Baking: 15 minutes

Freezing: excellent

TIP

Have lots of candies on hand to decorate. Some won't make it to the cookies!

- *Preheat oven to 350°F (180°C)*
- *Cookie sheet, greased*

Cookie

1½ cups	Robin Hood All-Purpose Flour	375 mL
2 tsp	baking soda	10 mL
1 tsp	salt	5 mL
2⅓ cups	Robin Hood Oats	575 mL
1 cup	shortening	250 mL
1½ cups	packed brown sugar	375 mL
2	eggs	2
1 tsp	vanilla	5 mL
1½ cups	semi-sweet chocolate chips	375 mL
1 cup	chopped walnuts	250 mL

Decoration

3	squares (each 1 oz/28 g) unsweetened chocolate, melted	3
2 tbsp	shortening	30 mL
2¼ cups	confectioner's (icing) sugar, sifted	550 mL
⅓ cup	milk	75 mL
	Candies, nuts, gumdrops, licorice, jelly beans, etc.	

1. **Cookie:** Combine flour, baking soda, salt and oats. Stir well to blend. Cream shortening, brown sugar, eggs and vanilla thoroughly. Add dry ingredients. Mix well. Stir in chocolate chips and nuts. Drop dough by ¼ cupfuls (50 mL) about 4 inches (10 cm) apart onto prepared cookie sheet. Flatten with floured hands into 3½-inch (8.5 cm) circles. Bake for 10 to 15 minutes or until golden. Cool for 5 minutes on sheet, then transfer to rack and cool completely.

2. **Decoration:** Beat together chocolate, shortening, sugar and milk to make smooth, spreadable frosting. Spread on cookies and use your favorite colorful candies to make faces or any other decorations you like.

Variation
Replace chips with raisins.

Character Cupcakes

Let your kids shine making yummy face cupcakes.

Makes 2 dozen cupcakes

Decoration time: All day!

Baking: 20 minutes

Freezing: excellent, undecorated

TIPS

Use lemon juice in place of vinegar in batter, if desired.

There's no egg in the recipe — a good choice if there are egg allergies in the family.

- *Preheat oven to 350°F (180°C)*
- *24-cup muffin pan, paper-lined*

Cupcakes

3 cups	Robin Hood All-Purpose Flour or 3⅓ cups (825 mL) Robin Hood Best For Cake & Pastry Flour	750 mL
2 cups	granulated sugar	500 mL
2 tsp	baking soda	10 mL
1 tsp	salt	5 mL
2 cups	water	500 mL
¾ cup	vegetable oil	175 mL
3	squares (each 1 oz/28 g) unsweetened chocolate, melted and cooled	3
2 tsp	vinegar	10 mL
2 tsp	vanilla	10 mL

Decoration

2 cups	chocolate or vanilla frosting	500 mL
	Candies, nuts, gumdrops, licorice, jelly beans, marshmallows, etc.	

1. **Cupcakes:** Combine flour, sugar, baking soda and salt in large bowl. Add water, oil, melted chocolate, vinegar and vanilla. Beat on medium speed of electric mixer for 30 seconds or with wooden spoon for 1 minute or just until smooth. Spoon batter into muffin cups. Bake for 15 to 20 minutes or until toothpick inserted in center comes out clean. Remove from pan. Cool completely.

2. **Decoration:** Spread about 1½ tbsp (22 mL) of the frosting on top of each cupcake. Use your favorite colorful candies and your creativity to make characters.

Mushroom, Asparagus and Pepper Quiche

Savories

Mushroom, Asparagus and Pepper Quiche

Here's a meatless meal everyone's sure to enjoy. Light but filling, it makes a delicious brunch, lunch or dinner.

Makes about 6 servings

Preparation: 15 minutes

Cooking: 5 minutes

Baking: 45 minutes

Freezing: not recommended

TIPS

Treat this as a vegetable side dish and serve with pork chops, chicken or ham. For a vegetarian meal, add soup, salad and rolls.

This quiche is a delicious way to get children to enjoy their vegetables.

- *Preheat oven to 425°F (220°C)*
- *9-inch (23 cm) pie plate*

Crust

	Pastry for 9-inch (23 cm) single-crust pie (see recipes, pages 247 to 249)	

Filling

1 tbsp	Dijon mustard	15 mL
1 tbsp	vegetable oil	15 mL
1	small onion, chopped	1
1 lb	fresh asparagus, trimmed and coarsely chopped	500 g
1 1/2 cups	sliced mushrooms	375 mL
Half	large sweet red pepper, cut in strips	Half
1 1/2 cups	shredded Swiss cheese	375 mL
3	eggs	3
1 cup	milk	250 mL
3 tbsp	finely chopped fresh dill (or 1 tsp/5 mL dried dillweed)	45 mL
1/2 tsp	salt	2 mL
1/4 tsp	black pepper	1 mL

1. **Crust:** Prepare pastry for unbaked pie shell. Roll out and fit into pie plate.
2. **Filling:** Spread mustard evenly over pastry. Heat oil in a large skillet over medium-high heat. Sauté onion, asparagus, mushrooms and red pepper until pepper is tender-crisp, about 5 minutes. Remove from heat. Spread evenly in pie shell. Sprinkle cheese over top.
3. Beat eggs, milk, dill, salt and pepper in a bowl until blended. Pour over vegetable mixture.
4. Bake for 10 minutes, then reduce heat to 350°F (180°C) and bake for 30 to 35 minutes longer or until filling is set and pastry is golden. Cool for 10 minutes, then slice and serve warm.

Variations

Replace asparagus with broccoli or green beans.

Omit red pepper; reduce asparagus to 12 oz (375 g) and add 1 cup (250 mL) diced cooked ham, smoked chicken, shrimp or salmon.

Chunky Ham and Vegetable Quiche

This delicious quiche is also good served cold. Chilled leftovers make wonderful picnic fare.

Makes about 6 servings

Preparation: 25 minutes

Cooking: 5 minutes

Baking: 45 minutes

Freezing: not recommended

TIPS

Bake pies on the bottom oven rack to ensure that the bottom crust browns before the filling soaks through.

Before baking, brush pastry with a lightly beaten egg white. This helps prevent a soggy crust.

For added flavor, spread a little Dijon mustard on the pastry shell.

Sauté vegetables in a hot pan to seal in the moisture and flavour. If the heat is too low, moisture comes out of the vegetables and they simmer, losing flavor.

- *Preheat oven to 425°F (220°C)*
- *10-inch (25 cm) pie plate or quiche pan*

Crust

Pastry for 9-inch (23 cm) single-crust pie (see recipes, pages 247 to 249)

Filling

2 tbsp	vegetable oil	30 mL
2 cups	sliced mushrooms	500 mL
¾ cup	sliced sweet red pepper (1 small)	175 mL
¾ cup	sliced sweet green pepper (1 small)	175 mL
½ cup	chopped onion	125 mL
1 cup	diced ham	250 mL
3	eggs	3
1¼ cups	half-and-half (10%) cream	300 mL
⅓ cup	grated Parmesan cheese	75 mL
1 tsp	dried basil leaves	5 mL
	Salt and pepper to taste	

1. **Crust:** Prepare pastry for unbaked pie shell. Roll out and fit into pie plate.
2. **Filling:** Heat oil in a large skillet over medium-high heat. Sauté mushrooms, peppers and onions until peppers are tender-crisp, about 5 minutes. Stir in ham. Spread mixture evenly over pastry.
3. Beat eggs, cream, Parmesan cheese, basil, salt and pepper in a bowl until blended. Pour over ham mixture.
4. Bake for 10 minutes, then reduce heat to 350°F (180°C) and bake for 30 to 35 minutes longer or just until filling is set and pastry is golden. Cool for 10 minutes, then slice and serve warm.

Variation

Replace ham with diced cooked chicken or eight slices bacon, cooked and diced.

Chicken Pot Pie

It's worth having leftover chicken or turkey so you can make this old-fashioned favorite. We've lightened it up by using only a top crust and lots of filling.

Makes about 8 servings

Preparation: 30 minutes

Baking: 30 minutes

Freezing: excellent

TIPS

Add a bit of sage or thyme to the pastry when you are using it with poultry.

Although this is only a single-crust pie, you'll need to make a double-crust recipe to fit the larger surface of the shallow casserole dish.

If you don't have leftover chicken, poach six to eight boneless skinless chicken breasts for this recipe.

To thaw frozen peas quickly, put them in a colander and run hot water over them.

- Preheat oven to 425°F (220°C)
- 12-cup (3 L) shallow casserole or baking dish, greased

Crust

	Pastry for 9-inch (23 cm) double-crust pie (see recipes, pages 247 to 249)	

Filling

2 cups	quartered potatoes (3 medium)	500 mL
1½ cups	chopped peeled carrot	375 mL
1 tbsp	butter	15 mL
2 cups	sliced mushrooms	500 mL
1 cup	chopped onion	250 mL
1	can (10 oz/284 mL) condensed cream of mushroom soup	1
2 tbsp	Robin Hood All-Purpose Flour	30 mL
1 tsp	dried thyme leaves	5 mL
¾ tsp	dry mustard	3 mL
½ tsp	dried oregano leaves	2 mL
4 cups	chopped cooked chicken	1 L
1 cup	frozen green peas, thawed	250 mL

Glaze, optional

1	egg yolk	1
1 tbsp	milk	15 mL

1. **Crust:** Prepare pastry for double-crust pie. Set aside.
2. **Filling:** Cook potatoes and carrots in boiling salted water just until tender, about 15 minutes. Drain, reserving ¾ cup (175 mL) cooking liquid for the sauce. Meanwhile, heat butter in a large skillet over medium-high heat; sauté mushrooms and onion just until tender.
3. Combine soup, flour, thyme, mustard and oregano and reserved vegetable liquid, stirring until smooth. Stir in chicken, mushroom mixture, potatoes, carrots and peas. Pour into prepared casserole.
4. Roll out pastry to fit top of casserole. Place over filling. Flute edges. Cut slits in the center to allow steam to escape.
5. **Glaze (optional):** Beat egg yolk and milk until blended. Brush over pastry.
6. Bake for 30 minutes or until crust is golden and filling is hot.

Variations

Use leftover holiday turkey to make a turkey pot pie.

If you prefer, divide the mixture between two casseroles (each 6 cups/1.5 L) and bake as per recipe. Or make six to eight individual pot pies. Decrease baking time by about 5 minutes.

Deep-Dish Lamb Pot Pie

A hearty lamb stew topped with a unique biscuitlike pastry makes a delicious, warming winter meal. This pie is also delicious made with veal, pork or beef shoulder.

Makes about 6 servings

Preparation: 30 minutes
Cooking: about 2 hours
Freezing: excellent

TIPS

The flavor of stews is usually better the next day, so prepare filling ahead and chill overnight.

Use only the white and very pale green parts of leeks. The dark green portion is tough and woody.

Leeks are usually quite gritty between the layers and need to be cleaned thoroughly. Cut in half lengthwise and wash well, separating the layers. Pat dry before slicing.

Pot pies are meals in themselves since the meat and vegetables are all in the same dish. Add a green vegetable or salad and bread to complete the meal.

- *Preheat oven to 375°F (190°C)*
- *8-cup (2 L) deep casserole*

Stew

2 tbsp	vegetable oil	30 mL
1½ lbs	boneless lamb shoulder, trimmed and cut in ¾-inch (2 cm) cubes	750 g
4	medium carrots, peeled and cut in ¼-inch (0.5 cm) slices	4
3	medium leeks (white and light green parts only) cleaned and cut in ¼-inch (0.5 cm) slices	3
2 tbsp	Robin Hood All-Purpose Flour	30 mL
2 cups	chicken stock	500 mL
3	potatoes, peeled and cut in ½-inch (1 cm) cubes	3
2	bay leaves	2
1½ tsp	salt	7 mL
1 tsp	dried rosemary	5 mL
¼ tsp	black pepper	1 mL

Pastry

1 cup	Robin Hood All-Purpose Flour	250 mL
½ tsp	each baking soda and salt	2 mL
3 tbsp	butter	45 mL
1	egg yolk	1
⅓ cup	buttermilk	75 mL

1. **Stew:** Heat oil in a large saucepan over medium-high heat. Add lamb. Cook, stirring, until well browned, about 10 minutes. Add carrots and leeks. Cook, stirring, until leeks start to brown, about 5 minutes. Sprinkle with flour and toss to coat. Stir in stock, potatoes, bay leaves, salt, rosemary and pepper. Bring to a boil, then reduce heat to low, cover and simmer, stirring occasionally, for 1½ hours or until meat is tender. Skim foam from surface, if necessary. Remove bay leaves. Transfer mixture to casserole or chill overnight (see Tips, left).

2. **Pastry:** Combine flour, baking soda and salt in a mixing bowl. Using two knives, a pastry blender or your fingers, cut in butter until mixture resembles coarse crumbs. Beat egg yolk and buttermilk together. Add to flour mixture. Toss with a fork until mixture comes together. Turn out on a lightly floured surface, knead briefly, then pat or roll out dough to fit top of casserole. Pastry should be about ½ inch (1 cm) thick.

3. **Assembly and baking:** Pour hot stew into casserole. Place pastry over top. Press to seal against inside rim of casserole. Bake for 30 to 35 minutes or until pastry is golden.

Multilayered Dinner

The leftovers, served cold, are almost as delicious as this pie when it is hot out of the oven.

TIPS

Prepare the parts the day before for easy assembly the next day.

Increase the vegetable layers and omit the ham for a meatless variation.

A quiche pan with straight sides produces an attractive result, but a pie plate works well, too.

- *Preheat oven to 400°F (200°C)*
- *9-inch (23 cm) deep-dish pie plate or quiche pan*

Crust

	Pastry for 9-inch (23 cm) double-crust pie (see recipes, pages 247 to 249)	

Filling

1	package (10 oz/300 g) frozen chopped broccoli, thawed	1
½ cup	chopped green onion	125 mL
3 tbsp	chopped fresh basil	45 mL
8 oz	sliced ham	250 g
8 oz	sliced Cheddar cheese	250 g
1	sweet red pepper, cut in strips	1
4	eggs, beaten	4
	Salt and black pepper to taste	

1. **Crust:** Prepare pastry for double-crust pie. Roll out bottom crust and fit into pan.
2. **Filling:** Combine broccoli, onion and basil. Lay ham slices over pastry. Cover with a layer of cheese, broccoli mixture, then the red pepper strips. Season with salt and pepper to taste.
3. Reserve small amount of egg (about 1 tbsp/15 mL) to brush over top crust. Slowly pour remaining egg evenly into pie. Roll out top crust and arrange over filling. Seal and flute edges. Brush with reserved egg. Cut slits in center of top crust to allow steam to escape.
4. Bake for 35 to 45 minutes or until pastry is golden.

Variations

Use any cheese or meat, keeping in mind the colors of the layers for an attractive pie, as well as the flavor combinations.

Replace frozen broccoli with 2 cups (500 mL) cooked and chopped fresh broccoli.

Tasty Traditional Tourtière

Tourtière, a French-Canadian meat pie traditionally associated with the holiday season, is so appetizing it has traveled well beyond the Quebec border. It freezes well, so keep a few in your freezer.

Makes about 6 servings

Preparation: 25 minutes
Cooking: 15 minutes
Baking: 30 minutes
Freezing: excellent

TIPS

Everyone who makes tourtière has his or her individual style. The combination of meat, spices and thickener varies from cook to cook. Try this recipe to start, then add your own touches, such as shredded carrot, tomatoes or a hint of cinnamon instead of cloves.

If you're making several pies at one time, make the filling the day before for convenience.

Serve tourtière with red or green chowchow (similar to chili sauce) or a good chutney.

- Preheat oven to 400°F (200°C)
- 9-inch (23 cm) pie plate

Pastry

Pastry for 9-inch (23 cm) double-crust pie (see recipes, pages 247 to 249)

Filling

1 lb	lean ground pork	500 g
8 oz	ground veal	250 g
1	onion, chopped	1
1	potato, grated	1
1/4 cup	water	50 mL
1 tbsp	beef bouillon concentrate	15 mL
1/2 tsp	salt	2 mL
1/4 tsp	ground savory or thyme	1 mL
1/4 tsp	black pepper	1 mL
1/4 tsp	ground cloves	1 mL

1. **Pastry:** Prepare pastry for double-crust pie. Set aside.
2. **Filling:** Combine pork, veal, onion, potato, water, bouillon concentrate, salt, savory and pepper in a large saucepan. Cook over medium heat, stirring constantly, until meat is no longer pink and liquid is absorbed, about 15 minutes. Stir in cloves. Cool slightly.
3. Roll out half of the pastry and fit into pie plate. Fill with meat mixture. Roll out remaining pastry and arrange over filling. Seal and flute edges. Slash center of top crust to allow steam to escape.
4. Bake on bottom oven rack for 25 to 30 minutes or until pastry is golden.

Variations

Use ground turkey or chicken in place of the veal.

Omit grated potato. Stir 3/4 cup (175 mL) mashed potato into the cooked meat mixture.

Tuna Soufflé

Light as a feather, this delicious soufflé makes a fabulous dinner. Serve with fresh asparagus and sliced tomatoes.

Makes about 6 servings

Preparation: 20 minutes

Cooking: 10 minutes

Baking: 55 minutes

Freezing: not recommended

TIPS

When beating egg whites, be sure the bowl and beaters are clean. Any trace of oil will prevent the egg whites from stiffening.

Beat egg whites just until they form stiff peaks but are still moist. If they become dry, they are difficult to fold into other mixtures.

Soufflés must be served as soon as they come out of the oven, as they immediately begin to collapse. Keep this in mind when you're planning your timetable.

As a safeguard, wrap a greased 3-inch (7.5 cm) foil collar around the top of your soufflé dish to support the soufflé as it rises above the rim of the dish.

- *Preheat oven to 375°F (190°C)*
- *7-inch (18 cm) soufflé dish, greased*

3 tbsp	butter	45 mL
1/3 cup	finely chopped onion	75 mL
1/4 cup	Robin Hood All-Purpose Flour	50 mL
1 cup	milk	250 mL
6	eggs, separated	6
2	cans (each 6 oz/170 g) tuna, drained and flaked	2
2 tbsp	lemon juice	30 mL
1 tbsp	tomato paste	15 mL
1 tsp	dried oregano leaves	5 mL
1/2 tsp	salt	2 mL

1. Melt butter in a medium saucepan over medium heat. Add onion and cook, stirring, until softened, about 3 minutes. Add flour and mix well. Gradually add milk, stirring until smooth. Cook, stirring constantly, until mixture comes to a boil and thickens. Remove from heat. Cool slightly, about 10 minutes. Add egg yolks, one at a time, beating well after each addition. Stir in tuna, lemon juice, tomato paste, oregano and salt. Mix well.

2. Beat egg whites until stiff but moist peaks form. Fold into tuna mixture. Pour into prepared dish.

3. Bake for 50 to 55 minutes or until puffed, set and golden. Serve immediately.

Variations

Serve the soufflé with hollandaise sauce or a creamy mushroom sauce.

Replace tomato paste with Dijon mustard.

Almond Cheese Gougère Wreath

Serve this tasty cheese-flavored puff as an appetizer.

TIPS

If they are available, use sliced almonds with the skins on to add color to the top.

Always use freshly ground pepper in savory dishes. You'll be amazed at the difference in flavor compared to the preground variety.

Check your oven temperature with an accurate thermometer. It's essential that these start at a high temperature to make them puff.

Always use large eggs when baking.

- Preheat oven to 450°F (230°C)
- Baking sheet, greased

1 cup	water	250 mL
1/2 cup	butter	125 mL
1/4 tsp	salt	1 mL
1/4 tsp	freshly ground black pepper	1 mL
1 cup	Robin Hood All-Purpose Flour	250 mL
4	eggs	4
1 1/2 cups	shredded Gruyère cheese	375 mL
1/3 cup	sliced almonds	75 mL

1. Combine water, butter, salt and pepper in a heavy saucepan. Bring to a boil over high heat. Remove from heat. Add flour all at once. Beat vigorously with a wooden spoon until mixture is smooth and pulls away from the side of the pan to form a ball. Return to low heat and beat for 1 minute longer. Remove from heat and let cool for 2 minutes.

2. Add eggs, one at a time, beating vigorously after each addition until smooth. Stir in 1 1/4 cups (300 mL) of the cheese. Drop batter by heaping spoonfuls (8 large or 12 smaller) onto prepared baking sheet to form a circle about 8 inches (20 cm) in diameter. (The edges of the drops should touch). Sprinkle remaining cheese and almonds over top.

3. Bake for 10 minutes, then reduce heat to 350°F (180°C) and bake for 30 to 40 minutes longer or until firm and golden brown. Remove from oven and immediately poke holes all around ring with a fork or the tip of a sharp knife to let steam escape. Cool for 10 minutes before serving.

Variation
Replace Gruyère with Swiss cheese.

Pizza in a Pan

This tasty dish has all the flavors of pizza without the bread crust.

TIPS

You can vary this versatile dish to suit your family's tastes.

Add crusty rolls for lunch and a green salad for dinner.

If your pasta sauce has lots of flavor, you may not need more seasoning, but if it doesn't you can always add herbs, such as oregano, garlic, basil and hot peppers, if you wish.

Use a pasta sauce that is thick and chunky. If it is on the thin side, decrease the amount slightly.

- Preheat oven to 400°F (200°C)
- 13- by 9-inch (3.5 L) baking dish, greased

1 lb	Italian sausage, mild or hot	500 g
1	onion, chopped	1
¾ cup	chopped sweet green pepper	175 mL
8 oz	fresh mushrooms, sliced	250 g
1½ cups	seasoned tomato sauce	375 mL
¾ cup	sliced pitted black olives	175 mL
8	slices mozzarella cheese	8
2	eggs	2
1 cup	milk	250 mL
1 cup	Robin Hood All-Purpose Flour	250 mL
1 tbsp	vegetable oil	15 mL
¼ tsp	salt	1 mL
⅓ cup	grated Parmesan cheese	75 mL

1. Remove casings from sausage. Crumble meat into a large skillet and cook over medium-high heat for 3 minutes. Add onion, green pepper and mushrooms. Continue cooking, stirring occasionally, for 10 minutes or until vegetables are tender and sausage is browned. Drain off fat. Stir in tomato sauce and olives. Spread evenly in prepared pan. Arrange cheese slices over top.

2. Combine eggs, milk, flour, oil and salt in a blender and process until smooth. (You can also do this in a bowl, with a whisk.) Pour evenly over cheese slices. Sprinkle with Parmesan cheese.

3. Bake for 25 to 30 minutes or until top is golden. Let cool for 10 minutes, then cut into squares and serve warm.

Variations

Replace sausage with ground beef, pork or chicken.

For convenience, replace fresh mushrooms with a can of sliced mushrooms, well drained.

Pizza Quiche Tidbits

These bite-size squares offer the best of both quiche and pizza: a flaky bottom and pizza toppings.

Makes about 5 dozen squares

Preparation: 20 minutes

Baking: 25 minutes

Freezing: excellent

TIPS

For easy entertaining, make these ahead, then reheat when ready to serve.

Prepared pasta sauce varies considerably. Choose one that is thick and flavourful.

Use a zesty pasta sauce that contains hot peppers if your guests like spicy foods.

Don't be surprised — these tidbits puff in the oven, then deflate on standing.

- Preheat oven to 425°F (220°C)
- 9-inch (2.5 L) square baking pan, greased

3	eggs	3
¾ cup	milk	175 mL
⅔ cup	Robin Hood All-Purpose Flour	150 mL
2 tbsp	finely chopped onion	30 mL
1 tbsp	vegetable oil	15 mL
½ cup	thick pasta sauce	125 mL
1 tsp	dried oregano leaves	5 mL
1 tsp	dried basil leaves	5 mL
½ cup	diced pepperoni	125 mL
½ cup	diced sweet green pepper	125 mL
1 cup	shredded mozzarella cheese	250 mL

1. Beat eggs, milk and flour until smooth. Stir in onion and oil. Pour into prepared pan.
2. Combine pasta sauce, oregano and basil. Pour over egg mixture to produce a marbled effect. Sprinkle pepperoni, green pepper, then cheese over top.
3. Bake for 25 minutes or until puffed and golden. Cool for 5 minutes, then cut into small squares. Serve warm.

Variations

Vary the toppings as you would for pizza: replace pepperoni with diced ham or chicken or add olives and sun-dried tomatoes. You can even combine Cheddar and mozzarella cheeses — the possibilities are endless.

Double-Crust Chicken and Cheese Pizza Sandwich

This tasty pizza is also easy to eat, which makes it ideal for those days when everyone is on the run.

Makes about 8 servings

Preparation: 35 minutes

Baking: 1 hour

Freezing: excellent

TIPS

For added fiber, replace half of the all-purpose flour with Robin Hood Whole Wheat Flour.

Prepare a few extra crusts. They will keep for up to 2 days in the refrigerator and freeze well, too.

Adjust the filling to suit your taste or to use up ingredients on hand — almost any kind of cheese will do. For a meatless version, you can replace the meat with 2 cups (500 mL) diced roasted vegetables.

For an attractive finish, sprinkle sesame seeds over the glaze before baking.

To prevent the dough from sticking to your hands, oil your fingers lightly before pressing it into the pan.

- Preheat oven to 400°F (200°C)
- Pizza pan or baking sheet, greased

Pizza Crust

2½ to 3 cups	Robin Hood All-Purpose Flour	625 to 750 mL
2¼ tsp	quick-rise yeast (1 envelope, ¼ oz/8 g)	11 mL
¾ tsp	salt	3 mL
1 cup	water	250 mL
2 tbsp	olive oil	30 mL

Filling

2	eggs, beaten	2
2 cups	shredded Gouda cheese	500 mL
2 cups	diced cooked chicken	500 mL
½ cup	chopped sweet green pepper	125 mL
¼ cup	chopped fresh basil	50 mL
	Hot sauce and black pepper to taste	

Glaze

1	egg	1
1 tbsp	milk	15 mL

1. **Pizza Crust:** Combine 2 cups (500 mL) of the flour, yeast and salt in a large bowl. Heat water and oil together until hot (125°F/50°C). Stir into flour mixture for about 2 minutes. Add enough remaining flour to make a soft dough. Turn out onto a lightly floured surface and knead for about 4 minutes, adding more flour as needed to make the dough smooth and elastic. Shape into a ball; cover and let rest for 10 minutes.

2. **Filling:** Combine eggs, cheese, chicken, green pepper, basil, hot pepper sauce and black pepper. Mix well.

3. Divide dough in half. Roll or press one half into a 12-inch (30 cm) circle on pan. Spread filling evenly over dough, leaving a narrow border. Roll or stretch remaining dough to same size. Place over filling. Seal and flute edges. Prick top with fork. Cover loosely with foil. Bake for 45 minutes. Remove foil.

4. **Glaze:** Beat egg and milk until blended. Brush over crust. Bake, uncovered, for 10 to 15 minutes longer or until crust is golden brown. Let stand for 10 minutes, then cut into wedges.

Variations

Replace chicken with roasted vegetables, ham, turkey or smoked chicken.

Quick-Fix Pizzas

Once you see how easy it is to make these delicious treats, you'll never order pizza again.

Makes one 14-inch (35 cm) thick-crust pizza (Two 12-inch (30 cm) thin-crust pizzas, four 8-inch (20 cm) individual pizzas or twenty 3-inch (7.5 cm) appetizer pizzas)

Preparation: 20 minutes

Rising: 1 hour

Baking: 20 minutes

Freezing: excellent

TIPS

Try the toppings called for the first time you make these pizzas, then use your favorites or be creative next time.

Baking times vary with the size of the pizza. The smaller the pizza, the less time it takes to bake; the larger, the longer. Watch carefully — the crust should be crisp and golden and the filling hot.

Letting the dough rise until it doubles in bulk produces a more "bready" crust.

Dusting pans with cornmeal gives a nice texture to the crust and prevents it from sticking. If you don't have cornmeal, parchment paper also works well.

- *Preheat oven to 400°F (200°C)*
- *Two pizza pans or baking sheets, greased and sprinkled with cornmeal*

Pizza Crust

1	batch Pizza Crust (see recipe, page 349)	1

Toppings
Zucchini Pesto Pizza

3 tbsp	basil pesto	45 mL
2	medium zucchini, thinly sliced and grilled	2
1	large sweet red pepper, roasted and sliced	1
1 tbsp	olive oil	15 mL
1/2 cup	feta cheese, crumbled	125 mL

Greek Pizza

1 tbsp	olive oil	15 mL
Half	red onion, sliced	Half
2	cloves garlic, minced	2
1 2/3 cups	diced fresh tomatoes	400 mL
1/2 cup	feta cheese, crumbled	125 mL
1/3 cup	sliced black olives, optional	75 mL
1/4 cup	chopped fresh basil leaves	50 mL

1. **Pizza Crust:** Prepare dough for pizza crust as per Step 1, page 349.
2. Cover with plastic wrap and let rise in a warm place for 30 to 60 minutes or until doubled in bulk. Punch dough down and turn out onto a lightly floured surface. Divide in half to prepare the two suggested pizzas, or in increments to suit size of pizza you want. Stretch or roll out dough. Place on pans.

Toppings

Zucchini Pesto Pizza: Spread pesto over dough. Scatter zucchini and red pepper over top. Drizzle with olive oil. Bake for 15 minutes. Sprinkle cheese over top and bake for 5 minutes longer or until crust is golden on the bottom.

Greek Pizza: Heat oil in skillet over medium heat. Add onion and garlic and cook, stirring, until tender, about 5 minutes. Stir in tomatoes, feta cheese, olives and basil. Spread over crust. Bake for 20 minutes or until crust is golden on the bottom.

Variations

The possibilities are endless. Vary the size of the crust and topping to suit the occasion and your tastes.

Supply each of your guests with an individual-size crust, set out a variety of toppings and let people create their own pizza.

Basic Crêpe Batter

This crêpe batter is versatile and can be used in both sweet and savory dishes.

Makes about eighteen 6-inch (15 cm) crêpes

Preparation: 10 minutes

Chilling: 1 hour or overnight

Cooking: about 3 minutes per crêpe

Freezing: excellent

TIPS

Make these crêpes in a blender, a mixer or by hand.

Prepare a batch of crêpes to have on hand. Cool completely, then stack between squares of waxed paper and refrigerate for up to 2 days or freeze for up to 3 months.

Don't stack warm crêpes or they'll stick together. To cool, turn out onto a tea towel in a single layer.

There are many ways to enjoy crêpes. Fill them (see recipes, pages 262, 264, 265 and 353), brush with butter and sugar and roll up, spread with jam and fold into quarters, or fold and serve with or in a warm sauce.

- *Crêpe pan or nonstick skillet, lightly greased*

3	eggs	3
1¼ cups	milk	300 mL
¾ cup	Robin Hood All-Purpose Flour	175 mL
2 tbsp	butter, melted	30 mL
1 tbsp	granulated sugar	15 mL
¼ tsp	salt	1 mL

Blender Method

1. Combine eggs, milk, flour, butter, sugar and salt in blender container. Blend until smooth, about 1 minute.

2. Cover batter and chill for at least 1 hour or overnight.

Mixer or Whisk Method

1. Beat eggs until light. Gradually add milk and flour alternately, making three dry and two liquid additions, beating until smooth. Beat in butter, sugar and salt, mixing until smooth.

2. Cover batter and chill for at least 1 hour or overnight.

3. **To cook:** Heat prepared pan over medium-high heat. Remove from heat; immediately pour heaping 2 tbsp (30 mL) of batter into hot pan. Lift and tilt pan to cover bottom with a thin layer of batter. Return pan to heat. Cook until bottom is lightly browned, 1 to 2 minutes. Turn crêpe over and brown other side. Repeat with remaining batter. Enjoy warm or let cool in a single layer on a tea towel to use in other recipes.

Chicken and Mushroom Crêpes

Because half of the preparation can be done ahead, crêpes make a particularly easy yet elegant dinner. Keep a stack of crêpes in the freezer to make entertaining easy anytime.

Makes about 12 crêpes

Preparation: 40 minutes
Baking: 25 minutes
Freezing:
not recommended

TIPS

Don't be afraid of crêpes. They look difficult but are really just pancakes made thinner.

You can buy special crêpe pans, but a small nonstick skillet works very well. A lightweight one works best because you have to pick it up and turn it so the batter coats the bottom evenly.

The batter recipe makes 18 crêpes. Freeze the extra for another use.

- Preheat oven to 350°F (180°C)
- Baking dish, buttered

Crêpes

1	batch Basic Crêpe Batter (see recipe, page 352)	1

Filling

3 tbsp	vegetable oil	45 mL
1	large onion, chopped	1
3 cups	sliced fresh mushrooms	750 mL
1½ cups	sliced celery	375 mL
2½ cups	diced cooked chicken	625 mL

Sauce

⅓ cup	butter	75 mL
⅓ cup	Robin Hood All-Purpose Flour	75 mL
2½ cups	milk	625 mL
2 tsp	Worcestershire sauce	10 mL
2 tbsp	finely chopped fresh parsley	30 mL
1 tsp	dried oregano or basil leaves	5 mL
1 tsp	salt	5 mL
¼ tsp	black pepper	1 mL

1. **Crêpes:** Prepare crêpes; set aside.
2. **Filling:** Heat oil in a large nonstick skillet over medium-high heat. Sauté onion, mushrooms and celery until celery is softened, about 5 minutes. Add chicken and stir until heated through. Keep warm.
3. **Sauce:** Melt butter in a medium saucepan. Add flour, stirring until smooth. Gradually add milk and Worcestershire sauce. Cook over medium heat, stirring constantly, just until mixture comes to a boil and thickens, about 5 minutes. Remove from heat. Stir in parsley, oregano, salt and pepper. Mix half of the sauce with filling; reserve remainder for topping.
4. **Assembly:** Fill crêpes with chicken filling, dividing evenly. Place, seam-side down, in a single layer in prepared baking dish. Cover with remaining sauce.
5. Bake for 20 to 25 minutes or until heated through.

Variations

Add 1 cup (250 mL) shredded Swiss cheese to the sauce.

Substitute cooked turkey or ham for the chicken.

Sesame Cheese Thins

These crispy wafers pack a whopping cheese flavor and make a delicious appetizer or snack.

Makes about 7 dozen thins

Preparation: 15 minutes

Chilling: 2 hours or overnight

Baking: 10 minutes

Freezing: excellent

TIPS

Prepare a few rolls of dough and keep them on hand in the refrigerator. You can quickly bake some thins and have a great appetizer to serve before dinner.

Use an old (sharp) cheese for the best flavor. Five- or six-year-old Cheddars are particularly good in this recipe.

For variety, use black sesame seeds instead of white, or a mixture of the two. Black sesame seeds are available in Asian grocery stores.

For a zestier result, add 1/2 tsp (2 mL) chili powder along with the paprika.

To store, let wafers cool completely and keep in airtight containers.

- *Preheat oven to 425°F (220°C)*
- *Baking sheet, ungreased*

1/4 cup	butter, softened	50 mL
2 cups	shredded old Cheddar cheese	500 mL
2/3 cup	Robin Hood All-Purpose Flour	150 mL
1/2 tsp	baking powder	2 mL
1/2 tsp	paprika	2 mL
1/4 tsp	salt	1 mL
2 dashes	hot pepper sauce	2 dashes
3 tbsp	sesame seeds	45 mL

1. Cream butter and cheese in a large bowl until smooth and creamy. Combine flour, baking powder, paprika and salt. Add to creamed mixture along with hot pepper sauce. Using two knives, a pastry blender or your fingers, blend mixture until it resembles coarse crumbs. Turn out onto a lightly floured board and knead lightly to form a smooth dough.

2. Shape dough into a log about 9 inches (23 cm) long and 1 inch (2.5 cm) in diameter. Roll in sesame seeds, pressing seeds firmly into dough. Wrap in waxed paper and refrigerate until firm, 2 hours or overnight.

3. Cut dough into 1/8-inch (3 mm) thick slices. Arrange on baking sheet. Bake for 8 to 10 minutes or until edges are lightly browned. Serve warm or at room temperature.

Sausage Rolls

Although sausage rolls are widely available in the frozen foods section of grocery stores, nothing can match the great flavor of homemade.

Makes about 30 sausage rolls

Preparation: 25 minutes

Cooking: 5 minutes

Baking: 20 minutes

Freezing: excellent

TIPS

The shredded Cheddar cheese adds flavor and eye appeal to the rolls, but you can make them plain, too.

Add dried herbs, such as basil and oregano to the pastry.

Making your own sausage rolls can be almost as convenient as buying them since they can be prepared ahead and frozen. Thaw, then warm to serve.

For a better seal, moisten the corners of the pastry square with water before pressing together.

- *Preheat oven to 450°F (230°C)*
- *Baking sheet, ungreased*

1 lb	pork or beef breakfast sausages	500 g
	Pastry for 9-inch (23 cm) double-crust pie (see recipes, pages 247 to 249)	
½ cup	shredded Cheddar cheese	125 mL
	Mustard	

1. Parboil sausages in boiling water for 5 minutes. Drain and set aside to cool. Cut in half crosswise.

2. Prepare pastry as directed in recipe, adding cheese to dry ingredients.

3. Roll out pastry, one half at a time, on lightly floured surface to ⅛ inch (3 mm) thickness. Cut into 2¼-inch (5.5 cm) squares. Spread a little mustard diagonally from corner to corner of the square. Place sausage half in the center of the square to cover part of the mustard. Fold the two corners on the other diagonal over to meet each other and seal. Place on baking sheet.

4. Bake for 15 to 20 minutes or until pastry is golden. Serve warm.

Variation
Use cocktail wieners for a change.

Mushroom Turnovers

These bite-size turnovers can be made ahead for easy entertaining. They are a good addition to cocktail party platters.

Makes about 30 turnovers

Preparation: 30 minutes

Cooking: about 10 minutes

Baking: 15 minutes

Freezing: excellent

TIPS

Use this cream cheese pastry for savory turnovers and tarts.

These turnovers can be frozen baked or unbaked. Choose the method that fits your schedule — both work well. To freeze baked turnovers, cool completely, wrap well with plastic wrap and freeze for up to 1 month. Reheat from frozen in a 300°F (150°C) oven for 10 to 15 minutes. To freeze unbaked turnovers, prepare up to and including Step 3. Freeze until firm in single layer on tray lined with plastic wrap, then transfer to airtight containers and freeze for up to 1 month. Bake at 400°F (200°C) for 15 to 18 minutes.

Line baking sheet with parchment paper for easy cleanup.

- Preheat oven to 400°F (200°C)
- Baking sheet, ungreased
- 3-inch (7.5 cm) round cookie or biscuit cutter, preferably fluted

Pastry

½ cup	butter, softened	125 mL
4 oz	cream cheese, softened	125 g
1½ cups	Robin Hood All-Purpose Flour	375 mL
½ tsp	salt	2 mL

Filling

2 tbsp	butter	30 mL
8 oz	fresh mushrooms, finely chopped	250 g
⅓ cup	finely chopped onion	75 mL
1 tbsp	Robin Hood All-Purpose Flour	15 mL
1	clove garlic, chopped	1
¼ tsp	each salt and black pepper	1 mL
¼ cup	sour cream	50 mL

Glaze

1	egg yolk	1
1 tbsp	water	15 mL

1. **Pastry:** Cream butter and cream cheese in a bowl until smoothly blended. Add flour and salt, mixing to form a stiff dough. Divide in half. Wrap and chill while preparing filling.

2. **Filling:** Heat butter in a large skillet over medium-high heat; sauté mushrooms and onion until mushrooms lose their liquid, about 5 minutes. Stir in flour. Add garlic, salt and pepper. Cook, stirring, until mixture is dry, about 2 minutes. Remove from heat. Stir in sour cream. Set aside to cool.

3. Working with half of the pastry at a time, roll out thinly, to scant ⅛ inch (3 mm) thickness. Cut out circles with cutter. Place a rounded teaspoonful (5 mL) of filling in the center of each pastry round. Fold in half to form a semi-circle. Press edges to seal. Place on baking sheet.

4. **Glaze:** Combine egg yolk and water to blend. Brush over tops.

5. Bake for 12 to 15 minutes or until golden. Serve warm, or cool completely and freeze (see Tips, left).

Variations

Use a mixture of white mushrooms and more-exotic varieties, such as shiitake, oyster and cremini for superb flavor.

Add 1 tbsp (15 mL) finely chopped chives to the pastry.

*Empire Cookies and
Swedish Butter Balls*

Holiday Baking

Empire Cookies

A long-time favorite cookie that's pretty for the holidays.

Makes about 3½ dozen cookies

Preparation: 30 minutes

Baking: 9 minutes

Freezing: excellent

TIP

A floured pastry cloth and rolling pin cover will make rolling out dough easy.

- *Preheat oven to 350°F (180°C)*
- *Cookie sheet, greased*

Cookie

¾ cup	shortening	175 mL
1 cup	granulated sugar	250 mL
2	eggs	2
1 tsp	vanilla	5 mL
2¼ cups	Robin Hood All-Purpose Flour	550 mL
1½ tsp	baking powder	7 mL
¼ tsp	salt	1 mL

Filling & Frosting

½ cup	raspberry jam	125 mL
1½ cups	confectioner's (icing) sugar, sifted	375 mL
¼ tsp	almond extract, optional	1 mL
1½ to 2 tbsp	hot water	22 to 30 mL
	Candied cherries	

1. **Cookie:** Cream shortening, sugar, eggs and vanilla in large bowl on medium speed of electric mixer until light and creamy. Combine flour, baking powder and salt. Add to creamed mixture, beating at low speed until well blended. If desired, refrigerate for 1 hour for easy rolling. Roll out dough, one portion at a time, on lightly floured surface to ⅛-inch (3 mm) thickness. Cut into 2-inch (5 cm) rounds. Reroll leftover pieces. Place on prepared cookie sheet. Bake for 6 to 9 minutes or until lightly browned around edges. Cool for 5 minutes on sheet, then transfer to rack and cool completely.

2. **Filling & Frosting:** Spread underside of half of the cookies with jam. Top with remaining cookies to form sandwiches. Combine confectioner's sugar, almond extract and enough hot water to make a thin frosting. Frost tops of cookies. Decorate with small piece of cherry. Store in airtight container overnight.

Swedish Butter Balls

A melt-in-your-mouth delight that's loaded with nuts.

Preparation: 20 minutes

Baking: 12 minutes

Freezing: excellent

TIP

Work dough with your hands to get it smooth.

- *Preheat oven to 400°F (200°C)*
- *Cookie sheet, ungreased*

1 cup	butter, softened	250 mL
½ cup	confectioner's (icing) sugar, sifted	125 mL
1 tsp	vanilla	5 mL
2½ cups	Robin Hood Best For Cake & Pastry Flour or 2¼ cups (550 mL) Robin Hood All-Purpose Flour	625 mL
1 cup	finely chopped pecans	250 mL
	Confectioner's (icing) sugar, sifted	

1. Cream butter, confectioner's sugar and vanilla thoroughly. Add flour. Mix well. Stir in nuts, mixing until smooth.
2. Shape dough into 1-inch (2.5 cm) balls. Place on cookie sheet. Bake for 8 to 12 minutes or until very light golden. Cool for 5 minutes on sheet, then transfer to rack and cool completely. Roll in confectioner's sugar.

Variation
Try hazelnuts or almonds.

Fruit and Nut Refrigerator Cookies

A colorful cookie to have in your refrigerator — ready to just slice, bake and serve.

TIP

Place cookies 2 inches (5 cm) apart on baking sheet to allow for spreading.

- Preheat oven to 375°F (190°C)
- Cookie sheet, ungreased

2½ cups	Robin Hood All-Purpose Flour	625 mL
1 tsp	baking powder	5 mL
½ tsp	baking soda	2 mL
¼ tsp	salt	1 mL
½ cup	butter or margarine, softened	125 mL
½ cup	shortening	125 mL
1 cup	granulated sugar	250 mL
2	eggs	2
1 tsp	vanilla	5 mL
1 cup	chopped candied cherries or fruit	250 mL
½ cup	chopped nuts	125 mL

1. Combine flour, baking powder, baking soda and salt. Stir well to blend.
2. Cream butter, shortening, sugar, eggs and vanilla thoroughly. Stir flour mixture into creamed mixture. Mix well. Add fruit and nuts. If desired, refrigerate for 30 minutes for easier handling.
3. Shape dough into two smooth rolls about 1½ inches (4 cm) in diameter. Wrap in waxed paper and refrigerate until firm, about 4 hours or overnight. Slice with sharp knife into ¼-inch (0.5 cm) slices. Place on cookie sheet. Bake for 8 to 12 minutes or until golden. Cool for 5 minutes on sheet, then transfer to rack and cool completely.

Hazelnut Shortbread Refrigerator Cookies

Prepare the rolls ahead so that they're ready to bake whenever you are.

Makes about 3 dozen cookies

Preparation: 15 minutes

**Refrigeration:
4 hours or overnight**

Baking: 12 minutes

Freezing: excellent

TIP

Leave skins on hazelnuts.

- *Preheat oven to 375°F (190°C)*
- *Cookie sheet, ungreased*

1 cup	Robin Hood All-Purpose Flour	250 mL
$1/2$ cup	cornstarch	125 mL
$1/2$ cup	confectioner's (icing) sugar, sifted	125 mL
$3/4$ cup	finely chopped hazelnuts	175 mL
$3/4$ cup	butter, softened	175 mL

1. Combine flour, cornstarch, confectioner's sugar and nuts in large bowl. With large spoon, blend in butter. Work with hands until soft, smooth dough forms.
2. Shape dough into smooth roll about $1 1/2$ inches (4 cm) in diameter. Wrap and refrigerate until firm, about 4 hours or overnight. Store rolls in refrigerator for up to 1 month.
3. Cut with sharp knife into thin slices. Place on cookie sheet. Bake for 8 to 12 minutes or until edges are lightly browned. Cool for 5 minutes on sheet, then transfer to rack and cool completely.

Variation

Cherry Pecan Shortbread: Omit hazelnuts. Mix dough until smooth, then mix in $3/4$ cup (175 mL) chopped candied cherries and $1/2$ cup (125 mL) chopped pecans until evenly distributed.

Place Card Sugar Cookies

An old-fashioned melt-in-your-mouth cookie that's great for the holiday season.

Makes about 4 dozen cookies

Preparation: 20 minutes

Baking: 10 minutes

Refrigeration: 3 hours

Freezing: excellent

TIP

Cookies can be prepared ahead and decorated as needed.

- *Preheat oven to 375°F (190°C)*
- *Cookie sheet, greased*
- *Cookie cutters*

3 cups	Robin Hood All-Purpose Flour	750 mL
1 tsp	baking powder	5 mL
$\frac{1}{2}$ tsp	salt	2 mL
1 cup	butter, softened	250 mL
$1\frac{1}{4}$ cups	granulated sugar	300 mL
3	eggs	3
1 tsp	vanilla	5 mL
	Colored sugar, nuts, candies colored icings	

1. Combine flour, baking powder and salt. Stir well to blend. Cream butter and sugar with electric mixer until light and fluffy. Beat in eggs and vanilla. Stir flour mixture into creamed mixture. Mix well.

2. Form dough into two balls. Wrap in plastic wrap and refrigerate for about 3 hours. Roll out dough on floured surface to $\frac{1}{4}$-inch (0.5 cm) thickness. Cut into desired shapes. Place on prepared cookie sheet. (If cookies are to be used as Christmas tree ornaments or as gift tags, insert toothpick through end of cookie and leave during baking.)

3. Decorate with colored sugar, nuts or candies before baking or leave plain and decorate with icing later. Bake for 8 to 10 minutes or until light golden. Remove toothpicks. Cool for 5 minutes on sheet, then transfer to rack and cool completely. When cool, decorate with colored icings, if desired. Personalize cookies with a name written in icing. Thread with colorful ribbon, yarn or cord.

Oatmeal Shortbread

Enjoy a unique texture and the flavor of oats in this melt-in-your mouth shortbread.

Makes about 2½ dozen cookies

Preparation: 20 minutes

Baking: 25 minutes

Freezing: excellent

TIP

Use quick oats, not instant.

- *Preheat oven to 300°F (150°C)*
- *Cookie sheet, ungreased*

Cookie cutters

¾ cup	Robin Hood All-Purpose Flour	175 mL
⅔ cup	Robin Hood Oats	150 mL
½ cup	cornstarch	125 mL
½ cup	confectioner's (icing) sugar, sifted	125 mL
¾ cup	butter, softened	175 mL

1. Combine flour, oats, cornstarch and confectioner's sugar in large bowl. With large spoon, blend in butter. Work with hands until soft, smooth dough forms. Shape into ball. If necessary, refrigerate for 30 minutes or until easy to handle.

2. Roll out dough to ¼-inch (5 mm) thickness. Cut into shapes with cookie cutters. Place on cookie sheet. Decorate if desired. Bake for 15 to 25 minutes or until edges are lightly browned. (Time will depend on cookie size.) Cool for 5 minutes on sheet, then transfer to rack and cool completely. Store in tightly covered container.

Variation

Cranberry Wedges: Add ⅓ cup (75 mL) chopped dried cranberries to dough. Roll out or pat dough into two 5½-inch (14 cm) rounds about ½ inch (1 cm) thick on cookie sheet or press into one 9-inch (23 cm) cake pan. Mark into eight wedges. Prick with fork. Bake for 30 to 40 minutes for small rounds or for 40 to 45 minutes for larger round.

Cherry Almond Macaroons

Moist, chewy and colorful; a new twist on an old favorite.

Makes about 45 cookies

Preparation: 15 minutes

Baking: 15 minutes

Freezing: excellent

TIP

Store soft cookies in airtight container with waxed paper between layers.

- *Preheat oven to 350°F (180°C)*
- *Cookie sheet, greased*

4	eggs, separated	4
¼ tsp	salt	1 mL
1½ cups	granulated sugar	375 mL
3 cups	flaked coconut	750 mL
1½ cups	Robin Hood All-Purpose Flour or 1⅔ cups (400 mL) Robin Hood Best For Cake & Pastry Flour	375 mL
1½ cups	chopped red or green candied cherries	375 mL
1½ tsp	almond extract	7 mL

1. Beat egg whites and salt in small bowl on high speed of electric mixer until foamy. Gradually add sugar, beating until very stiff, about 4 minutes.
2. Beat egg yolks in large mixing bowl. Stir in coconut. Add flour, cherries and almond extract; mix well. Stir in egg white mixture thoroughly. (Mixture will be very stiff.)
3. Drop dough by tablespoonfuls (15 mL) about 2 inches (5 cm) apart onto prepared cookie sheet. Bake for 10 to 15 minutes or until set and edges are very light golden. Cool for 5 minutes on sheet, then transfer to rack and cool completely.

Variation
Substitute 1½ cups (375 mL) slivered almonds or a mixture of cherries and almonds for candied cherries.

Raspberry Pinwheel Refrigerator Cookies

Keep a roll handy in the refrigerator to bake whenever you need them.

Makes about 3 dozen cookies

Preparation: 25 minutes
Refrigeration: overnight
Baking: 16 minutes
Freezing: excellent

TIP

Rolls can be frozen. Thaw overnight in refrigerator before slicing.

- *Preheat oven to 375°F (190°C)*
- *Cookie sheet, greased*

1¾ cups	Robin Hood All-Purpose Flour	425 mL
2 tsp	baking powder	10 mL
¼ tsp	salt	1 mL
½ cup	butter or margarine, softened	125 mL
1 cup	granulated sugar	250 mL
1	egg	1
1 tsp	vanilla	5 mL
½ cup	raspberry jam	125 mL
½ cup	flaked coconut	125 mL
⅓ cup	finely chopped pecans or walnuts	75 mL

1. Combine flour, baking powder and salt.
2. Cream butter, sugar, egg and vanilla thoroughly. Add dry ingredients, mixing well. Work with hands to form smooth dough. Roll out dough between two sheets of lightly floured waxed paper into 12- by 9-inch (30 by 23 cm) rectangle.
3. Combine jam, coconut and nuts. Spread evenly over dough, leaving ½-inch (1 cm) border. Roll up tightly, jelly roll fashion, using waxed paper to help, starting from long side. Press edge to seal and shape into roll. Wrap in plastic wrap. Refrigerate overnight.
4. Cut into ¼-inch (0.5 cm) thick slices. Place on prepared cookie sheet. Bake for 12 to 16 minutes or until golden. Cool for 5 minutes on sheet, then transfer to rack and cool completely.

Variation
Replace raspberry jam with apricot.

Festive Fruitcake Cookies

Chock-full of fruit and nuts, these taste like mini fruitcakes.

Makes about 3 dozen cookies

Preparation: 15 minutes

Baking: 15 minutes

Freezing: excellent

TIP

Store cookies at room temperature for a day to let flavors mellow before eating.

- Preheat oven to 350°F (180°C)
- Cookie sheet, greased

1 cup	raisins	250 mL
1 cup	candied cherries, coarsely chopped	250 mL
1 cup	candied pineapple, coarsely chopped	250 mL
1 cup	Brazil nuts, coarsely chopped	250 mL
½ cup	shortening	125 mL
¾ cup	granulated sugar	175 mL
1	egg	1
1 tsp	vanilla	5 mL
½ tsp	almond extract	2 mL
1¼ cups	Robin Hood All-Purpose Flour	300 mL
½ tsp	baking soda	2 mL
½ tsp	salt	2 mL

1. Combine raisins, candied fruit and nuts. Mix well.
2. Cream shortening, sugar, egg, vanilla and almond extract in large bowl on medium speed of electric mixer until light and creamy.
3. Combine flour, baking soda and salt. Add to creamed mixture, beating on low speed until blended. Stir in fruit mixture. Mix well.
4. Drop dough by heaping tablespoonfuls (20 mL) about 2 inches (5 cm) apart onto prepared cookie sheet. Bake for 10 to 15 minutes or until golden. Cool for 5 minutes on sheet, then transfer to rack and cool completely.

Variation

Replace cherries and pineapple with mixed candied fruit.

Fabulous Fruitcake

Prepare a few months in advance to let flavors mellow.

Makes 3 loaves

Preparation: 20 minutes
Baking: 2½ hours
Freezing: excellent

TIP

Don't overbake. Cakes continue baking a little after removing from oven.

- Preheat oven to 275°F (140°C)
- Three 9- by 5-inch (2 L) loaf pans, greased, lined with aluminum foil and greased again

Fruits & Nuts

3 cups	raisins	750 mL
2 cups	candied pineapple, coarsely chopped	500 mL
2 cups	candied cherries, halved	500 mL
2 cups	mixed candied peel	500 mL
2 cups	coarsely chopped pecans	500 mL
1 cup	chopped dried apricots	250 mL
1 cup	slivered almonds	250 mL
1 cup	Robin Hood All-Purpose Flour	250 mL

Batter

1½ cups	Robin Hood All-Purpose Flour	375 mL
1 tsp	baking powder	5 mL
1 tsp	ground cinnamon	5 mL
½ tsp	salt	2 mL
½ tsp	ground nutmeg	2 mL
¼ tsp	ground cloves	1 mL
1¼ cups	butter, softened	300 mL
1½ cups	liquid honey	375 mL
1 tbsp	vanilla	15 mL
6	eggs	6

1. **Fruits & Nuts:** Combine raisins, pineapple, cherries, candied peel, pecans, apricots, almonds and flour. Mix well to thoroughly coat fruits with flour.

2. **Batter:** Combine flour, baking powder, cinnamon, salt, nutmeg and cloves. Mix well. Cream butter, honey and vanilla on medium speed of electric mixer. Add eggs, one at a time, beating well after each addition. Add dry ingredients on low speed, mixing just until blended. Stir in fruit and nut mixture. Mix well.

3. Spread batter evenly in prepared pans. Keeping pan of hot water in oven, bake for 2 to 2½ hours or until toothpick inserted in center comes out clean. Cool in pans. Remove foil. Wrap well and store in cool, dry place.

Variation

Vary the candied fruit and nuts to suit your own tastes. Keep the total amount the same as the recipe recommends.

Cherry Bundt Cake

A colorful cake for the holiday season but enjoyable all year round.

TIP

A white icing drizzle is a pretty alternative decoration.

- Preheat oven to 350°F (180°C)
- 10-inch (3 L) Bundt pan or 10-inch (4 L) tube pan, greased and floured

1¼ cups	butter, softened	300 mL
2¾ cups	granulated sugar	675 mL
5	eggs	5
1 tsp	almond extract	5 mL
3 cups	Robin Hood All-Purpose Flour	750 mL
1 tsp	baking powder	5 mL
¼ tsp	salt	1 mL
1 cup	undiluted evaporated milk	250 mL
2 cups	quartered maraschino cherries, well drained	500 mL
	Confectioner's (icing) sugar, optional	

1. Beat butter, sugar, eggs and almond extract in large bowl on low speed of electric mixer until blended, then on high speed for 5 minutes until light and fluffy. Combine flour, baking powder and salt. Add dry ingredients to butter mixture alternately with evaporated milk, mixing lightly after each addition. Fold in cherries. Pour batter into prepared pan.

2. Bake for 75 to 85 minutes or until toothpick inserted in center comes out clean. Cover with foil for first 10 minutes if becoming too brown. Cool in pan for 20 minutes. Remove from pan and cool completely. Dust with confectioner's sugar before serving, if desired.

Variation
Replace half the cherries with candied pineapple.

Holiday Mincemeat Cake

Enjoy the moist, delicious flavor of mincemeat all year.

Makes about 12 servings

Preparation: 15 minutes

Baking: 50 or 60 minutes

Freezing: excellent

TIP

Mincemeat not only keeps baked goods moist but also adds a unique flavor.

- Preheat oven to 350°F (180°C)
- 10-inch (3 L) Bundt pan or 13- by 9-inch (3.5 L) cake pan, greased and floured

3½ cups	Robin Hood All-Purpose Flour	875 mL
3½ tsp	baking powder	17 mL
1 tsp	baking soda	5 mL
¾ tsp	salt	3 mL
¾ cup	butter, softened	175 mL
4 tsp	grated orange zest	20 mL
1½ tsp	vanilla	7 mL
1 cup	granulated sugar	250 mL
3	eggs	3
3 cups	prepared mincemeat	750 mL
¾ cup	milk	175 mL
1 cup	chopped walnuts	250 mL
	Confectioner's (icing) sugar	

1. Combine flour, baking powder, baking soda and salt. Set aside.

2. Cream butter, orange zest and vanilla in large bowl on medium speed of electric mixer until light. Beat in sugar. Add eggs, one at a time, beating well after each addition. Blend in mincemeat. Add dry ingredients to mincemeat mixture alternately with milk, beginning and ending with dry ingredients. Stir in nuts. Pour batter into prepared pan. Bake for 55 to 60 minutes for Bundt pan, 45 to 50 minutes for rectangular pan, or until toothpick inserted in center comes out clean. Cool in pan for 20 minutes. Remove from pan; cool completely. Dust with confectioner's sugar before serving.

Chewy Cherry Bars

A colorful addition to your holiday cookie tray.

TIP

For bars with frosting, cut, place on foil tray and freeze to harden frosting. Then wrap in plastic bags to store in freezer. Remove individual bars as needed.

- Preheat oven to 350°F (180°C)
- 13- by 9-inch (3.5 L) cake pan, greased

Crust

1 cup	Robin Hood All-Purpose Flour	250 mL
1 cup	Robin Hood Oats	250 mL
1 cup	packed brown sugar	250 mL
1 tsp	baking soda	5 mL
½ cup	butter	125 mL

Filling

2	eggs	2
1 cup	packed brown sugar	250 mL
½ tsp	almond extract	2 mL
2 tbsp	Robin Hood All-Purpose Flour	30 mL
1 tsp	baking powder	5 mL
¼ tsp	salt	1 mL
1 cup	flaked coconut	250 mL
1 cup	maraschino cherries, drained and coarsely chopped	250 mL
½ cup	chopped pecans or walnuts	125 mL

Frosting

¼ cup	butter, softened	50 mL
½ tsp	almond extract	2 mL
2 cups	confectioner's (icing) sugar, sifted	500 mL
3 to 4 tbsp	milk or cream	45 to 60 mL

1. **Crust:** Combine flour, oats, brown sugar and baking soda in mixing bowl. Cut in butter until crumbly. Press into prepared pan. Bake for 10 minutes.

2. **Filling:** Beat together eggs, brown sugar and almond extract. Combine flour, baking powder and salt. Stir into egg mixture. Mix well. Stir in coconut, cherries and nuts. Spread evenly over crust. Bake for 25 minutes or until lightly browned. Cool completely.

3. **Frosting:** Beat together butter, almond extract, sugar and milk until smooth and creamy. Spread over top. Chill until icing is firm, about 30 minutes. Cut into bars.

Cranberry Orange Bubble Bread

Prepare the dough in a bread machine, then finish baking in a conventional oven.

Makes about 10 servings

Preparation: 15 minutes

Rising: 45 minutes

Baking: 25 minutes

Freezing: excellent

TIP

For an attractive finish, drizzle with a white icing or sprinkle with confectioner's sugar. Leftovers make wonderful bread pudding and French toast.

- Preheat oven to 375°F (190°C)
- 9-inch (23 cm) springform pan, greased
- Bread machine

Dough

1 cup	milk, at room temperature	250 mL
1	egg	1
1 tbsp	butter or margarine	15 mL
3 cups	Robin Hood Best For Bread Homestyle White Flour	750 mL
1 tbsp	granulated sugar	15 mL
2 tsp	grated orange zest	10 mL
1 tsp	salt	5 mL
¾ cup	dried cranberries	175 mL
2 tsp	bread machine yeast	10 mL

Glaze (optional)

1	egg, beaten	1

1. **Dough:** Add all ingredients to bread machine according to manufacturer's directions. Select Dough cycle.

2. Divide dough into 16 pieces. Shape each piece into ball. Place in prepared pan. Cover with tea towel. Let rise in warm place (75° to 85°F/24° to 29°C) until doubled, about 45 minutes.

3. **Glaze (optional):** Brush lightly with beaten egg for a shiny, golden top.

4. Bake on lower oven rack for 20 to 25 minutes or until golden. Cover top with aluminum foil if becoming too brown. Remove from pan immediately. Cool on rack.

Variation

Replace cranberries with dried cherries, chopped apricots or raisins.

Cranberry Chocolate Orange Rounds

Soup cans make ideal baking pans for round cranberry loaves. These make wonderful holiday gifts.

Makes
10 mini loaves

Preparation: 15 minutes

Baking: 40 minutes

Freezing: excellent

TIPS

These make wonderful hostess gifts any time of the year.

For two 9- by 5-inch (2 L) loaves, use 2 tsp (10 mL) baking powder and bake for 70 minutes.

- *Preheat oven to 350°F (180°C)*
- *Ten 10-oz (284 mL) cans, well greased*

2 cups	fresh or frozen cranberries, coarsely chopped	500 mL
2 cups	granulated sugar, divided	500 mL
3½ cups	Robin Hood All-Purpose Flour	875 mL
1 tbsp	baking powder	15 mL
1 tsp	baking soda	5 mL
1 tsp	salt	5 mL
2	eggs	2
1 tbsp	grated orange zest	15 mL
1⅓ cups	orange juice	325 mL
¼ cup	vegetable oil	50 mL
2 cups	miniature semi-sweet chocolate chips	500 mL
1 cup	chopped nuts, optional	250 mL

1. Combine cranberries and ½ cup (125 mL) sugar. Set aside.
2. Combine flour, remaining 1½ cups (375 mL) sugar, baking powder, baking soda and salt in mixing bowl. Stir well to blend.
3. Beat together eggs, orange zest, juice and oil. Add to dry ingredients, stirring just until moistened. Fold in cranberry mixture, chocolate chips, and nuts, if desired. Divide batter among prepared cans. Bake for 35 to 40 minutes or until toothpick inserted in center comes out clean. Cool for 10 minutes, then run thin-blade knife around sides of cans to loosen. Turn out onto rack to cool completely. Wrap and store overnight before slicing or freeze for later use.

Index

(v) = variation